Perfection of Exile:
Fourteen Contemporary Lithuanian Writers

Henrikas Radauskas

Antanas Vaičiulaitis

Jonas Aistis

Antanas Škėma

Algirdas Landsbergis

Kostas Ostrauskas

Alfonsas Nyka-Niliūnas

Algimantas Mackus

Henrikas Nagys

Kazys Bradūnas

Albinas Marius Katiliškis

Jonas Mekas

Aloyzas Baronas

Bernardas Brazdžionis

PERFECTION OF EXILE:

Fourteen Contemporary Lithuanian Writers

by Rimvydas Šilbajoris

Norman
University of Oklahoma Press

By Rimvydas Šilbajoris

Russian Versification: the Theories of Trediakovsky, Lomonosov, and Kantemir (New York, 1968)

Perfection of Exile: Fourteen Contemporary Lithuanian Writers (Norman, 1970)

International Standard Book Number: 0–8061–0907–6
Library of Congress Catalog Card Number: 72–108798

Composed and printed at Norman, Oklahoma, U.S.A., by the University of Oklahoma Press.
First edition.

Contents

Illustrations

Perfection of Exile:
Fourteen Contemporary Lithuanian Writers

1 Brief Survey of Lithuanian Literature

THERE was no significant Lithuanian literature until the middle of the eighteenth century. The reasons for this late development are Lithuania's small population and its remote geographical position, in northeastern Europe, far from the Mediterranean centers of culture. The ancient Hebrews and Greeks accomplished what they did in part because they looked upon their civilizations as the center of the universe, and the world they knew was too small to convince them otherwise. The Lithuanians, on the other hand, have been only too well aware throughout their history of their small numbers, their isolation, and of the overwhelming power and influence of their huge neighbors, the Russians, the Germans, and the Poles. Practically all their energies were spent in a fierce, at times desperate, struggle for survival, and there was no time left for an indigenous cultural development. National identity simply meant stubborn commitment to the traditional, ancient ways of life against the encroaching more powerful and more advanced civilizations, especially against the strong pressure of the crusading Teutonic knights who came to baptize the country by fire and sword. Having successfully resisted the military machine of salvation, the Lithuanians became the last European people to be converted to Christianity, at the end of the fourteenth century. By then Lithuania had already conquered or otherwise acquired large areas of Russia and established close dynastic and military ties with Poland which eventually grew into a complete political union. The Lithuanian nobility thus became absorbed into the Polish and, to some extent, Russian cultures, so that there was little left to identify the Lithuanians as a separate nation, except for the continued adherence of the peasantry to its ancient mother tongue and its rich folk heritage.

When, at the end of the eighteenth century, the political and military power of the Polish-Lithuanian state collapsed, both peoples became subject to foreign rule. Most of Lithuania found itself under the Russian tsars, and its nobility and educated classes made common cause with the Poles, adopting the Polish national aspirations for their own. Consequently, there was little or no interest in developing an indigenous literature in the Lithuanian language, except for an occasional poem by a provincial landowner or compilations of religious texts. This is where matters pretty much remained until Lithuania became caught up in the general European surge of nationalism in the nineteenth century.

The situation was different in East Prussia, where the Lithuanian element was still strong in the seventeenth and eighteenth centuries. The Prussian state, in comparison with the Russian empire, was quite enlightened in its own authoritarian way, and efforts were made to prepare the Protestant clergy to work among the Lithuanians in the villages, bringing the word of God to them in their native idiom. Some of the clergy were Lithuanians themselves, and from this group emerged the monumental figure of Kristijonas Donelaitis (1714–80), the pastor of the tiny parish of Tolminkiemis and the first, and greatest, Lithuanian epic poet.

Donelaitis' fame rests on a single narrative poem, *Metai* (*The Year*, or better, *The Seasons*), a rural epic describing the joys and sorrows, work and leisure of the Lithuanian peasants walking the treadmill of the four seasons. The poem consists of a series of episodes from the lives of several peasants with differing fortunes and personalities strung together on the thread of time, the principal structural element. The hero is, perhaps, nature itself, for it is the only constant, all-pervading presence, depicted in vivid detail. The struggles between the changing seasons—the careful labors of the summer sun and the grim forays of howling winter—are depicted almost as if every natural phenomenon were a person playing out a complex and splendid drama that makes the people's lives seem small and humble by comparison. This constitutes the proper setting for the moral intent of the poem, which is to teach the peasants humility, patience, fidelity to their simple Lithuanian ways, love of sobriety and hard work, and, most important, faith and confidence in God. Indeed, the poem in some ways resembles a long sermon given by the pietist cleric that Donelaitis was, replete with parables and homilies, inspiring and horrible examples, richly adorned with the beauties of nature as well as of the vigorous, expressive, often earthy, poetic language itself, running smoothly in stately hexameters along the course of the narrative.

A literary historian accustomed to seeing everything in terms of influences, cross-fertilizations, and developments will be hard put to explain the sudden appearance of this grand poem in the cultural desert of Lithuanian literature in the eighteenth century. Because of Donelaitis' good classical education, his work has been compared with Vergil's *Georgics* and Hesiod's *Works and Days*, but Donelaitis, unlike Hesiod, does not use mythology in his poem at all. Hesiod's deprecation of *hybris*, however, could be likened to Donelaitis' own exhortations to humble and patient labor. The relationship to Vergil could be seen in the fact that, like the *Georgics*, *The Seasons* concerns itself with the social and political conditions of the given time. The relationship can also be seen in the metaphorical language describing the processes of nature, which shows anthropomorphic tendencies similar to those in Vergil. Donelaitis does not, however, use the elevated style of the Roman classic. Some comparisons have also been made with James Thomson's *The Seasons*, but there is little resemblance between the two works.

Donelaitis' *The Seasons* did not exercise any formative influence on the further development of Lithuanian literature, primarily because it was not published until 1818. By then the focus of literary activity had already shifted to Lithuania proper, in particular to the old University of Vilnius. This institution had become an important European center of learning at the beginning of the nineteenth century, when the more liberal rule of Tsar Alexander I permitted it to develop with a large degree of independence. The intellectual climate at the university was almost exclusively Polish, but the winds of romantic nationalism blowing in from western Europe aroused the curiosity of some of the Lithuanian students in the past of their own people, their language, their identity. They became aware of themselves as members of a once great nation which had played a historical role out of all proportion to its numerical strength.

One outstanding graduate of the University of Vilnius was Simanas

Daukantas (1793–1864), a steady, determined worker, who followed the trail of the Lithuanian past through archives and corridors of history and came up with a romantic, idealized image of his people which he then embodied in several large historical works. Although studded with scholarly references, these works are in essence colorful yarns about the sterling virtues and greatness of the Lithuanian people, dwellers in deep woods, builders of a huge medieval empire stretching from sea to sea. More important as literature than as history, these works made a significant contribution to the resurgence of Lithuanian nationalism several decades later.

Simanas Stanevičius (1799–1848), another alumnus of the University of Vilnius, made an important collection of western Lithuanian folk songs and wrote original fables in which the allegorical personages symbolized the aspirations of Lithuanian people and their present lot.

Motiejus Valančius (1801–75), the Bishop of Western Lithuania, represents a different aspect of the Lithuanian struggle for national consciousness. He was primarily interested in the present, in the spiritual welfare of his charges. In his realistic, practical mind the work of salvation took the form of concrete measures to enhance popular education, increase the sobriety, knowledge, and skills of the peasants, and to organize the printing and promotion of Lithuanian books. He wrote moral and educational stories intended to delight and instruct his readers, full of realistic details and amusing incidents. These works are not outstanding literature, but they did contribute to the development of a clear, realistic style in later works.

A much more important writer was Antanas Baranauskas (1835–1902), the Bishop of Eastern Lithuania. Although his life span overlapped both Daukantas' and Valančius', he was not their spiritual contemporary but belonged to a later generation with a different world view. He was educated not in the University of Vilnius but mostly in St. Petersburg and, for a year abroad, in western Europe. His interest in Lithuanian matters had little to do with historical romanticism or with any great concern for the enlightenment and education of the peasantry. A lonely, talented misfit, he liked to immerse himself in the study of "esoteric" topics, such as mathematics or Lithuanian dialectology, for the sheer joy of mastering the subject. It was probably his joy in the richness, flexibility, and expressiveness of the Lithuanian language that inspired him to write his single *magnum opus*, the lyrical poem *Anykščių šilelis* (*The Pine Grove of Anykščiai*) during the summers of 1858 and 1859. (He said he wrote it to prove that Lithuanian is no whit inferior to the magnificent Polish of Adam Mickiewicz, the author of *Pan Tadeusz*, the greatest epic poem in Polish literature.)

The poem starts out as a kind of elegy, a lament for the bygone beauties of a pine grove near his native village, cut down by ruthless and greedy timber merchants. After a brief survey of the bleak present landscape, the poet starts in on a rhetorical figure of praise to the grove's former charms and soon loses himself completely, gloriously, amid the countless splendors of the sylvan beauty remembered. He describes in great detail and with high-spirited enthusiasm all the sounds, smells, and movements, the plants and the animals, in sentences seemingly as interminable and inexhaustible as the forest itself, moving along in an emotional rhythm that corresponds exactly to the changes of day and night, noise and silence, wind and stillness in the glade. Baranauskas' Lithuanian is indeed rich and beautiful, handled with great instinctive skill, building up emotion by means of image, enhancing the image by intense feeling growing naturally out of the poetic context. The poem also has an allegorical level of meaning, referring to the sufferings of the Lithuanian nation. Like Donelaitis' *The Seasons*, *The Pine Grove of Anykščiai* is a unique achievement with no literary tradition to explain its magnificence and little or no direct influence on later developments.

In his later years Baranauskas dissociated himself from the cause of Lithuanian nationalism and remained a passive observer of events which led to the creation of a separate Lithuanian literature, contributed to by writers who were fully conscious of belonging to an established indigenous tradition. The efforts of Bishop Valančius and many other members of the Roman Catholic clergy and provincial intelligentsia to educate the people resulted in the formation of a new class of intellectuals stemming from the village and owing little or nothing to the aristocratic, Polish-oriented ideology of the ruling classes. Perhaps the last significant effort made by this Polonized gentry to guide the destinies of their country was their participation in the unsuccessful Polish uprising of 1863. When the revolt was crushed, the tsarist authorities punished the landowners by more strict enforcement of the abolition of serfdom, proclaimed in 1861. This policy increased the material well-being of the peasants and allowed a more rapid development of the new Lithuanian intelligentsia.

The next logical step in this chain of events was a further rise in national consciousness and an inevitable conflict with the Russian rule. The new struggle became especially intense after 1865, when the Russians prohibited the use of the Latin alphabet in all books written in the Lithuanian language. A vigorous movement for freedom of the press grew up immediately. Books in Latin letters were printed in East Prussia and brought across the border with the help of a well-organized underground network composed of selfless patriots as well as professional smugglers interested in the material rewards of this enterprise.

Cultural development became closely identified with the political struggle for freedom. An especially important role in this "national resurrection" movement was played by two of the illegal magazines, *Aušra (The Dawn)*, published by Dr. Jonas Basanavičius (1851–1927), and, later, *Varpas (The Bell)*, edited by Dr. Vincas Kudirka (1858–99), a devoted idealist, relentlessly driven all his life by the categorical imperative of patriotism. Kudirka was also the most talented writer among the initiators of the "resurrection" movement, famous for his vicious anti-Russian satires and impassioned articles calling for a militant nationalism that would direct its efforts toward more and more popular education, higher standards of living, and unyielding opposition to the Polish and Russian overlords of the country.

The awakened national consciousness produced a number of writers whose works, while still dominated by some political or social ideology, managed to achieve a respectable literary standard. Julija Žemaitė (1845–1921), a self-educated rural writer, painted realistic pictures of everyday life in the countryside, emphasizing the efforts of a vigorous new peasant generation to improve their lot and acquire more education. Her stories are written in a vigorous, straightforward manner. Marija Pečkauskaitė (1878–1930), writing under the pseudonym of Šatrijos Ragana ("the

Witch of Šatrija"), produced the novel *Sename dvare* (*In the Old Manor*). It is a series of semiautobiographical sketches of family life in a Lithuanian nest of gentlefolk caught up in the spirit of changing times. Gabrielė Petkevičaitė-Bitė (1861–1943) also wrote about landowning gentry faced with the need to commit itself either to the Polish cultural heritage or to the new nationalist movement.

Jonas Biliūnas, perhaps the most important writer of this group, wrote short stories from the life of ordinary folk in the spirit of social protest and great humanitarian sympathy for the oppressed. His stories are remarkable for their psychological insight into the mentality of the common people as well as for their passionate intensity. One story, "The End of Brisius," has been translated into English in *Selected Lithuanian Short Stories* (Voyages Press, 1959).

While Lithuanian literature continued to develop in this relatively quiet corner of the Russian empire, the tsarist regime itself was shaken to its foundations by the Russo-Japanese War and by the ensuing revolution of 1905. These events did not produce any great direct literary response among Lithuanian writers, because they had lost all sense of spiritual commitment to the affairs of Russia and were interested in the revolution only insofar as it promised greater freedom to their own country. In the political sphere, matters were somewhat different. Many Lithuanian intellectuals tried to take advantage of the turmoil to promote their national aspirations. Their efforts culminated in the Great Assembly of Vilnius in 1905—a conference of the leading Lithuanian cultural figures which presented a number of demands to the Russian government. They won at least the recognition that Lithuania was indeed a separate ethnic entity, as well as the right to teach Lithuanian in the schools. The ban on printing Lithuanian books in the Latin alphabet had already been lifted a year earlier, in 1904. All these changes further encouraged the growth of *belles lettres*, to which an important contribution was made by two patriotic Catholic priests, Juozas Tumas-Vaižgantas (1869–1933) and Jonas Mačiulis-Maironis (1862–1932).

Both Vaižgantas and Maironis were, in a sense, behind their time, because their ideological convictions were already formed before the events of 1905 and because they devoted their greatest efforts to the awakening of national consciousness—to a degree an already accomplished fact—instead of looking forward to new horizons for Lithuanian cultural life. What they did achieve, however, was the popularization of their ideas throughout the countryside, thus helping to create a genuine patriotic mass movement. Maironis, in particular, is quite deservedly called "the bard of national resurrection." His sonorous, highly emotional poetry, burning with great love for the country's past and unyielding hope for the future, captured the imagination of his readers with compelling force. Many of his poems became popular songs among the people, sustaining their spirit not only in his own day but even now, through all the adversities and tragedies of recent Lithuanian history.

The student of literature, however, will be particularly interested in Maironis' accomplishments as an artist. In this sphere he was certainly not behind his time; on the contrary, his work constitutes a major breakthrough in the development of Lithuanian poetic diction and prosody. Except for the hexameters of Donelaitis, most Lithuanian poetry before Maironis was written in rather awkward imitations of the Polish syllabic meter, based not on a regular recurrence of stresses, but on an equal number of syllables in each line. Only the great talent of Baranauskas was able to make this syllabic verse move harmoniously, with a musical lilt. Maironis seems to have grasped instinctively the natural affinity between the Lithuanian language, with its strong but variable word stress, and the syllabo-tonic system of versification, in which the units of scansion are the classical verse feet of Greek and Latin poetry in which stress is substituted for syllable length. Both bisyllabic and trisyllabic meters are used in Maironis' verse with sure hand and great sensitivity to the fine nuances of relationship among emotion, rhythm, and idea. His poetic language, although not distinguished for richness of vocabulary, is pure and vigorous and highly sophisticated in the use of syntactic structures and rhetorical intonations for maximum emotional effect.

After Maironis, truly modern Lithuanian poetry, capable of reflecting all the complexities and profundities of recent poetic trends in Russia and western Europe, became possible. The modern poets, however, tended to regard Maironis himself as an old-fashioned bard who had outlived his age. Tumas-Vaižgantas, although not quite the equal of

Maironis as an artist, was better accepted. His sparkling, entertaining prose works, especially the novel *Pragiedruliai* (*Cloud Breaks*), 1918–20, describing the rise and development of national self-consciousness in all of Lithuania, continued to be highly regarded even after the country became politically and culturally independent.

National independence was won in 1918, partly because of favorable political changes after World War I. Lithuanian literature, however, had already achieved its own independence from the dominant patriotic themes and was in the midst of a highly complex and rapid development in which the old ideas of national resurgence alternated with new concepts and influences of a purely literary nature. Some writers used a variety of styles and trends in their works; some became interested in contemporary European literary movements such as symbolism; and others again sought to develop a realistic direction in literature. But all this turmoil clearly pointed to the ever-increasing prevalence of art itself over social or political ideology. The Lithuanian muse had just about laid down her war trumpet and was turning to the cultivation of her own garden.

In prose, the two outstanding writers of the early period of independence who continue to loom large even to the present day were Vincas Krėvė-Mickevičius (1882–1954) and Antanas Vienuolis (1882–1957). Krėvė, a prolific and complex writer, developed his art in several genres. At the beginning of his career he was particularly interested in Lithuanian folklore, ancient songs, and legends. His imagination reworked them into highly stylized and poetic tales of the country's past in the collection *Dainavos šalies senų žmonių padavimai* (*Tales of the Old Folks of Dainava*), 1912. Some of these tales have a historical background and others are pure inventions, but the achievement of Krėvė's art was to fuse both fact and fancy into a special kind of lyrical-heroic universe where every word trembles on the verge of song and every brave deed turns into a hyperbole of itself, acquiring grandiose, poetic proportions.

Quite different from these heroic legends are the short stories of Krėvė. They present pictures of country life in realistic detail, creating a series of fascinating village characters, such as the old Jew Kušlius in "The Herrings," who must bear the burden of primitive Christian prejudice and contempt while himself being a very harmless, tired, and desperately poor individual, eking out a living by selling all sorts of odds and ends. Another picturesque character is Lapinas in "The Herdsman," a strong and healthy ancient who seems to have outlived entire generations of village folk until, finally, he too dies when a neighbor cuts down a huge, ageless linden tree. What relates these realistic stories to the romantic legends is their tendency to acquire a hidden mythological dimension, discernible in the presence of intimate ties between man and nature and between nature and some unknown, deep sources of strength which have sustained the Lithuanian through countless ages. The human being seems somehow as poetic and inexplicable as nature itself, whether he appears as a legendary hero, a poor Jew, or as the peculiar, shaman-like herdsman Lapinas.

The mystery of man acquires another aspect in Krėvė's dramatic works. He wrote a series of plays dealing with Lithuanian history in which the central characters are strong and lonely figures, tragically aware of what they must do to fulfill the laws of history even if, at the given moment, their deeds must cause bloodshed and sorrow, making them appear as ruthless tyrants. Again, like the legendary founder of the Lithuanian state in the play *Šarūnas* (1911), the heroes acquire a mythological aspect, becoming personifications of some unknowable forces in nature and history.

The intensity of human passions at a fateful moment in Lithuanian history is depicted with special force in the play *Skirgaila* (1925), in which Krėvė analyzes the human and political complexities of the struggle between paganism and Christianity in Lithuania soon after its baptism. The play has Shakespearean overtones in the handling of action and in the portrayal of human emotions in conflict between inner conviction and the pressure of necessity.

Man as rebel, prophet, and tyrant is also the central figure in the biblical epic *Dangaus ir žemės sūnūs* (*The Sons of Heaven and Earth*), on which Krėvė worked from about 1907 to his death in exile in 1954. The work investigates the turbulent, tragic, and poetic period in the history of Palestine from the birth of Christ to the death of Herod. In a number of conflicts between man and God, truth and the selfish greed for life, humanity is seen desperately trying to understand itself and its relationship to the absolute.

Antanas Vienuolis was also interested in the legendary and the exotic, but his inspiration came from travels in foreign lands, notably the Caucasus. His *Kaukazo legendos* (*Legends of the Causasus*), 1907, consists of original tales suggested to his imagination by the wild beauty of the Caucasus mountain landscape. Vienuolis' most important contribution, however, resides in his short stories and, to some extent, his novels in which we see Lithuanian life, from the poignant individual tragedy of a seduced village girl in the story "The Drowned Girl," to the decay of the landowning class which has lost touch with the realities of the new Lithuania in "Cancer," and finally, to the struggles, errors, and achievements of the awakened nation in various works, of which the largest is the novel *Prieš dieną* (*Before Daybreak*), 1925. A great admirer of Chekhov, Vienuolis often tried to achieve the Russian writer's keen critical insight into the hidden tragedies of ordinary lives and to emulate his powerful portrayals of the slow dissolution of human integrity and idealism under the relentless pressure of gray everyday reality.

In poetry, there was a rapid and many-sided development drawing its inspiration from a variety of sources. At the beginning, significant influences came from Russian poetry, ranging from the nineteenth-century classics of Russia's "golden age" to the futurism of Mayakovsky. Vincas Mykolaitis-Putinas (1893–1966) responded in his early poetry to the clear, lyrical beauty in the verse of Afanasy Fet. Like Fet, he paid homage to the esthetic of "pure art" derived from the elevation of nature to the realm of calm, harmonious beauty. Somewhat later, Putinas became attracted to the complex, brooding, philosophical poetry of Fedor Tyutchev. In the poetry of Putinas the basic dichotomy between cosmos (the ordering, rational principle of the universe) and chaos (the primeval, dark, turbulent realm from which both creativity and destruction are born) became transformed into an expression of man's passionate struggle against the inert and deadening forces of ordinary life which gradually exhaust the soul and leave us confused and defeated by the countless questions surrounding the mystery of existence which the poet cannot resolve. Yet the philosophical despondency that fills one cycle of his poems called "The Hymns of Pessimism" was soon replaced by a rebellious, Promethean spirit in later works, notably the long poem "The Slave," depicting the revolt of a slave surrounded by his master's luxury who leaves the endless crystal palaces in search of an unknown destiny. The poem perhaps reflects the inner struggle of Putinas' own life—described in detail in his novel *Altorių šešėly* (*In the Shadow of the Altars*), 1933—his painful but inevitable decision to leave the calling of the Roman Catholic priesthood, to which he had already been consecrated. This work met with great success because it seemed the first "modern" Lithuanian novel. It influenced a number of writers to take up working in this genre.

Profound inner conflicts and the spirit of rebellion combined with intense desire to comprehend and to serve the mystery of being brought Putinas' poetry close to the Russian symbolists, particularly Vladimir Soloviev and Vyacheslav Ivanov. His own verse became filled with symbolic conceptions among which the powerful, sensual, and, in essence, chaotic pull of the earth plays a dominant role.

Faustas Kirša (1891–1964) also contributed to the development of symbolism, but the most "pure" Lithuanian symbolist poet was Jurgis Baltrušaitis (1873–1944). Most of his poetry was written in Russian, during years of close personal association with the Russian symbolists. He conveys a stern message of man's insignificance in the universe, which man comes to understand as his cosmic consciousness expands. His duty therefore, is to consent with quiet fortitude to the sorrows he must bear and to accept every little flower by the roadside as his equal in the vast total scheme of things.

The poetry of Balys Sruoga (1896–1947) also contains elements of symbolism. A highly individualistic, restless spirit, he revolted vigorously against vapid patriotic verse and turned for inspiration toward neo-romanticism and the symbolists. Sruoga was less interested in the philosophical aspects of their poetry than in their experiments with form, style, and the musical qualities of words. His own symbolic and metaphorical devices, however, came mostly from the rich store of Lithuanian folklore.

After 1924, Sruoga shifted his interest from lyrical verse to verse drama, as if in search for more significant content in his poetry. His most important work is *Milžino paunksmė* (*The Shadow of the Giant*), 1932, a play about the Grand Duke Vytautas under whose rule Lithuania had reached the summit of its power, in the fifteenth century. Vytautas himself never appears on the stage, but his unseen presence dominates the fierce political struggle between him and his brother Jogaila, the king of Poland. Actually, Jogaila is not much more than a figurehead in whose name his advisers are advancing their designs to keep Lithuania subordinate to and in union with Poland. Helpless to influence events and achieve reconciliation with his brother, Jogaila presents the tragic figure of a man placed in opposition to the country of his birth, for which he yearns with great lyrical sorrow. The play is written in dignified five-foot iambics and shows no trace of Sruoga's earlier exuberant experimentations with verse form and diction. *Kazimieras Sapiega*, published in Soviet Lithuania in 1947 and in the United States in 1951, is a serious, brooding play about the destinies of the Lithuanian nation at a critical period of its history.

The influence of Russian futurism and West European expressionism manifested itself in the so-called Four Winds movement. Its guiding spirit was the poet Kazys Binkis (1893–1942), editor of the literary magazine *Four Winds*, which came out intermittently between 1922 and 1927. The movement's manifesto contains all the brash and brave statements typical of futurism: worship of the dynamic age of machines, determination to forge poetry like iron by the effort of rational will, and contempt for "insipid romanticism" and "starry-eyed symbolism." The paradox of Lithuanian futurism, however, was that the country had no industry and no huge cities for the poets to worship; it was a place of quiet lakes and green meadows, just beginning to emerge from centuries of isolation. If the movement was to exist at all, it had to find another basis in reality. Binkis and his fellow futurists then turned again to the village, as other literary movements had done, this time, however, seeking out those elements of peasant culture and folklore which were expressive of crude, even vulgar, dynamic strength—the promise of the future.

Nevertheless, Kazys Binkis was not a poet of ruthless, explosive power.

Rather, his talent tended toward spontaneity and elegance of form and youthful bravado in content. With all this, his verse remained very lyrical and very Lithuanian in essence, but enriched by bold metaphors, wild humor, and breathless flights of fancy. Other important members of the Four Winds movement were Juozas Petrėnas-Tarulis (born 1889), a novelist and journalist, and Teofilis Tilvytis (born 1904), a satirical poet and humorist.

After the Four Winds movement died down, it became apparent that the group had indeed broken new ground in the development of Lithuanian literature, especially by stimulating fresh ideas and new literary trends. One new movement was the Third Front, organized around a literary magazine of the same name which came out briefly in 1930 and 1931. The group consisted of young writers with leftist leanings, interested in fighting social and economic injustice and fond of glorifying the figure of the strong, honest, brave young peasant, simple and pure in heart, who was to come from the soil and break up the bourgeois order to build himself a new and happy country.

The strongest representatives of the Third Front in terms of artistic achievement were the poet Salomėja Neris (1904–45) and the novelist and short-story writer Petras Cvirka (1909–47). Salomėja Neris was drawn into the movement more or less by mistake, since her deeply lyrical and feminine poetry, vibrant with warm personal feeling, had little to do with the political tenets of Marxism. Cvirka, on the other hand, did commit himself, both ideologically and as an artist, to class struggle, to impassioned social protest. His novel *Frank Kruk*, for instance, depicts the adventures of a ruthless and amoral young peasant who emigrates to the United States, makes a fortune by bootlegging and other chicanery during the Depression, and finally returns to Lithuania only to be cheated out of all his money by the vulgar and unscrupulous new Lithuanian bourgeoisie. Important members of the Third Front were also the literary critic Kostas Korsakas (born 1909) and the poet Antanas Venclova (born 1906). Korsakas, Cvirka, Venclova, and also Teofilis Tilvytis formed, in effect, the nucleus of the new Soviet Lithuanian literature after the Russians returned in 1944.

The Four Winds and Third Front were the strongest explicit literary movements in which some central ideological, social, or political conception of the purposes of art played a dominant role. There were other groups and other publications, but the people who belonged to them made their mark more as individuals than as representatives of some clear-cut ideology. Literature had come of age in the sense that art itself, as an embodiment of a personal vision of reality, became a matter of primary concern. Strong talents came to the fore in both prose and poetry, which were inspired for the most part no longer by the Russian literary movements but by the accumulated indigenous tradition and by current trends in western Europe.

An interesting blend of these two elements, plus a very personal propensity for a kind of Christian medievalism, can be seen in the poetry of Bernardas Brazdžionis (born 1907), now living in the United States, whose work is discussed in Chapter 15. The folk heritage gives his verse an aura of romantic lyricism in which patriotic motifs grew especially dominant after he was forced to contemplate the tragic fate of his country from the perspective of exile. Western romanticism and expressionism introduced an element of exalted, impassioned rhetoric, combined with the tendency, especially at the beginning, to seek unusual, even mannered, modes of poetic expression.

The central core of Brazdžionis' poetry, however, concerns his intimate portrayals of religious experience. The frequent biblical references in his books create a feeling not only of Christian devotion but also of an exotic, romantic longing for some dimly perceived, intensely desired, ultimate home for the soul. This mood is especially strengthened by his skillful handling of rhythm, syntax, and word repetitions, and by fine sensitivity for the musical qualities of words. Brazdžionis seldom tries to discover what are the poetic qualities of "unadorned" reality, as it presents itself to the observing eye. Instead, he treats both broad landscapes and minute details of nature as stage settings for his poetic drama of faith and longing. It is this faith—the fundamental conviction that the process of living is but a journey toward eternity—that fills his verse with the wonder and beauty of existence made meaningful by the all-pervading, hidden presence of God. Loving the earth with a gentle nostalgia for eternity, he loves his country, too, almost as if it were a wayside chapel, hundreds of which dot the Lithuanian countryside, built by peasant hands. His tragedy in exile is that, having always believed, when he was still at home, that the brief span of a man's life has meaning and purpose leading to God, he is now forced to wander aimlessly among alien roads that go nowhere in particular. For this reason, his late poetry becomes filled with bitter, unyielding sorrow and desperate longing to return to Lithuania, which, his faith tells him, will one day be free again. His earlier poetry, collected in such books as *Ženklai ir stebuklai* (*Signs and Wonders*), 1936, *Kunigaikščių miestas* (*The City of Princes*), 1939, or *Per pasaulį keliauja žmogus* (*A Man Goes Traveling Through the World*), 1943—a collection representing selected poems from the total body of his verse up to that time—continues to hold the reader by the magic of humble and lyrical faith. But his efforts to meet the new and, to him, incomprehensible reality of exile, in *Svetimi kalnai* (*Alien Mountains*), 1945, or in *Šiaurės pašvaistė* (*The Northern Lights*), 1947, or in later books, have found relatively little response in the new generation of Lithuanian writers abroad, whose young age and early contact with world-wide literary movements have endowed them with a more philosophical and universal point of view.

Antanas Miškinis (born 1905) brought to perfection a special quality of Lithuanian lyric poetry which comes from highly personal and creative adaptation of the poetic texture of folk songs combined with romantic and patriotic love for the homeland and with faith in its future. He preferred the pure, instinctively lyrical and humble qualities of the soul ascribed by loving poets to the Lithuanian peasant, to the presumed amoralism, surface sophistication, and essential vulgarity of the urban bourgeoisie. The main collections of Miškinis' poems are *Varnos prie plento* (*Crows by the Highway*), 1935, and *Keturi miestai* (*Four Cities*), 1938. Miškinis remained in Lithuania after 1944 and made no effort to hide anti-Soviet feelings. As a result, he was deported to Siberia. He came back a broken man and the little he now writes is in the conforming spirit of "socialist realism."

Jonas Aistis (born 1904), who is discussed in Chapter 4, is certainly one of the most outstanding poets of what was the younger generation in independent Lithuania between the two world wars. Having spent considerable time in western Europe, especially France, he absorbed many of the techniques of modern French poetry, combining these with his own adaptations of the spirit and diction of Lithuanian folklore. Among the Lithuanian poets he is perhaps the most painfully aware of the agonizing distance between poetic conception and the actual written word—an awareness that often leads him to brood darkly upon the seeming helplessness of the artist when confronted with his own inner worlds demanding expression in the idiom of art.

Another significant poet is Kazys Boruta (born 1905), a friend of freedom and bold singer of human dignity. His clear and firm convictions have gotten him into trouble with both the Lithuanian regime and the Soviets (he has been imprisoned by both), but Boruta remains even today in full possession of his personal integrity.

Turning again to prose, one might acknowledge first of all a new voice coming from the so-called Lithuania Minor—the Lithuanian ethnic minority living in East Prussia and in the Klaipėda (Memel) district—in the work of Ieva Simonaitytė (born 1897). This area had not contributed anything more of importance to Lithuanian letters since Kristijonas Donelaitis, except for the contemplative writings of Vilius Starosta-Vydūnas (1868–1943). Vydūnas was a spokesman for the principle of "inner light" in man, that is, the perfection of human self-awareness sought especially by the oriental philosophers. Vydūnas also wrote historical drama in verse which, however, is not particularly distinguished for its literary qualities. Ieva Simonaitytė achieved recognition for her novel *Aukštujų Šimonių likimas* (*The Fate of the Šimonys of Aukštujai*), 1935, in which she traced the life of several generations of a noble Lithuania Minor family through wars and natural calamities. The family is under the constant pressure of the German element, which ultimately engulfs and absorbs its last remnants. The novel could be called an example of "regional romanticism." It contains all the patriotic sentiments seen in the work of writers in Lithuania proper, but presents them from a local point of view and with a tragic sense of ultimate defeat and extinction instead of the resurrection that illuminates the future of other Lithuanians. Simonaitytė writes with great sensitivity to the idiom and spirit of her own people and with a kind of somber, aristocratic dignity of style that elevates the lives of her characters to the dimension of poetic experience filled with the dark beauty of sorrow.

Perhaps the most western-oriented Lithuanian novelist of the independence period was Ignas Jurkūnas-Šeinius (1889–1959). Most of his life was spent abroad, mainly in Sweden. The Scandinavian impressionism, seen in the work of Knut Hamsun, for instance, was close to Šeinius' spirit even before he went to Sweden. Under its influence he became the foremost Lithuanian impressionist. His most important work is the short story "Kuprelis" ("The Hunchback"), first published in the United States in 1913. It tells the tale of a gifted dreamer, disfigured by nature, who is devoted to the life of the mind but doomed to vegetate as a mill-keeper in a remote province. The romantic appeal of the story thus issues from the double tension—between the desire for personal happiness and the physical deformity that prevents it and between intellectual yearning and gray reality.

In the novel *Siegfried Immerselbe atsijaunina* (*Siegfried Immerselbe Rejuvenates Himself*), 1934, Šeinius bitterly ridiculed the Nazi theories of racism. The plot line concerns an old Nazi who, feeling that his vitality is gone, rejuvenates himself by accepting, unknowingly, a transfusion of blood from a young, vigorous Jew. This operation not only makes him young again but improves all his mental and physical capacities much beyond the level of his own former youth. It is interesting that Šeinius attacked the Nazi movement at this early date, when by no means all European intellectuals had as yet fully understood its nature.

After the war Šeinius remained in Sweden to his death, writing a number of short stories in both Lithuanian and Swedish and a large novel, *Raudonasis potvynis ateina* (*The Red Deluge Is Coming*), 1941, depicting the Soviet takeover of Lithuania, in a manner approaching the current "nonfiction" novel in America.

A special place in the development of Lithuanian literature belongs to the novelist and short-story writer Antanas Vaičiulaitis (born 1906) and the poet Henrikas Radauskas (born 1910). Both are discussed in the present book. They have been called, somewhat inaccurately, the representatives of "estheticism" because the perfection of form in their art supposedly takes precedence over content. Actually, it might be better to say that content, for them, is a function of form; that is, an idea has no recognizable identity until it acquires precise outlines in its expression. To put it another way, the manner of saying something constitutes the core of what is being said. This means that utmost care is required in the choice of words and of every artistic device in order not to distort, or diminish, the original creative conception. Vaičiulaitis strives for such perfection through the symmetry of design and clear, classical simplicity of style in his prose, and Radauskas, through perfect balance in the interplay of subtle and complex shadings in the rhythm, thought, image, and melody of his poems.

In prose one should mention especially the contribution of Jurgis Savickis (1890–1952), by profession a diplomat who had spent considerable time in western Europe. His short stories are noted for their sardonic elegance of style and clear, cool understanding of both the weaknesses of men and the excellence of some of their aspirations. The stories "The Red Shoes" and "A Battle" have been translated into English. Juozas Grušas (born 1901) published among other things an excellent collection of short stories called *Sunki ranka* (*The Heavy Hand*), 1937, and a novel *Karjeristai* (*The Careerists*), 1935. After the Second World War, Grušas turned his attention to drama and has now become the most prominent playwright in Soviet Lithuania. Other prose writers are Liudas Dovydėnas (born 1905), a realistic critic of life, Jurgis Jankus (born 1906), a master storyteller, and Vincas Ramonas (born 1905), a novelist and delicate craftsman of landscapes with children playing in them.

There was, on the whole, no great development in the genre of drama in the pre-war period after the plays of Vincas Krėvė and Balys Sruoga. New and original playwrights such as Kostas Ostrauskas and Algirdas Landsbergis appeared only in exile, after the war.

This discussion has now reached the point where Lithuanian literature splits, as it were, into two separately functioning entities, one of them being the literature of exile, and the other the literature of Soviet Lithuania. This latter body of literature will not be described here, not because there are no talented and significant writers but because the

Soviet situation presents a set of topics and issues best discussed in another context. The majority of the important expatriate writers have been included in the following collection of essays, so not much else remains to be said, except, perhaps, for a few remarks concerning the basic situation of the Lithuanian émigré writer.

The most important, overwhelming fact to which every writer must in some way respond is the fact of exile itself. It represents a traumatic experience of tremendous magnitude not only in personal terms but also in terms of literary work, because a writer cannot escape the knowledge that he no longer stands on his own soil, where he would belong in a historical continuum with what had been accomplished before. He knows he is working in a context in which the written Lithuanian word is, in an important sense, an irrelevance. His readers are his fellow exiles; as they die off or become absorbed into the foreign culture, the whole body of expatriate literature begins to disintegrate, for literature is actually not so much a poem, novel, or story, but communication—that which happens when the minds of the author and the reader meet.

On the other hand, if the writer is willing to fling the act of creation, like a challenge, into the very teeth of oblivion, the experience of exile may well contribute new dimensions to his art. There is a resemblance between home and prison; they both surround a person with four walls, encouraging the illusion that the world ends where they do. The holocaust of war blew down the walls of home, making us both naked and free. It was a tragic liberation, but it did open new horizons, new countries, new civilizations, new ways of perceiving and understanding things.

Some writers refused this challenge and remained safely inside the walls of what they persist even now in believing is their home, although it has lost all material substance. There are many novels, short stories, and poems being written now, amid the noise and bustle of the great American cities, in which the quiet brooks of the homeland keep on flowing, and the trees rustle, and old neighbors from a village, not knowing that they have become mere ghosts, come over and shake your hand.

Other writers, however, decided to face the new reality as well as they could and to search for new forms and ideas which would make their work meaningful in terms of the new situation. Most of these writers were still relatively young when they compiled, in 1951, an anthology of their works called *Žemė* (*Earth*) and, somewhat later, created the literary journal *Literatūros lankai* (*The Literary Folios*), published in Buenos Aires between 1952 and 1959 but representing almost exclusively authors living in the United States. They did not proclaim any manifestoes; what they did was to explain that their work must now be concerned with deep existential questions, that it must respond to those currents in Western thought which profess that not only members of small downtrodden nations but the world as a whole is facing spiritual exile from all the systems of values that up to now have constituted civilization. Among these writers were Kazys Bradūnas, Alfonsas Nyka-Niliūnas, and Henrikas Nagys, all discussed in this book. But the person who contributed most to bringing this group together is Juozas Kėkštas (born 1915), a poet of the pure sorrow of exile who later went to live in Poland. Actually, the new philosophical directions in Lithuanian art had their beginnings at home, with the work of Vytautas Mačernis (1920–45), the author of a profoundly contemplative cycle of poems called "Visions." He was known personally by most members of what later became the *Žemė* collective. One might venture to say, therefore, that even without the shock of exile Lithuanian literature might have entered upon some radically new path, although the nature of it can only be guessed.

Among the writers discussed in the present book who, although they did not originally belong to the *Žemė* collective, have followed similar directions in their art, are Algirdas Landsbergis, Antanas Škėma, Kostas Ostrauskas, and Algimantas Mackus. All of them, especially the first three, did contribute to *The Literary Folios*. Others are Liūnė Sutema (born 1927), a contemplative and lyrical poet immersed in painful redefinitions of her own identity and her relationship with the alien universe; Julius Kaupas (1920–64), an author of charming, whimsical, but also deeply probing fairy tales who also wrote short stories and perceptive literary criticism; and, possibly, Kazys Kęstutis Almėnas (born 1935), although he represents a much younger generation which, being no longer subject to the trauma of exile, not really feeling itself a stranger in the adopted land, has been able to regard both its Lithuanian heritage and the new surroundings with a more detached view.

Others have taken different directions in writing in exile. Jurgis Gliauda (born 1906) has been well received by American readers with his novel *House Upon the Sand*, 1951, translated into English, which deals with life in Germany under the Nazis. His latest significant work is the "nonfiction" novel *Agonija* (*The Agony*), 1966, which describes the tragic events that culminated in the loss of Lithuanian independence. Nelė Mazalaitė (born 1907) is popular with her readers for her sentimental, poetic novels, short stories, and legends in which great and tragic love of her homeland is expressed in beautiful, emotionally intense language. Jurgis Blekaitis (born 1917), an actor, director, and prolific playwright, popular for his lively plays dealing with various facets of the pre-war Lithuanian society, continues to produce both drama and literary criticism. Vladas Šlaitas (born 1920) is a contemplative poet concerned with the tragedy of war and with golden memories of home in Lithuania. Antanas Gustaitis (born 1907) is widely known for his humorous verse ruthlessly criticizing the assorted human frailties of the exiled Lithuanian community.

Many more writers are continuing their work in exile, often along the same lines they had followed at home, sometimes striking out in new directions. The literary life in exile is, in fact, very rich and varied in spite of the adverse conditions surrounding it. Whatever its ultimate destiny may be, the expatriate Lithuanian community, at least for the present, shows a good deal of vitality and a strong sense of cultural identity.

2 Henrikas Radauskas—the Passion of the Intellect

Henrikas Radauskas was born April 23, 1910, in Cracow, Poland. After the war, when his family returned to Lithuania, Radauskas attended high school and a teachers' institute, then took up the study of Lithuanian, German, and Russian literatures in the University of Kaunas, 1930–34. In 1936 he was a radio announcer in Klaipėda (Memel), then, between 1937 and 1941, an editor in the Commission on book publishing of the Lithuanian Ministry of Education.

Having spent the war years in Berlin and Reutlingen, Germany, Radauskas came to the United States in 1949. After a decade of manual labor, he joined the Library of Congress in 1959 and remained there until he died in August, 1970. He was a member of the PEN International Writers' Club.

His poetry has been collected in: *Fontanas* (*The Fountain*), 1935; *Strėlė danguje* (*Arrow in the Sky*), 1950; *Žiemos daina* (*The Winter Song*), 1955; and *Žaibai ir vėjai* (*Lightnings and Winds*), 1965. Selected poems from all the above books came out under the title *Eilėraščiai* (*Poems*) in 1965. Radauskas' poetry has been translated into Latvian, English, German, Finnish, and Estonian. He himself has translated Jurgis Baltrušaitis, Boris Pasternak, Anna Akhmatova, Julian Tuwim, Heine, Goethe, and Verlaine into Lithuanian.

THERE is poetry for which the reader must reach out, which becomes rewarding only if we are willing to confront reality on the poet's own terms. In Lithuanian literature, such poetry is written by Henrikas Radauskas. By reputation he is a highly respected but somewhat remote figure, inhabiting the ivory tower of an intellectual estheticism. An attentive look at his work, however, will reveal the insufficiency of such a notion. The distinguishing characteristic of Radauskas' verse, one that ultimately makes the greatest impact, is not the intricacy of abstract design, at first so striking to the eye, but the intense and vibrant emotion at all levels of structure and meaning. Radauskas combines his firm commitment to formal esthetic values with a great concern for the emotional immediacy of communication. A conventional attitude, which holds these two purposes in art to be opposed to each other, no longer presents an adequate approach to Radauskas' poetry. We must learn to understand that there exists in poetry a passion of the intellect, very similar to that of a theoretical physicist pressing against the edge of the unknown, and that the white heat of this passion throws another light upon the nature and function of art.

The question seems to be, how can one believe in art for its own sake without denying its relevance to life in general? One answer might be that the question itself is false, that art can only be relevant to human reality if it is accepted as an independent, self-determining value. This requires a second look at the traditional and still widely accepted description of art as an imitation of life. Such an idea tends to relegate art to the inferior status of a game, a fictional, "esthetic" variant of the direct, and therefore presumably authentic, experience of reality, which is then understood to be the proper concern of all "serious" human activity. It also carries with it the implication that art, in order to be meaningful, must contribute something to this "real" life, that it must serve some purpose other than its own. A different way to think of art would be to regard it as a function of the human mind fully equivalent to such disciplines as philosophy or science, since it also translates the given facts of outside reality into the inner, specifically human, categories of thought and feeling, working, as these disciplines do, with concepts and images, seeking both knowledge and vision. A philosopher, for instance, does not imitate reality but subjects it to logical processes of thought in the hope of attaining the knowledge of truth. This same knowledge is also the aim of art, but what matters to the poet is less the objective existence than the poetic significance of fact. This means that truth, for him, is a unique personal experience, created in his own mind from the interplay among beauty, feeling, and thought, between form and content. Such an attitude toward his task sets the poet free from servitude to truths or assertions proclaimed in spheres other than his own. He may thus produce art which ignores political events, refuses the consolations of faith, seems at times insane when judged by what we know of the laws of nature and logic, and still constitutes an achievement valid in all aspects of life, consistent with and true to itself.

Henrikas Radauskas strives in his poetry toward such personal experience of truth, toward the creation of a special universe relevant to but separate from outside reality, effecting this separation first of all by means of imagery. An observed fact of nature, for instance, may become important not in itself, and not even because of an idea or a feeling it might evoke, but as the nucleus of an esthetic creation of the imagination. Thus the lines "And trees are weighing molten gold / On scales of shimmering emerald" neither distort nor imitate nature but create instead a gold and emerald glory of their own, built on the precise observation that the sun, enmeshed in tree branches, will suffuse the leaves with gold on a summer day made magic by the touch of wind. In another image, "All through the garden runs the rain / On thin and brittle legs of glass," the illusion of fine streaks that seem to follow each raindrop deceive the poet's eye long enough to be transferred by him into the realm of his art, where they acquire their own permanent reality as the component parts of a very special rain conjured up in the poet's fancy.

The short poem "Landscape," from the collection *Strėlė danguje* (*Arrow in the Sky*), uses the round heads of trees as the starting point of an expanding poetic image that ultimately rolls up the whole landscape into a kind of glass ball and smashes it with catastrophic force against its own reflection in the water:

> In dense, Italian heavens blue
> Two trees are rolling, round as balls,
> And glassy, slippery winds are ringing
> Around the two trees, singing green.
> The landscape rolls downhill to river
> And splashes into sun and sky,
> While in the leaves, a lost ray of sun,
> Like a yellow chicken, chirps alone.

The observed phenomena of nature—the glassy transparence of a clear evening sky and the moving, round-headed treetops—create their own music in the wind, expressed in the counterpoint of blue and green. Because of this, they cease to belong to outer reality; the poet has transferred them to his own domain, enriching the indigenous universe of his art. Similarly, the river's face, rippled by the breeze, becomes an image of the world's destruction, complete with its orphans, and as such it is again subject to the poet's own destructive whim and not to nature's laws.

The same transference is effected in terms of emotion. Feelings known to us in daily life do not enter Radauskas' verse unchanged but are transformed into component parts of the general artistic design. Thus in the poem "Shepherd's Pipe," from *Žiemos daina* (*The Winter Song*), the nostalgic memory of childhood and the sad understanding of the language of death become integrated into the visual descriptions of a landscape dominated by the symbolic presence of a shepherd's pipe:

> How morning stone is glittering!
> How time is running down the branches!
> Thus speaks an unknown shepherd boy
> To us, through music of his pipe.
>
> These are the songs of branches cut
> That come in swarms of springtimes past.
> The cries of willows, to whose tune
> You danced in youth on river's edge,
> Have worn you out; there was a wave,
> Though barely felt, which pushed you on:
> Another pipe, just freshly cut
> From warm and blooming bark of trees.

This poem, like the one quoted before, is enveloped in its own kind of music, which helps define the quality of the emotion assimilated into the poet's own reality.

At other times the nature of the feeling is determined by sharp and cutting images which slash and tear the fabric of life in the process of transferring it into the realm of art. The night sky, for instance, becomes poetic because of the wounds inflicted upon it by the author's imagination: "The incurable wounds of the stars / Through the springtime are looking at us." The pine trees in the morning "impale each dewdrop on their needles." And the red reflection of the sunset on a puddle just beginning to freeze over in the autumn produces the following image: "With the first knives of silver, the autumn / Has slaughtered itself in the puddles." One poem, "The Harbor," from *The Winter Song*, is a sort of study of the various ways in which the sunlight in a harbor on a bright day can be made to appear as an inexhaustible source of glittering, cutting, wounding instruments of pain. Part of the first stanza will serve as an example:

> Enclosed in midday, like a diamond,
> My eyes on seashore lose their sight.
> A holiday of cruel light—
> Replete with nails and glass and daggers—
> Who will extend a helping hand?

In this way, fear and pain become integrated with material objects in the poetic image. (Some have also seen the frightened loneliness of an exile in this poem.) At times the cutting, wounding images are further elaborated by the introduction of literary or mythological dimensions. Thus the poem "Epilogue," from the collection *Žaibai ir vėjai* (*Lightnings and Winds*), combines landscape, emotion, and Goethe's *Faust* to conjure up the troubled face of death. In the first stanza the atmosphere of evil and mourning is spun from purple clouds and the names of Faust and Mefisto:

> Devil took the morning cloud,
> Studded it with purple fire.
> Mephistopheles and Faust
> Walked in spirit by my side.

Thus conceived, the landscape proceeds in the next stanza to develop into an image of violence, recalling the death of Marguerite's brother Valentin, pierced by the devil's power and the sword of Faust. The sunrise then becomes an ironic symbol of an inevitable though inadvertent tragedy brought forth by man's love and yearning:

> Faust is seeking Marguerite,
> Will go on for a hundred years.

> Morning dies like a wounded soldier,
> Crying, stabbed by a piercing branch.

The visual source of this image is a naked tree branch against the backdrop of a large and blood-red sun. The poem thus seems to acquire an element of fatalism, for the sun must rise, and the branches will be there, and therefore (the point of the image) men will murder in their search for love, or at least the devil will make sure they do. As the poem proceeds, the devil's dark power conquers nature completely, changing the very same sun and trees into an image of the triumph of evil, which calls to mind some terrible pagan deity of ancient Egypt, its head adorned by the solar disk between the horns:

> Devil's work has now been done,
> Sunrise hangs between the horns,
> Multicolored, like a parrot,
> Morning jumps from branch to branch.

In Radauskas' poetry the parrot is occasionally used as an ominous, ironic, and, in a way, repulsive symbol representing the many-hued disintegration of the bright hopes of men and even sometimes of their lives. The parrot seems to embody the raucous stupidity and gaudiness of evil, as if it were a modern image of the mythological harpies. After such parrot-mocked and devil-borne landscape, the poem shifts its emphasis to Marguerite, her shame, and finally her death. Again the content fulfills itself in the image:

> Marguerite is calling God,
> Fearful of the sins of love.
> God gives a meadow to the maiden,
> Blossom-stained and spotted all.

The final stanza introduces one more medium of poetic expression. In addition to landscape, feeling, and literary allusion, we now have a foreign language. Unlike T. S. Eliot or Ezra Pound, for instance, who will weave single words or expressions from various languages into the texture of their poems, Radauskas constructs the whole final stanza entirely in German:

Auf der Wiese tanzen Maedchen,
Jedes wiegt ein totes Kind.
Glaubst du wirklich, liebes Gretchen,
Dass die Toten froehlich sind?

There might be several ways of responding to this sudden introduction of a completely alien idiom. First of all, it intensifies the shock caused by the emergence of the *danse macabre* of death as the dominant theme. Death is, in a sense, quite unthinkable in words that are "our own," that is, words which fill our living consciousness. An altogether different language seems necessary to convey the reality of nonbeing to us, because we consist entirely of our own existence. In modern literature (for instance, in Samuel Beckett) a similar effect is sometimes achieved by artists using their own language in ways which suddenly seem nonsensical but precisely through the destruction of logic convey the imponderable with dreadful clarity. Secondly, becaue of the fact that German was Gretchen's own familiar and native idiom, we are made to understand the most terrible thing of all about death—that, unthinkable and absolutely alien though it may be, it is also the most intimate and constant, the most personal presence in our lives. In the light of all these thoughts, the final question of the poem, "Do you really think, dear Gretchen, that the dead are happy?" pierces the mind with a peculiar, indescribable force of irony.

Occasionally, in assimilating objects and emotions into the special domain of art, Radauskas combines vocabulary and references which belong to well-established tradition of poetic diction with those taken from ordinary "nonpoetic" language. A small-town hardware shop may in this way become the scene of a truly classic tragedy of human solitude. The short poem "The Salesgirl," from *Arrow in the Sky*, describes the sorrow of a young girl forsaken by her lover. In the second stanza there is a sudden blending of "poetic" and "prosaic" imagery:

The castles fell, the legends died.
The town is flooded by the autumn.
And in the shop—just horseshoes, ropes,
And nails, and nails, and nails, and nails.

The sharp pain of these pointed nails, piercing every moment of the girl's existence, not only provides a counterpoint to the romantic world of ruined castles and dreams but also fills the poem with tragic cadences comparable, perhaps, in their own way, to Shakespeare's "Never, never, never, never, never." An earlier book of Radauskas' verse, *Fontanas* (*The Fountain*), contains a similar poem, called "The Old Maid," in which the conventional "elevated" language of lyric poets is combined with down-to-earth expressions in such stanzas as the following:

> I am alone. O star-borne spears!
> Do kill my painful longing!
> Ah, I should have gotten married
> At least to that bald-headed oldster.

There is a note of cruel humor in this "inappropriate" juxtaposition of clashing images. Radauskas makes repeated use of such effects in his verse. In the poem "The Record Player," from *Arrow in the Sky*, the sweet and tragic strains of *La Traviata* are combined unmercifully with the noise of the primus stove. The result is lines such as these:

> Each evening, when the lady of the house
> Starts boiling tea on the little primus stove—
> Consumptive Violetta, in the opera *La Traviata,*
> Together with the primus, sings of death.
>
> This puts the master of the house in a pleasant mood;
> He likes strong tea and gentle music.

On a different plane, these contrasts are worked out into Radauskas' own restatement of the ancient theme of sacred and profane love. "Evening in Naples," from *The Winter Song*, combines the two loves by means of a landscape suffused with the reddish color of passion and blood:

> Having drunk of Lacrimae Christi,
> He goes out and falls through misty
> Depths of red-stained evening sky,
> Where the winds are walking high.
>
> O bella Napoli!

He's to Venus coming back now,
He's forgotten amore sacro.
Reddish lips, and reddish boats,
Reddish smoke from mountain floats.

O amore profano!

In his ascent and his decline
Touches he the limbs divine.
Through the nails and through the thorns
Gently, reddish fire returns.

O amore sacro e profano!

The whole poem is a series of contrasts on several levels, held together by the constant color of red which, as it passes through multiple realities, acquires a number of different meanings. To begin with, the pink Italian landscape suggests both blood and roses and is itself an embodiment of the combined pagan and Christian heritage of the land. Only such a country could innocently conceive of the irony of naming a wine the "tears of Christ." The fall of man intoxicated by both the wine and the meaning of its name includes the idea of heaven stained in turn by the red clouds rising from volcanoes of passion as carnal as it is divine. The rise and fall of man become united in a single experience, literally embodied in the pagan limbs of the profane love goddess Venus, which then become transfigured into the bleeding limbs of Christ, burning with the fire of heavenly love. In a way, this poem is reminiscent of Dmitry Karamazov's passionate commitment to the idea of Sodom as well as that of the Madonna, except that Dostoevsky's intense and rather rambling argument is here replaced by the disciplined structure of a poem designed to incorporate the given landscape within the idea.

Radauskas perfects his transformation of life into art by the formal devices of prosody, especially by subtle and melodious organization of sound repetitions combined with rhythmic effects. It is very difficult to discuss these aspects of his poetry in English because, even if it were possible to translate the poems in such a way as to make the patterns of sound significant, the effects would pertain only to the translation. What we often see in the original is an interplay of meaning and sound not unlike the one accidentally achieved in translating the line quoted previously, "And trees are weighing *molten gold* / On scales of *shimmering emerald*," although in the original the sound pattern is different:

> O medžiai *sver*ia aukso lydini
> *Svar*styklėm *vir*pančio *smar*agdo.

The interrelationship among meaning, rhythm, and sound organization might be illustrated by another line from Radauskas:

> Mane *nuliūd*ino ta *ru*denio diena.

There are two main progressions of sounds. The first one can be identified by the consonant *n* and the vowels surrounding it:

> Mane nuliūdino ta rudenio diena.

As the line goes on, this cluster is strengthened by the additional consonant *d*. This consonant provides the link with the second progression characterized by the vowel *u* and its surrounding consonants:

> Mane *nuliūd*ino ta *rud*enio diena.

This second progression dominates the sound of the line, because in two positions the vowel *u* carries a strong stress. Therefore, the complete disappearance of this vowel in the final word, dieną́, although the "connecting consonant" *d* is still there, results in a sudden emphasis on an entirely different vowel, *a*, thus changing the sound "color" completely at the end of the line. The stress pattern, in formal scansion is a six-foot iambic

> Mané / nuliū / dino / ta rú / denio / dieną́

in which the third and fifth feet are pyrrhic. These pyrrhic feet contain the clusters of the first sound progression:

> -dino, -denio.

The final stressed word, dieną́, also represents the same sound cluster. Consequently, this first progression increases in importance, while the second, consisting of the "*n* cluster," is subject to atrophy. The same atrophy can be perceived in intonational groupings. Notwithstanding the formal iambic scansion, there are in actuality only three dominant stresses, each organizing around itself a regularly diminishing group of syllables:

mane nuliū́dino (6 syll.)

ta rúdenio (4 syll.)

and, finally,

dieną́ (2 syll.).

These groups also constitute three sense units. The first one means "I was made sad," the second, "by this autumn," and the third, "day."

The translation contains nothing of the intricate interplay among formal and intonational meters, the two progressions of sounds, and the meaning of the line. What we get in English is a flat, one-dimensional statement, weakening both the sense and the emotion to the point of insignificance. Yet it is precisely this integration of feeling with sound, image, objects, and rhythm which constitutes one of the main achievements of Radauskas' poetry. To try another example, the two lines

Lelíjų línijoms lengvóms prilýgt galí,

Ó melanchólija šio vákaro tylí

might, with some distortion of sense, be rendered in English as "Light lines of lilies may be likened to your lilt. / O melancholy over silent evening spilt." The concept of "melancholy" is important not as an emotion with a meaning circumscribed in reality existing outside of art but as a poetic feeling that continues into the sound of other words and therefore passes on to them some of its own quality, while, in turn, acquiring the properties of all the words that constitute the esthetic entity of the line. Therefore it becomes possible to speak of melancholy having the physical outlines of a lily, belonging to the silence of the evening, and embodied phonetically in the repeated liquid sound of *l*.

Thus the sounds of words, their meanings, the emotions they evoke, and the objects described by them become something other than themselves as they enter through the gates of the author's imagination into his special poetic universe. It is a universe in which all images can become interchangeable because they are all directed toward the central purpose of naming the new insight which changes the nature of reality. The description by Boris Pasternak of the special experience from which art is born may also be applicable to the poetry of Radauskas:

> We cease to recognize reality. It appears to us as some new category. This category seems to be a condition inherent in reality itself and not in us. Aside from this condition, everything in the world has its name. It alone has no name. We try to give it a name. The result is art.

What are the names given by Radauskas to the new condition of reality made manifest at the moment of inspiration? Or, to put it differently, how many aspects of itself does the world reveal when observed through the prism of his poetic medium? In a sense, such a question is so broad as to be practically meaningless, for obviously each poem is a reality unto itself, containing in its turn a multitude of concepts and emotions, so that there is, potentially, an infinite variety of experiences. Nevertheless, it might be possible to generalize these multiple impressions into several related, but distinct, visions of the world in Radauskas' poetry. Some of them are explicitly described in a poem called "Arrow in the Sky" from the collection with the same title. The poem presents three different self-portraits of the artist, each of them connected with the others by the image of the flying arrow. The first stanza (in the translation by Theodore Melnechuk) reads as follows:

> I am an arrow that a child shot through
> An apple tree in bloom beside the sea;
> A cloud of apple blossoms, like a swan,
> Has shimmered down and landed on a wave;
> The child is wondering, he cannot tell
> The blossom from the foam.

The general impression here is one of pure beauty in which things have lost their own properties to become part of an esthetic continuum. Such an experience requires a child's ability to wonder at the world, at the marvelous, unsuspected things that can happen to reality when it is touched or pierced by the light of imagination. The "game" of art here returns to its original premises of magic and of play. This particular vision in Radauskas' poems is often enveloped in a soft, lyrical haze; images and feelings blend imperceptibly in the smooth and melodious flow of the verse. Beauty reveals itself to us in the metamorphosis of given outside facts into the inner music of the mind, while, in turn, idea and emotion themselves become esthetic categories as they are shaped into the created fact of a poem.

The second stanza continues the connecting image of the arrow, but now the effect is altogether different:

> I am an arrow that a hunter shot
> To hit an eagle that was flying by;
> For all his strength and youth he missed the bird,
> Wounding instead the old enormous sun
> And flooding all the twilight with its blood;
>   And now the day has died.

The comparison of poetic inspiration with a hunt implies an essentially catastrophic vision—that art is the result of a violent encounter between reality and the imagination in which the world becomes the poet's victim, his prey. Like a hunter, the poet pursues beauty and, like a hunter, he can take possession of it only by destroying its embodiment in the world around him. In this kind of artistic experience creation must of necessity resemble destruction, because there is no way to build an image without obliterating the perception of reality which suggests it—thus do the evening colors turn to blood. These "catastrophic" poems do not, however, convey a mood of failure and despair. Instead they are full of wild, Dionysiac, sometimes cruel, more often both cruel and joyful, passion for life. It seems as if the poet, in profound agreement with nature, has gladly embraced the inevitability of death as one of the processes by which new life is produced and sustained, even if, in art, new life must exist in a different, and perhaps imaginary, dimension.

A different kind of death—a barren presence, the visage of cosmic solitude—meets us in the final stanza of the poem:

> I am an arrow that was shot at night
> By a crazed soldier from a fort besieged
> To plead for help from mighty heaven, but
> Not having spotted God, the arrow still
> Wanders among the frigid constellations,
> Not daring to return.

In many of Radauskas' poems we can read the implication that beauty, conceived in lyrical dreams, born of a metamorphosis resembling destruction, is a lost and lonely thing. He dismisses the illusion that the insights of art can reveal the presence of any ultimate metaphysical truth. Art may speak the language of faith, as well as of despair, but actually it is something else altogether, and there is no way to be comforted or reassured by the miracle of its word.

We can see that in all three of its aspects Radauskas' poetry consists, in essence, of a complex series of transformations in which we witness art "describing its own birth," as Pasternak once put it. The visions of art as beauty, as violence, and as the empty image of death are all connected by the dynamics of the creative impulse—the flight of the arrow. We should think of Radauskas' poetry primarily as an expression of movement, even when a particular poem seems, at the first glance, concerned only with reproducing static images of "pure beauty." We may take as an example the poem "The Midday of Babes," from *The Fountain*, which describes a quiet lake in the midday sun:

> Sparkling, shimmering spirals of the sun
> Walk around in depths of the quiet lake,
> Where, with green and tender hands of grass
> Wave to us the secrets of the babes.
>
> In the zenith, blue and blinded eyes
> Hover over shivers of the deep,
> Where the spirals of the molten gold
> Spread and sparkle, meaningless and slow.
>
> All the reeds, and midday, and the deer,
> Watch with blank, uncomprehending eyes
> How so slow the golden millstone turns
> In the midst of secrets light and green.

This description is poetic mainly because it contains a movement of image and emotion, a hidden tension with an implied significance that far exceeds the possibilities of the landscape itself. The dynamics of the poem begin with the choice of the spiral rather than, say, a circle as the image describing sunlight penetrating the surface of the lake. A circle is static, self-enclosed, but a spiral leads us either up or down, through a potentially infinite number of levels, each of which may signify a new dimension of experience. Here the movement is downward, into the depths, and its implied infinitude creates the aura of some dark, unfathomable mystery toward which we are descending along the golden, spiral stairway of the sun. At this point Radauskas confronts us with the irony of surprise; instead of some awesome presence, perhaps a mythical monster of the depths who would become the terrible fulfillment of all our secret fears, we meet the gently waving hands of babes, soft and innocent, the keepers of the mystery. If the poem were to proceed to the revelation of some reassuring truth, the image of the babes would blend with perfect logic into the euphoria of happiness and knowledge that the world is good. Instead of this, however, we are confronted with another paradox; there may be mystery, but there is no meaning. And meaninglessness is precisely what every instinct of man cries out against. A babe thus becomes the embodiment of the unthinkable; its very sweetness is now grotesque almost beyond imagination.

We realize with a shock that Radauskas has used this image to suggest that there are secrets which a babe will know but for which the figure of a monster is not a terrible enough representation. Innocence knows the truth, and this truth, in the poem, resides in the disappointment of our essential need for meaning, even if it were too terrible to bear. The romantic imagination would much prefer to conceive of life as being evil and dreadful rather than simply meaningless. It would therefore impose its own monsters upon nature; hence the weird and bloody creatures of the Gothic tales. Radauskas, however, is a realist in the sense that he lets the facts themselves provide the starting point and determine the nature of his idea. There are no dragons at the lake—only the gently swaying weeds, like childrens' hands. So, then, this is the shape of the ultimate horror.

The whole inner tension of the poem thus resides in the contrast between the descending golden spiral of hope, one might say, and the blank and empty eyes in heaven and on earth, watching it without comprehension because there is simply nothing to understand—the stairway of the sun leads down to nowhere. Curiously, the slow and inexorable turning of the millstone, to which the spiral is transformed in the final stanza, suggests the destructive force of time and also evokes the visions of the golden galaxies turning forever in the endless void, so that the lake—a little spot on tiny earth—becomes the symbol of the universe.

A different kind of movement exists in another poem, "The Sailor's Departure," from *Arrow in the Sky*. The first impression is again one of "pure beauty," but there is also tension underneath. This time, however, it becomes embodied in soft and fluid lines of images, carrying the central emotion through a series of transformations toward the abrupt and tragic final statement:

> Lonely lindens are rustling in night without shore.
> Moon is young as it shines through the veil of your hair.
> I hold on unto you. And I fall down to bliss
> As to sea. But today, like a river, you flowed
> Toward me; now you speak of your mother who's dead
> And of skylarks and storm shutters . . . talking to me
> You start waving to the moonbeam that runs toward us
> To stop by, and you turn into tremulous light
> Made of glass. The good May puts a cloud under you
> To protect you from breaking. Above, yellow star,
> In the fragrance of legends and marigolds, dies.
> The anchor is rising. Don't cry. Adieu.

Everything in this poem aims toward a fluid, continuous movement in which there are tightening knots of emotion breaking the pace in the flow of words only to emphasize still more the basic rhythm of the verse, as an irregular crashing wave would underscore the rhythmic breathing of the sea. This can be seen in the meter itself, which this translation has endeavored to reproduce. The poem scans in four-foot anapests, but in the first two lines the words "lonely" and "moon" have a strong stress on the initial syllable that is impossible to ignore. The effect of this is to slow down the beginning of each line so that it seems to turn into a five-foot, trochee and dactyl combination:

Lonely / lindens are / rustling in / night without / shore.

The fundamental anapestic beat can be re-established in our consciousness only after a deliberate effort to "push through" the obstacle of the first trochaic foot. This results in a stronger commitment on our part to the dominant rhythm of the whole poem and we try to suppress the rhythmic disturbance by reading the line as follows:

Lonely lin / dens are rust / ling in night / without shore.

And as we do so, we understand how the rhythm has reproduced exactly the basic movement of feeling, consisting of outbursts of sorrow controlled by the deliberate effort of will. The meter disintegrates only in the final line, thus emphasizing the catastrophic reality of the lovers' parting—a reality they try nevertheless to overcome by their tight, laconic statements.

In the phrasing, the enjambments, arching over the stanzas, reach out to contain the whole poem within a single frame of thought, while inside each stanza short sentences or breaks in the continuity of a long one seem to threaten a breakdown of the whole syntactic structure. The contrast is then reflected exactly in the imagery itself, as when the girl becomes fragile, like glass, while a soft cloud is spread under for her protection. Similarly, the infinitudes of boundless sea and night and river are counterbalanced by the seemingly inconsequential, very human, very desperate chatter of the girl about mother and skylarks and storm shutters. Throughout the poem the images move in two opposite directions, avoiding a catastrophic encounter and explosion of feeling only because the poet was able to walk the tightwire of his art by the most precise calculation of the effect of every image, every movement and idea. Thus a lyrical landscape is transformed, in the interplay between reality and the artist's imagination, into a tense, dynamic, and even potentially explosive depiction of the secret forces which move and press and strain inside the soul. The "pure beauty" of this poem is the result not of a vague lyrical reverie but of precise balance in the tension of its component parts aimed at suspending the tragedy of a brief moment in the perfection of eternity.

Actually, of course, it is not the lovers but the poet who achieves this effect. Human emotion as such is not significant if not transcended by the power of art. In both poems discussed above we can see that it is the presence of creative and ordered imagination that counts. Precisely the same discipline controls those poems by Radauskas in which we see a vigorous thrust of the imagination into the fabric of reality, tearing it asunder with catastrophic force. Sometimes, as in "Three Lines," from *Lightnings and Winds*, the world appears in its apocalyptic aspect, and the poet's relationship to it resembles the relationship of the writing finger to the mad feast of Babylon. The poem describes the destruction of a city in three stages, told in three stanzas, each governed by the last line. These lines state, quite simply, that a poem is being written, but they hover over the tumultuous events in the stanzas like some terrible power which determines the fate of the world without itself being of it. At first we see the city as a noisy, cheerful marketplace in which the presence of art, in the guise of trees set on fire by the evening sun (the flames "rise toward heaven like a song"), already seems to promise doom to the people who laugh and feast and "trade in weapons, pots, in love and horses," paying no attention to this image of the burning bush. Over the trees are the words "And he wrote the first line." In the second stanza the gates of hell burst open, and a prophet screams destruction "in howling fire" upon the city, while the finger writes the second line of its poem. Finally, the city is dead and it moves through the seasons in its own bleak eternity of ruin. All this remains under the shadow of the third line of that "other" poem, as it were, and although we never see its words, their effect is the image of total destruction.

In the poem "The War's Beginning," also from *Lightnings and Winds*, the power of art gathers a number of different symbols from all aspects of life around the central fact of war:

The tiny serpent was sleeping, an orphan, lost, without parents,
Thin tongue of the prophet was sowing joy all around in the foliage,
Evening fell under the lindens, having sprinkled the hope of the plowman,
Chlorine and carbon, and oxygen, were resting in coffin of glass.

The tiny serpent woke up, a cry ran over the market,
The explosion put down its red hand on top of the continent,
The fishermen pulled out a siren, shrieking, happy and drunk,
The oxygen, also the hydrogen, started enormous work.

We can see that the texture and movement of this poem are much rougher, more "angular," than those of "The Sailor's Departure." Of course, the inadequacies of the translation increase the "awkward" effect even more, but the fact remains that the very principles of construction here are different. In the previous poem the author's task was to turn explosive emotion into a melody; here he attempts to translate a huge and catastrophic fact of life into the language of art primarily by an effort of the intellect. The result is an intricate pattern, replete with symbols, allusions, and cross-references—a kind of net in which art has trapped the precipitous events of reality.

One of the most clearly visible structural devices is the symmetrical distribution of images. The main lines, lines which constitute the basic frame of the poem, are the first and last in each stanza. The first stanza begins with the description of the sleeping serpent, and the implicit threat of this image is fulfilled in the first line of the second stanza—the serpent wakes up. The last lines of both stanzas refer to some of the basic elements in nature, productive of both life and death. At first they are resting in their glass coffin, like Snow White in the fairy tale—a reference which endows these elements with the power, indigenous to all myths and fables, as well as to science, to sustain the dreams of mankind. The "enormous work," suggestive of an atomic holocaust, which these elements begin in the final line of the poem mocks our human dreams with the terrible irony of violence. Snow White, too, has waked up, and we all shall die forever after.

Within this frame, the images continue to mirror each other with the same ironic effect. The image of the thin tongue of the prophet is a direct reflection of the preceding image of the serpent. The poisonous threat of the latter is augmented by all the biblical and literary memories of the deadly deceptions of false prophets who had imbued mankind with joyful visions of eternal bliss while arousing the unyielding passions leading to death and destruction. In the second stanza both images come together; the serpent strikes, like the tongue of the prophet in the market square, and the world explodes in the mass hysteria of war. A further structural connection exists between the serpent-prophet and the implied image of Snow White in her glass coffin. Both present a picture of weakness, innocence, and beauty wronged, downtrodden and forgotten by men. This points up the irony of one of our most vicious illusions, that man the destroyer is really Prince Charming, a knight in shining armor, fighting and killing in order to re-establish justice, protect the weak, and revenge oppression.

The deadly oxygen and hydrogen resting in the coffin are the elements in life-giving water, the same water that "sprinkled the hope of the plowman." Thus the poet obtains another restatement of the same irony of man's hopes and aspirations leading to his destruction. The final embodiment of the irony is in the image-symbol of the siren, which contains a double meaning. First, it is the mythological siren who has always lured men to their perdition with the beauty of its song—a beauty, one might add, that resembles the enchantment of lyrical, poisonous prophets. Secondly, it is also the screaming sirens of war, singing cities to their death.

We must understand, however, that the significance of the poem is not in the ironies themselves but in the art which made them manifest. Any historian or political commentator could say as much about war and peace and the nature of man; for the poet these things are but the means toward an esthetic construction. The power of the poem—its effect upon the reader—resides primarily in its intricacies of construction and symbolic reference, not in the idea as such. What matters, again, is the presence of art transforming reality by means of an image. What shocks the reader in the poetry of Radauskas is the violent intrusion of his images upon the precincts of our fond illusions, for instance, that joy of life is a creative emotion or that beauty is a gentle thing or that love is a sweet and tender emotion. In the above poem we saw the drunken, Dionysiac ecstasy of the siren amid the holocaust. In another poem, "Kornelija," from *Arrow in the Sky*, a young and gloriously beautiful witch flogs the sea until it rises like a fearsome wild stallion, sinking the fishermen's boats and making their widows and orphans "cry and howl louder than the storm." Kornelija, the terrible and beautiful witch, is only one of the many deadly apparitions of the muse in Radauskas' poetry. Almost always an appearance of the muse represents an inner storm that breaks into the world of things like some ruthless marauder and then departs, leaving behind nothing but shambles, carrying off the world's greatest treasure, the poem itself.

An interesting poem from this point of view is "The Muse," from *Lightnings and Winds*, because it not only depicts the birth of art as a catastrophe but also shows how things, through their destruction, cross over into another dimension of existence where they become radiant with beauty. Some think this way of death as merely a passing to the glory of eternity, but there is no eternity in the poem, only art:

> The seamstress muse from Denis' painting
> Now leaves her sewing on the bench, stands up,
> Walks down the empty street of summer
> Which has turned yellow, like a Chinese face.
> The spotted dress starts climbing up the stairway,
> And underneath her feet, the voice of oak
> Begins to scan the running words in pure iambics.
>
> She passes through the heavy, sleeping door
> Like unsubstantial wind, and then, at once,
> Inside the room, springs up like a statue.
> When they perceive the sightless face of stone,
> The children screech and start to thrash about,
> But she throws all the children out the window,
> And pellargonium, and the canary.
>
> And little babies, beating with their wings,
> Like angels, settle down upon the square.
> The flower starts to sing like little bird,
> And the canary starts to bloom

> With pure and yellow blossom. But the stone
> Hands to the man a tablet and a stylus
> And, without hurry, starts its own dictation.

Two sets of transformations lead up to the act of creation. The first is of the muse herself who, up to the critical point of confrontation with the poet, keeps losing material substance to the reality around her, turning from the solid and prosaic seamstress into a spotted dress and finally dematerializing herself entirely, becoming wind. As she goes through these changes, the things around her become steadily more poetic in the sense that they acquire properties not inherently theirs. The street takes on the aspect of an oriental mystery, and the oaken stairway starts to echo the iambics of the poem—the measured steps of the evanescent muse. It seems as if reality presents a barrier to inspiration which can be penetrated only by the complete dissolution of the muse in everything that exists, so as to make the world itself the substance of art. After this point is reached, it is the muse alone who has any reality; in fact, she becomes a very solid substance indeed—a stone. We should note here that in Radauskas' poetry we often see this complex and paradoxical relationship between dead stone and the life of art. In a way it expresses the paradox of sculpture, which uses stone to make immortal the perishable shape of human flesh; on a deeper level, it reflects the passionate desire of the artist, who is always in some sense a Pygmalion, to make this stone alive again, more perfect than men as they are made by nature could ever be. In any case, the very idea of shaping stone in imitation of a living form does violence to the natural order of things and is, like art itself, a specifically human property.

In recognition of this violence, there is the second set of transformations: Everything that surrounds a poet's daily life, the reality in which a poet ordinarily exists, must itself change into art; the children become angels, the flowers become birds. Some critics have seen an element of surrealism in this aspect of Radauskas' art, but this is, perhaps, not true. Radauskas does not deliberately choose the surrealistic mode of expression. It is his purpose not to make the world grotesque but to construct imagery expressive of his conception of the relationship between life and art. At times the laws of nature must surrender to the poet in order that this relationship can be depicted, and at other times this may not be necessary.

In the violent collision between reality and the creative imagination the poet emerges victorious to the extent that he can master the tumultuous, kaleidoscopic swarms of images which arise from this encounter. Radauskas does succeed, at times magnificently, in ordering the chaos of impressions and ideas, but he must also pay the price of victory, which is solitude. Having created his own universe, he stands in it alone, confronted with new questions that have no answers within the limits of his art. Communication with his readers is, of course, rewarding when it occurs, but all readers are mortal, and so are the poets, and what is creative striving worth if it does not, in some way, become an aspect of eternity? The ultimate question is not one of art and life but one of art and death. Death is another name for time, and time is the real enemy besieging an individual's existence, that lonely fortress of *cogito, ergo sum*, from which the arrow makes its final desperate flight in search of God. To be sure, the arrow conquers time because it flies forever in the cosmic void, but such a victory carries with it its own irony of pointlessness. The question will always remain, but what if the mind that asked it is no longer there?

This final issue, its ironies and paradoxes, occupies a large place in Radauskas' poetry. His images and metaphors, the music of his words, invade the precincts of time and death just as they did those of life and beauty. This might explain his fascination with sculpture. A marble statue is an exquisitely ironic symbol of the conquest of time; it remains immortal, but only because it is dead. Another similar image is that of the phonograph record. In the prose poem "Domenico Scarlatti," from *Lightnings and Winds*, the recording of Scarlatti's music is also his tomb, and the listener can only resurrect the sounds by submitting to the grotesque lunacy of dead, mechanical processes:

> The emaciated hand of the record changer rises up, remains suspended for a fraction of a second and then, with indifferent accuracy, sets down the needle on the disk which shines like polished granite and is the tomb of Domenico Scarlatti.

The resurrection itself is mechanical and therefore false. Scarlatti, the artist of the sound, has now achieved the perfection of silence, and no amount of repetition of what was once his life can ever destroy it:

> . . . and the sonata, having lasted three minutes and nineteen seconds, returns to the indestructible and perfect silence which Domenico Scarlatti had promised to it alone.

In this way a poetic image becomes the mask of death. This mask acquires an especially terrible aspect in another prose poem by Radauskas, called "The Land of the Lotus-Eaters," from *The Winter Song*, because in it the poet has conceived of eternity without the loss of consciousness—precisely the highest hope of any mortal individual—and this eternity turns out to be too dreadful to bear contemplation:

> The careless nurses tell them tales in the cradle about the sweet land of the Lotus-Eaters, and they spend their childhood as if in a dream, waiting for the hour when they will be able to depart on the distant journey.
>
> The ship rocks them like a cradle in the gentle hands of the Nereids (gods are well disposed toward such journeys), and the camels rock like cradles, moving from oasis to oasis.
>
> Upon reaching the land of the Lotus-Eaters, they start eating the lotus fruit and are satiated immediately, but they go on eating and soon forget their homeland. And, having spent a hundred or a thousand years in the land of the Lotus-Eaters (the sun never goes down there, and no one keeps the time), they grow old and weak and can no longer raise their hands to pick the fruit, and then they fall on the sand, next to the lotus trees.
>
> The Lotus-Eaters carry them out of the lotus forests and lay them down, dying, in the sun, and they scream in voices barely audible, tortured by hunger and by thirst, and they never die (the sun never goes down in the land of the Lotus-Eaters, and no one there keeps the time).

The formal meter of verse lines has been replaced here by the rhythmic recurrence of images and phrases signifying eternity: the cradle, the sands, the gentle, hypnotic swaying of the sea, the sun that never sets. The barrenness of the sea and the sand contrasts with the abundance of the lotus fruit, in the same way as reality opposes myth and the cold eye of reason disperses illusions. We understand that lotus is a monstrous lie, and that the only ones who will believe in it are those who never grew up to leave the cradle of their dreams. The terrible thing is that one can grow old without reaching maturity, without ceasing to be helpless like a babe. Maturity is fulfillment, and fulfillment needs death. Here, however, the spiral of one's life passes the point of death and descends into infinity, carrying with it the deathless horror of inextinguished consciousness. Immortality may suddenly reveal itself as the most dreadful of all illusions, and no philosopher or man of God could ever argue us out of this horror, because what the poet has communicated through the devices of his art is not a thesis or conviction but an experience.

The bearer of the death mask, the artist himself, cannot remain immune to its meaning. The act of creation requires total sacrifice and is therefore an experience which, in that sense, resembles death. This point is made by Radauskas in the poem "The Actors," from *Lightnings and Winds*:

> Now you were told to go and play. The gong
> With blows of steel is throwing you onstage,
> Where piercing spotlights, falling from the ceiling,
> Like harpies, take possession of your heart.
>
> You start to shout; the wind that is your voice
> Sweeps off the dust from darkness of backstage
> And from the sets—the castles and the trees.
> This dust then settles on your weary hearts.
>
> You need some rest, and so, the functionaries
> Of anonymity then put you on the table.
> The gentle undertaker carries off your heart,
> As if a baby, in an urn of tin.

Particularly striking is the violence of imagery in the first stanza. The actors are being sent to the performance as if to their deaths, and the assumed passion they portray tears their own hearts with the terrible claws of harpies. The deliberate choice of such images to depict the opening of the performance makes the actors symbolic of the deadly crucible of their creative art. They seem not mere imitators of invented lives, able to remain safely behind an assumed identity, but true embodiments of the heroes they portray and, as such, vulnerable to the blows of the same destiny. In this they resemble the poet who never has time, as J. Alfred Prufrock did, "to prepare a face to meet the faces that you meet." Like the poet, they must present their own naked faces, twisted into the semblance of a tragic mask. Walking onstage for them is a fatal step, like that of a gladiator or toreador coming out to meet his moment of truth. Indeed, the strange attraction we feel toward both the tragic actor and the toreador resembles our feeling toward the poet, in that all three give us the vicarious experience of our ultimate destiny, which, for them, is real and is now. Therefore, what we demand from actors, poets, and toreadors is not merely that they should face our own terrors but that they should do it in a manner befitting our wishful dreams, with elegance of line and movement, with beauty of design and with nobility of posture, as if they were merely toying with the dreaded enemy. To be sure, the poet and the actor face only the images of death, but this does not make their task any the less real for us, since death itself is only as terrible as our conception of it.

The violent flood of light in the opening lines evokes the image of a fire; the actors' hearts seem to burn up in their tragic passion. The rest of the poem then consists of ashes. Ashes and dust blend into a single substance, just as the illusion of death merges with the reality of its experience on the stage. The relationship between the actor and his audience is the same as in the first stanza. We contribute the ashes that have settled on the cardboard trees and castles—romantic illusions born in the minds of the quintessence of dust—and the artist turns them into the ashes of his own burning heart. We are then ourselves the faceless mass, the "functionaries of anonymity," upon whose altars the artist dies. The whole poem is in an ironic sense a kind of play or ceremony—an enactment of death—mock sacrifice for an illusion of salvation to which we give the exalted name "catharsis."

Radauskas extends the presence of death, consisting of the images of his art, from the mythical land of lotus-eaters and the illusions of the stage into the actual world of nature. In *The Winter Song* there is a poem entitled "In the Hospital Park" which depicts the effects of spreading chloroform on the surrounding flowers, birds, and trees:

> Through the hospital window, the chloroform
> Runs from the broken bottle
> To the garden of evening,
> And the poplar's legs go numb,
> And his hands are lost in dream.
>
> And the cups of wild rose blossoms
> Gasp for air like fish—
> The bush quivers, leans down,
> Still holds on with its branches
> To the low cloud, then sinks.
>
> And the nightingale no longer
> Can count to three:
> In the third trill the melody falters,
> Falls into the yellow pond,
> And the garden then suddenly bursts into light:
>
> I am burning like funeral candle
> At the side of my hanging coffin
> And I float into bottomless box.
> On the tower, the weathervane,
> Gone mad, is thrashing and screeching
> Prayers to lift the chloroform
> On behalf of the nightingale, the rose, and the poplar,
> And, not remembering my name,
> It whirls in hysteria and squeaks,
> And chokes off.

The three introductory stanzas are, in a way, reminiscent of a poem by the nineteenth-century Russian poet Fedor Tyutchev. The poem, called "Malaria," depicts the limpid beauty of an Italian landscape permeated with the mysterious evil of death. Tyutchev, however, uses abstract categories—"I love this anger of God, this invisible / All-pervading, mysterious evil"—while Radauskas chooses to embody this secret presence in the concrete image of chloroform spilling into the night. This preference for communicating what is actually a spiritual experience in terms of material objects supplies the key to the images of the rose, the nightingale, and the poplar. These are but three different metaphors of the poet himself; what happens to him is an event in nature. The poplar suggests the ancient myth of metamorphosis, made more profound in this poem by a further transition, on the level of eternity. Having been turned into a tree by his own imagination, the poet then takes nature with him through the second metamorphosis of death. The rose—always a symbol of beauty—must then also enter oblivion along with the poet who created, or, rather, himself became, that image. The closest symbol of the poet is the nightingale, and therefore its dying song accomplishes the transition into the second part of the poem, in which the nature masks of the artist fall off and we see him in a sudden illumination as himself in the process of being transformed again into direct symbols of his own death—the candle and the coffin.

At this point Radauskas introduces two related ironies centering around the notion of eternity as oblivion, a dissolution of the self in an unconscious (hence, the chloroform), nameless Nirvana. This oriental concept is suggested by the turning weathervane, like a Buddhist prayer wheel. Its irony is that it can pray only for images and not for the substance. If the world is an illusion, as Buddhists say, then only illusions —the rose, the nightingale, the tree—can be saved from death. The human mind, the individual "I," however, is reality, and in the world of dreams it has no name. Hence, the second irony—having saved the visions of his art, the poet cannot save himself.

A glance at the three basic aspects of Radauskas' imagery reveals in the end that the common factor in his visions of beauty, violence, and death is the presence of art as power. The true content of his poems is the self-portrayal of this power in a multitude of ever-changing, subtly interconnected images which do not really represent separate categories of experience but are instead no more than different facets of one another and ultimately of the creative impetus in the mind of the poet. There is beauty in violence as well as in death, while the beauty itself is the result of turbulent emotions and deadly terrors controlled, directed, and brought to fulfillment in images by the force of art. What we see, then, is the dynamic movement of this force, under the guise of an image, a symbol, or an idea, passing through reality like an arrow and changing the nature and meaning of everything. We can observe this process taking place in a number of poems in which the basic structure consists of a given framework being altered by some force going through it. One such poem, from *Lightnings and Winds,* is called "The Angel of Death":

> He's coming now across the granite yard,
> Gray feathers shining bright in his black wings.
> He strokes the tree, the cat, he touches water,
> He glances at the mirror of the day.
>
> The pond's aquiver, though the wind is gone,
> The cat jumps up from threshold, grasping air
> As if a mouse. The blood of tree congeals,
> The day's brown spots are scattered on the grass.
>
> Like newborn baby, cries the heavy door
> Of ancient oak. And through the yellow fog
> The sick man sees: the rainbow's brilliant stripes
> Fall down to earth like cackling raucous parrots.
>
> The clock is keeping time for those who live,
> The spider hangs a net between the stars,
> The angel, having entered the hearth,
> Transforms himself to smoke, and fire, and ash.

The images chosen to depict the change in reality are not limited to the immediate setting but connect by implication with ideas, myths, and symbols related to the processes of art as well as the totality of human condition. The angel of death is a complex figure because he is, in essence, dynamic; that is, he not only fatally alters the fabric of reality but is himself subject to the forces of decay which he serves. The first description of him as a black-winged presence in the granite yard somehow brings to mind black statues of angels over granite tombstones in cemeteries. He does not, however, possess the permanence of such statues, but is subject to time—his wings are turning gray. He is a tired angel, come not only to kill but also to die. The impression is that death is not some nameless outside force but something essential within ourselves which, in dying, carries us as well into oblivion. The manner of the angel's death—by fire—recalls the legend of the Phoenix, but with an ironic reverse twist; the angel may rise in order to die again, instead of dying for the sake of resurrection.

The impermanence of the angel is further suggested by the manner in which he touches things as he passes. Invisible to the creatures he meets (the cat is clawing empty air), brushing past them, he becomes like wind. Stone and wind, discussed in an earlier poem, are also attributes pertaining to the metamorphosis of the muse. Hence, once more, death and art seem to blend into a single mysterious entity, permitting the thought that in the present poem the angel's passage is equivalent, in some sense, to the passing of art through reality. An even more complex idea is suggested by the fact that the angel looks at the day—the world surrounding him—as if it were a mirror. This not only reminds us that art has been thought to hold a mirror up to nature (here the reverse is true) but also implies that being and nonbeing are but mirror images of each other. This, in turn, leads to unanswerable questions concerning the nature of life, death, and eternity.

The effects of the angel's passing are also complex because they seem to comprise several dimensions of experience. The pond, trembling without wind, is reminiscent of the pool of Bethesda, waiting for the angel to descend so that the sick can be healed. The moving waters of this poem, however, will only open the blind men's eyes to the fact of death. Perhaps the most ironic image is the disintegration of the rainbow—the symbol of hope—into mocking, cackling parrots who have always been the mindless imitators of human sounds. This is how death answers our prayers. The irony is completed by the image of the spider's nest between the stars (quite contrary to Dylan Thomas' notion that "time has ticked a heaven round the stars"), a trap for all our hopes of eternity.

The intricacies of design in Radauskas' verse, the complexity of his imagery and symbols, and the subtle underlying interplay between rhythm and sound, combined with irony and profundity of thought, make him perhaps the most intellectual poet writing in the Lithuanian language. Yet the work of his intellect is clearly inspired by passion—not a passion to preach or to proclaim some eternal verities but passion for life itself, in all its transmutations, including that of death. His is a free intelligence, informed with feeling, not committed to any limited system of thought. Precisely for this reason his talent can open insights deeper, if more disturbing, than those accessible to the men of blurred vision who think that meaning in art can only come from outside its limits.

3 Antanas Vaičiulaitis—the Gentle Master of Design

Antanas Vaičiulaitis was born in Vilkaviškis, southern Lithuania, June 23, 1906. He studied Lithuanian and French literatures in the Lithuanian State University in Kaunas, then continued his work on French in the University of Grenoble and the Sorbonne. In 1934–35 he taught high school in Kaunas, then joined the Lithuanian news agency Elta (1938–40), and also lectured in the University of Kaunas. In 1940 he entered diplomatic service at the Lithuanian embassy in Rome and, after a brief time, was forced to emigrate to the United States. Having served for a while in the U.S. Armed Forces, he returned to academic life, teaching French in Scranton University, 1947–51. Since 1951 he has been associated with the Voice of America and with the United States Information Agency.

Vaičiulaitis has written one novel and many short stories. The novel, *Valentina*, came out in 1936 and again in 1951. His short stories are collected in *Vakaras sargo namely* (*Evening at the Watchman's Cottage*), 1932; *Vidudienis kaimo smuklej* (*Noon at a Country Inn*), 1933, published in English by Maryland Books in 1965; *Pelkių takas* (*Path Through the Marsh*), 1939; *Kur bakūžė samanota* (*Where the Thatched Cottage Is*), 1947; *Pasakojimai* (*Stories*), 1955; *Auksinė kurpelė* (*The Golden Slipper*), 1957; and *Gluosnių daina* (*The Song of the Willows*), 1966. Vaičiulaitis is also known as an important literary critic and author of many articles and a book on naturalism and realism in Lithuanian literature. In 1942 he published an *Outline History of Lithuanian Literature* in English.

THE great and dramatic passions of men, their fierce hunger for love, their violent onslaughts upon the world's nameless mystery or upon one another, have in the past been very useful to writers talented enough to transform the strong, raw stuff of life into artistic achievement. In our day, people of infinite capacity for irony and for despair have conjured up, in words as meaningless and subtle as magic incantations, the total downfall of the whole structure of reality, including power, mystery, and love. At all times, however, there have been others who did not require that man be measured in Promethean dimensions and who felt that the colors, shapes, and sounds of everyday life were genuine and meaningful enough to serve as the building blocks of the artist's own universe. Believing in the possibility of beauty, they were interested in recognizing and augmenting it in their works. Willing to assume that man's perceptions can be true and his imagination fruitful, they tried to express their own vision of reality through the consciousness of a created character. They did not necessarily speak in the language of their own day, but what they said has retained its relevance to the human experience of any given time, perhaps because their concern was not only the experience itself but also the art with which it is conveyed.

In Lithuanian literature one such writer is Antanas Vaičiulaitis. A member of the older generation, he developed his profile as an artist while the country was still at peace and one could work unhurriedly and with great care on the transformation of ordinary people and events into an artistic design that would capture and make manifest the iridescent beauty of the human soul, as if it were like a dewdrop on the rough surface of life. The catastrophic events which destroyed Lithuania as an independent political entity and drove many of its people into exile made the voice of Vaičiulaitis seem small and remote amid the doomsday noises of history. The people listened much more eagerly to the violent and tragic voices among them and professed to recognize in what they said a genuine image of themselves and of their fate. Yet, even in exile, Vaičiulaitis maintained his confidence in the veracity of his artistic vision, because he understood, long before any had tasted the bitter bread of dispossession, that the fragile texture of the human soul does not really belong among the harsh realities of life. Man has never been at home in the real world but only inside the worlds he has created for himself. There is no need of a catastrophe to make him an exile; the shock of disappointed love, the urgent pressure of hard and personal decisions will be enough to tear the fabric of his dreams and make him feel a stranger and alone in the very places which, a moment earlier, seemed so much like paradise.

Vaičiulaitis' main work, *Valentina*, a delicate portrayal of a woman's withdrawal from the challenge of love, does not confront the reader with any of the grand existential conceptions of cosmic solitude but simply tells the story of an unhappy love which ends in death. The plot is very slight. A young man named Antanas comes to a small town in search of a girl, Valentina, he has seen once and cannot forget. They meet and fill the world around them with their love, but when Antanas proposes marriage, Valentina becomes frightened by the decision she must make. She has to choose between him and Modestas, a strong and vulgar construction engineer who had loaned money to her parents and thus is now in the position to demand her loyalty as a reward. Torn between these two demanding realities, Valentina flounders helplessly without deciding anything at all, until Antanas, convinced that she has betrayed his love, insults her bitterly, not from malice but because he cannot bear his own pain. When he comes to his senses, it is too late; all of Valentina's problems have been solved forever in the stormy waters of the lake.

In telling this story, Vaičiulaitis relies much more on mood and atmosphere than on conventional interplay of causes and effects. A reader who is accustomed to hard, clear lines of plot, to issues and conflicts arising directly from strong internal drives, will find himself groping vaguely for the main thread of events, since nothing much seems to happen from one chapter to another. Practically everything the people do and say appears peripheral to the situation they are in, and thus there is no buildup of tension leading up to the tragedy. What we find instead is a greatly expanded and refined self-awareness which seems to include the whole universe as if it were but a variation of an individual's consciousness. We see everything not from our own perspective but through the eyes of Antanas, the main hero, who is extremely sensitive to every detail of his surroundings and to every nuance of feeling evoked in him by the changing shapes, colors, and sounds of reality. Thus the novel unfolds not by means of narrative—a chain of events related to and influenced by the protagonist—but through poetic experience; that is, a simultaneous inner relationship with a multitude of perceptions and emotional stimuli which gradually accumulate certain knowledge of inexorable destiny.

Instead of describing a linear course of action, the novel becomes a study in interrelated patterns of lyrical composition. The author's purpose is not so much to describe a tragic love affair as to use it as a component part of an artistic whole—the novel—which must fulfill itself not only in terms of human experience but also in terms of the esthetic function of all aspects of reality.

This manner of writing leads naturally to the introduction of symbols corresponding to the protagonists and the things surrounding them, since both are equal integral parts of the author's general design. Thus the physical setting in which the lovers meet—a small town close to nature—is in itself an expression, an embodiment, as it were, of their love and destiny. An especially important symbol is the lake separating Valentina's home from the rest of the town where Antanas is staying. Its ever-changing, fluid element is not only a barrier between the lovers but also a medium of their communication; it is on the lake that they first meet on a soft summer night filled with cheerful human voices and lanterns and fishermen's boats and the lonely, passionate song of the nightingale. The waters of the lake also become the instrument of destiny at the end of the novel, capsizing Valentina's boat in a raging storm on the day when Antanas, in his own violent fury, replete with jealousy and injured love, refuses her shelter in his home and in his heart. The lake is like their love. Its mirror-smooth surface can play with little clouds when Antanas and Valentina go boating on sunny afternoons, talking happily of unimportant things, and yet, in the murky depths of the lake grow tangled weeds, like the lovers' confused emotions, and there are the ugly claws of crayfish crawling along the bottom, like the hand of fate. The image of the crayfish, in particular, recurs as an ominous symbol of impending doom. Long before the outcome of the love affair can otherwise be foretold, on the first night the lovers meet, Antanas comes to the lake to watch people fishing for crayfish. The creatures, hypnotized by the light of the lanterns piercing their dark, muddy world, run about helplessly until they are caught one by one. Antanas looks at them in a kind of mindless trance of his own, when his boat is suddenly touched by another. It is Valentina, who has come to meet the engineer Modestas, who already holds her parents in his power. There is an implicit threat of misfortune in this accidental encounter and mistaken identity, containing both the beginning of love and the cause of its bitter end.

In this way the action acquires a complex logic of its own, in which conventional human motivations are determined not only by inner psychological factors but also by certain parts of the landscape to which the author, working through the consciousness of his main hero, has assigned some definite symbolic meaning. There are oblique as well as direct reasons for things to happen in the novel. Antanas' love is doomed not only because Valentina cannot make up her mind but also because the threatening image of the crayfish and a number of other images have reinforced one another to condition him to accept the tragic aspect in every situation. In this atmosphere many otherwise neutral objects acquire the quality of grim prophecy and foreboding, even before any connection is established between them and the protagonists. One such object is the dark, ominous outline of a monastery tower which looms across the lake throughout the novel, as if in waiting for its victim. When Antanas first comes to the lake shore, he is met by several unhappy portents at once. A lonely old man, owner of the boat in which Valentina drowns, talks to him about how he feels himself growing smaller and smaller as he watches the stars every night until, he knows, he will not be there at all anymore. Antanas listens to him, watching with vague revulsion a bucket of crayfish on the ground; at this moment there comes the heavy sound of bells from the faraway tower. The old man crosses himself and says, "Someone has died there tonight." Later Antanas finds out from Valentina that her sister is in the monastery and that she herself has often felt the hidden pull of its tower—to go there and be safe from the disturbing challenge of happiness and also from pain. In the closing pages of the book the bells sound again, announcing the death of Valentina.

Another symbol is the bee. In a sense, there is something defeating about the labors of a bee—working tirelessly from day to day collecting honey, as if it were the sweet quintessence of all the beauty of nature, only to have it all taken away by the beekeeper. We get a similar impression of Valentina. She seems at times an ephemeral creature, a child of the sun, the fields, and the winds of summer, a gentle vision which could at any moment be destroyed by the harsh impact of passion, like a wasted treasure. The symbolic relationship between the bee and Valentina becomes explicit and acquires material presence in the story when her father starts gathering honey from his beehives and notices, with superstitious worry, the strange shape of the honeycombs:

> "The honeycombs are so strange, my child, so strange . . . as if a misfortune . . ."
>
> "Oh, what are you . . ."
>
> "I know, daughter, I know . . . But still, I feel there's something wrong about it, as if a blow of fate was in store for you . . ."

The skies are sunny on that particular day. Antanas and Valentina are still in the initial stage of their relationship, marked by clear and innocent happiness, and yet their future is already taking shape in the things around them.

The correlation between the objective reality and the human dimension is also manifest in contexts other than those relating to evil omens. As a compositional principle, it is used to enrich the emotional texture of the novel with a series of symmetrical patterns in which human situations and states of mind are balanced by corresponding landscapes, objects, and details of nature. At the very start of the novel the landscape contains a series of movements gently tinted with lyrical sadness. There is a blue ribbon of sky, winding its way through an opening in the forests and then suddenly swooping down overhead. Two storks are turning slowly in wide circles, and we seem to hear their clatter, which is then answered by the melancholy song of a group of peasants, swaying rhythmically to their tune, as if they were boatmen rowing along a wide, calm river. This movement of the landscape has its counterpart in Antanas' thoughts, which travel back to the time he first saw the dainty, unforgettable figure of a lovely girl. Only then do the two movements blend: we are told that Antanas is traveling by bus to a little town to search for the living counterpart of his vision.

Similarly, in the middle of the book there is a passage of delicate interplay between the physical, intellectual, and emotional textures of reality. Antanas comes to the village church to hear the parish priest—a talented, lonely misfit—play his beloved organ. Valentina is coming, too, as she has done so often before: she is the only person in the town with a good knowledge of and deep love for music, able to appreciate the priest's enthusiasm and his great skill. Thus we have three people, three strangers in the world, living somewhere on an intermediate level between their dreams and the rugged realities of life, coming together to share a moment of intimacy. The quality of this moment is defined in terms of the priest's thoughts as he sits on the granite steps of the church, watching their rough texture and musing sadly about those who can neither totally commit themselves to the earth, rejecting God, nor become God's children in all eternity. Will Christ truly conquer the world? When Antanas reminds him of the invincible rock of Peter, they both lift their heads and see the slender figure of Valentina coming to greet them. Dead granite, the rock of faith, the weak spirit of man, and a fragile angel in human form—all blend together in a composition evocative of both sadness and beauty.

This compositional balance is carried through to the smallest details. At nearly every moment there is something around Antanas which corresponds either to his mood or to the situation he is in. It might be, for example, a bumblebee in his room, making its home under the floor as Antanas dreams of possible family happiness with Valentina. There is also a somewhat humorous episode in which a little boy deliberately steps on a cat's tail because the animal is so ugly. This act furnishes a counterpoint to an incident between Antanas and an unpleasant woman who hypocritically tries to press her attentions upon him. There is, again, a little bird bouncing among the branches of pine trees as Antanas walks through the forest in excited expectation of meeting Valentina. Sometimes the little things in nature seem to take a direct part in Antanas' life. So, at the end when, having lost Valentina, he lies in the grass weighed down by his despair, an ant comes and stings him sharply, as if trying to bring him back to his senses. At that moment he also hears an intense, continuous chirping of a cricket in the stuffy heat before the storm, concentrating all of the hero's suffering in one sharp, unending, desperate sound.

The unbroken continuum between man and nature in the novel is not a reflection of the author's philosophical claim to such a continuum in actuality, outside the realm of fiction, as is the case, for instance, with Pasternak. Vaičiulaitis' concern is with the unity and inner logic of the special world which is the work of art itself. For this reason he uses not only nature and human emotions but also those aspects of the intellectual dimension of life which can contribute to the fulfillment of his artistic purpose. The novel as a whole aims toward a fluid movement of feeling in which sense impressions, events, and various human choices and experiences lose their hard and clear outlines, blending into one another imperceptibly, like the colors of an impressionist painting. Consequently, the protagonists themselves seem to lack the solid core of character that comes from lucid, rational thinking combined with an effort of will to implement one's decisions. A person who does not have such qualities will also tend to rely more on emotional attitudes when confronted with intellectual issues.

To emphasize this aspect of Antanas' personality, the author introduces a semi-paralyzed, elderly scholar, retired professor Žiobras, a specialist in Lithuanian ethnography. Antanas had actually come to the little town for two reasons: to find Valentina and to assist the professor in the writing of his book. His personality therefore emerges from the interplay of these two aspects of his life in the given setting. The important thing to understand is that Antanas agrees completely and wholeheartedly with the professor's views, which are quasi-intellectual at best, full of nineteenth-century romanticism in scholarship. The professor is a great lover of his country; therefore his aim is not to pursue objective truth about its people, wherever it might lead, but to proclaim their ancient virtues, to inspire his students with his own poetic ideal. This ideal, being at least to some degree a substitute for reality, in a way resembles the exalted image of Valentina which Antanas carries in his heart. "I do not adduce proofs at all," says the professor. "I affirm, I proclaim—only in this way can great things be communicated to people." An ironic counterpoint to this is provided by the disintegrating smoke rings from the professor's cigarette. He watches them happily and then asks Antanas, "Do you smoke?" "No," answers Antanas. "Well, don't start," advises the old man. But Antanas does not follow this advice; in his relationships with Valentina he does "smoke"—allows himself to be guided by cloud dreams and misgivings. This, of course, contributes to the final tragic outcome. It is, in fact, the professor who brings the lovers together, for Valentina also serves as his assistant. In writing down the professor's dictated emotional effusions, Antanas and Valentina, in a sense, "write" the book of their own destiny.

We might go even further and say that Antanas is the "author" not only of his own life but also of Valentina and of everything contingent upon their love. This means that for him nature, ideas, people, and events can have no meaning, cannot "exist," except as aspects of Valentina or, rather, of his vision of her. This is the essential quality and nature of his love. Valentina's image, as seen through Antanas' eyes—something fragile, something graceful, childish, clever, sunny, and sad—is in actuality the concentration of the whole atmosphere of the book in a single luminous point. When this light goes out, the whole world becomes dead and meaningless. When Antanas feels he is in danger of losing Valentina, all connections between him and his surroundings break off at once and everything becomes lifeless, pointless, of no concern to him at all. At one point, Antanas, Valentina, and the parish priest are having dinner at the professor's home. Completely absorbed in his love, Antanas does not seem to notice anyone else, except for a warm, grateful awareness that her presence makes all the other people belong together in mutual understanding of the goodness of life. Then the engineer Modestas comes in unexpectedly and addresses Valentina with the familiar pronoun "thou." This little word smashes the whole radiant evening like a bullet shattering glass, and Antanas is left among the broken pieces of his happiness, wondering why on earth these strangers, unnecessary to him or to one another, have to come here and destroy his love.

At another time, Antanas comes to Valentina's house and finds it empty. It is a beautiful, idyllic afternoon, full of flowers, sleepy farmyard animals, and sunshine, but none of this lazy rustic summer beauty can reach him now that Valentina is missing:

> Antanas felt that the tie between things and his soul had been broken, that there was no echo in his heart to answer the clatter of the stork, the slow flight of the rook, or the humming of the bees. Everything sang and glittered before his eyes, but did not penetrate inside him, as if he had broken off from the world, as if time had stopped its course, and he himself had been separated from things by a large glass cover.

Thus it is not an actual woman, a small part of the surrounding world, that Antanas loves, but his own conception of the essence of all things as a great and luminous feminine vision. His love has, in fact, created a world; he writes in a letter to his friend that Valentina exists in all the living things around him. Then he adds:

> All my movements, every thought, have meaning only in connection with her, in her light. . . . This is why I am even inclined to think that love is more powerful when I am separated from her, from this girl. When we see each other, we see only ourselves; when we are separated, our imagination begins to see still greater things.

Valentina herself recognizes this feeling in Antanas, and because of it she fears to commit her life to him in marriage. She understands that he sees another, ideal Valentina in his dreams, and knows that between this image and herself there is not much in common. So, paradoxically, she refuses him because of the frightening intensity of his love.

It is this same intensity that makes Antanas so fearful and tender, so happy and yet ready to see omens of misfortune everywhere. The tower, the crayfish, the dark and blood-red clouds in the evening—everything seems like a threatening alien presence that might at any time break into his dream and destroy it. Again, this very fear contributes to the inevitability of the disaster. And when Valentina dies, only a few words are needed to convey the dreadful emptiness of a world gone blank: "In all this earth there was nothing left for him to look at."

These are practically the last words of the novel, as if the author himself had also nothing more to see, nothing else to say. There is a very close proximity between his own point of view and that of Antanas—not that Vaičiulaitis would himself resemble his hero or be in love with Valentina, a creature of his fancy, in the same way that Antanas loved her as a vision, but in the sense that the whole novel is intended to be the fruit of an intimate collaboration between the author's own consciousness and that of his main hero. This is why we have trouble grasping Antanas as a separate personality except at those moments when the author steps back from his creation far enough to see him in perspective. Antanas is like the author's own eye—everything and nothing in the novel. This can be extended, of course, to all the other characters; to the degree that everything happens only in the mind of Antanas, the others are his visions, while Antanas himself, in turn, is but the main motif in the intricate, gentle, and lyrical interplay of colors, forms, and the music of the heart which constitutes the novel.

Similar principles of composition are carried over to Vaičiulaitis' shorter works. In a collection of short stories and fairy tales called *Kur bakūžė samanota* (*Where the Thatched Cottage Is*), the landscape is again much more than an ornament or a "setting" for action. It has dynamic qualities. In depicting nature, the author manages to convey also the mentality and spirit of his protagonists, to develop their fate and to communicate his own ideas. Thus the events taking place in the short stories unfold before the reader more as an image than a line of action. In one of the stories, "The History of Two Villages," a little girl named Uršulytė, having discovered the terrible fact of her illegitimate birth, begins to withdraw from the world into herself, as if apologizing to both men and God for her existence. Her life becomes a descending curve, falling across the limpid beauty of village landscapes and through the dark, tearful regions of the soul filled with repentance for her mother's sin, all the way down to death. This basic deathward movement is captured in a single paragraph that combines in itself the nearness of nature, the course of time, and the girl's own fate—to lay down her little life at the threshold of heaven:

> A year went by, and then another. The blossomtime of lilacs was all gone; the birds flew south and then came back again. Uršulytė stepped out into the world. She played with children in the Žvirbliai [the name translates as "sparrows"] yard and in the garden patch, among the vegetable beds. When vespers came in May, she went to the crossroads chapel with some posies in her hand and laid them down at the feet of the dear God.

In a different type of short story, the psychological motivations of the girl's suicidal leaning toward God might present an interesting and complex topic for development, but this story is an essentially poetic composition, in which such problems are not subject to analysis or judgment. What counts is the dynamics of the image, its movement, the sad and lyrical beauty of the descending curve of feeling.

In another story, "Kriokininkų Ievutė," we meet again this gradual downward flow describing a person's life in terms of little things and feelings interwoven in the texture of the landscape. Ievutė is an old and tired woman, a very humble, pious creature whose whole life passes unnoticed by anyone, in the shadows of the village church. The beauty of her soul is conveyed to us by means of a small event—the giving of alms—in which, somehow, nature itself becomes a crucial presence. Ievutė passes by a blind beggar and drops a silver piece into his bowl. The beggar listens for the sound of some more coins and, not hearing any, is disappointed. Only later, when he touches the coin, does he realize that it is worth much more than two or three copper pieces:

> Juozelis' heart joyfully skipped a beat. Again it felt good to be sitting in the sun and listening to the cock crowing in the parson's yard, to the noisy bunch of sparrows fluttering by, and to the drowsy hush of the afternoon, when everything quiets down and one can hear a leaf, falling through the silence, rustling slightly overhead, and settling near one's feet. No, Kriokininkų Ievutė is a good woman—she had it in her to part with a whole silver coin.

This leaf, falling through the silence, contains the basic theme of the story, the quiet fall of Ievutė into the arms of death. Her entire old age progresses in only one direction—toward the graveyard and toward her place in it, bought and reserved well in advance. This goal is, so to speak, her greatest ambition; it even led her to the sin of vanity. She had wanted to have her tombstone inscribed, in beautiful Latin letters, with "*beati mortui qui in Domino moriuntur*." She does, of course, die in the Lord, but just the same, the parson convinces her that it would be more proper and helpful toward salvation simply to say, "Kriokininkų Ievutė."

Vaičiulaitis is particularly interested in such humble people, quiet pilgrims in this world who do not seem worthy of much attention, except to those who are impressed by the stately grandeur of a falling leaf. They are generally poor farmers, people who work, live, and die in close touch with nature and seem to have acquired nature's own unhurried ways. They are conservative, as is nature itself when it takes long centuries to consider a change in the shape of a flower. Their very conservatism, in time, inevitably dulls their minds and keeps them poor, but, on the other hand, their humility speaks to all ages in a language more significant than the loud noises of a passing fancy. Yet they can hurt those among them who, while willing to accept their lot, do nevertheless cherish some dream, take some step to give it body and presence. In the story "Father's Fence" such a man is Motiejus, a farmer and the village fiddler, who commits the "crime" of putting up a beautiful new fence. This makes him vain, "uppity," in the eyes of his neighbors; it disrupts the shabby dignity of their accustomed ways. So the neighbors come with axes and chop the fence down, leaving Motiejus a broken man, like his old, cracked violin, which he will never again take out of its worn and ancient case.

Sometimes in these stories we can see a different "fence"—a wall of alienation—growing up between the generations. The young men wish to build and search and achieve things, while the old ones just shake their heads in bitter sadness; they have seen it all before. While clearly on the side of the future, the author does not assume that everything new is good and everything old is rotten and worthless. Quite the contrary, he finds much that is of value and dear to his heart in this ancient, dying spirit of the past, even while he agrees that it must all make room for the coming season. The last story of the collection, "Where the Thatched Cottage Is," concentrates his love for living relics of the past in the figure of an old grandmother who understands that her time to die has come when her grandsons build themselves a bright new cottage next to the old one. The woman drags herself wearily into the rotting, empty hut, where long generations of her forefathers had lived, and prepares herself for death, talking to a little boy about the olden days:

> See how it is, my boy: neither my mother nor myself had an easy time of it, walking this earth. . . . Quiet, child, quiet. . . . As if I didn't know

> that many tears and beatings are in store for us, and little joy. . . . Such is our land, such are we ourselves.

This seems light years away from the spirit of the younger generation; at least, the grandson had not the slightest intention of ever bending his back to another man's whip. Yet, the independent Lithuania, built by cocky young men, was crushed under the wheels of history once more, and today some of us realize that there might have been more to the old woman's words than seemed at first. In the light of events—exile, genocide, slavery—we can again perceive the outlines of the grim old specter of Lithuania, the land of sorrows, which the ancients accepted with calm and humble dignity. In these terms, the woman's death acquires a kind of awesome, earnest beauty, like a restatement of an old and tragic truth:

> Listening to her lonely words, the child began to feel as if he saw those strong and ancient men who used to come to this house to hold council or to pay respects to their dead. It seemed that these people were gathering here once more, serious and grim, taking their seats on the invisible benches. They then remained so—silent—as if prepared for a grand ritual.

The tragic undercurrent in the life of the Lithuanian countryside also makes itself felt in another collection by Vaičiulaitis, *Noon at a Country Inn*. One of the stories, "The Woman From the North," describes the suicide of a young woman who committed bigamy as much through the force of circumstances as through her own choice. Given away in marriage to a man she did not love, she went to another part of Lithuania to work as a maid when a severe flood caused famine in her own village. The husband gave his consent and even helped her to assume the identity of her unmarried sister, since a married woman would not be hired as a maid. He, of course, expected her to remain faithful to him and to come back when things got better at home. Two years later he comes down to the place where she is working only to find that she has in the meantime married her employer's son, and even has a child by him. When her true situation comes to light, the employer insists that she leave her unlawful second husband and the baby and go back with the man she had first married. The girl cannot bear the thought of this misfortune and of having to live with a man who is a stranger to her in every way, even though he has both human and divine law on his side. She commits suicide, leaving behind her two ruined lives.

The basic situation is reminiscent of the novel *Valentina*. In both cases there is an unloved man with strong claims upon a weak and essentially childlike woman, a helpless second man whom she truly loves, and a resolution of the ensuing conflict by the woman's retreat into death. The concrete circumstances are, of course, different. Valentina is not yet married, and she dies because she cannot make up her mind, while in this story the issue is not one of choice but of bearing the lot that fate has already imposed upon the girl. The stronger outlines of plot in the short story also tend to make the protagonists more realistic, giving the work the character of a human story rather than an artistic design in which humanity is but a component element. Nevertheless, the presence of nature in the story is overwhelming, creating the impression that it is the force which actually governs people's lives. The floods up north which forced the young woman to seek work elsewhere seem to follow her husband when he comes to bring her back. It is autumn, and unmerciful rains turn the whole place into a dismal, muddy swamp. When we first see the man, he is wandering through unknown crossroads and flooded fields in search of the farm where his wife is working. There is not yet any reason for him to expect trouble, but the pressure of the rain and mud and autumn darkness upon the consciousness of the reader precludes any possibility of expecting a happy ending. Heavy fog covers everything, making it difficult for the man to find his way. This, too, amounts to a commentary upon human helplessness in situations requiring moral clarity and just decisions. People decide either upon a sudden impulse, as the young woman did, or on the basis of established law which stands beyond human judgment. Nevertheless, in both instances the seemingly personal act of will is actually the fulfillment of an inevitability. What appears to the woman as an impulse was in reality the sum total of her life, in turn a conglomeration of character and circumstance. On the other hand, the submission to God's law, as when the master of the house says that he must act according to the biblical precept, presupposes a lifelong avoidance on his part of any troublesome thoughts about the measure of his personal responsibility for his life or about the difference between law and grace. In his old age, the man is no longer able to form a judgment requiring the exercise of his own conscience and humanity. Thus, both people might feel that they can disclaim any guilt for the tragedy, saying, as the young woman does, "God sees me for what I am." This statement, however, cuts like a two-edged sword.

In spite of the impression produced by this story, the over-all mood of *Noon at a Country Inn* is not one of somber realism in the face of human weakness confronted with the enormity of fate. On the contrary, in most of the stories Vaičiulaitis tends toward playful fancy, intertwining the works of man and nature in a rich baroque composition, delicately controlled by the artist's instinct for measure and proportion and by his good taste. The tone of a story is often set by what might be called an "exuberance of detail," of little things in nature cheerfully cluttering up the world of men. "The Sledge," for instance, is a simple, gently tragic story about a bishop and some humble, devoted monks who greatly desire to make a magnificent sledge for His Holiness to ride in. The carpenter monk works and works all through Lent until he produces a true masterpiece of great beauty. In the meantime, there is an outbreak of the plague and other misfortunes, but the monks go on with their project, while their good bishop prays to God. The blacksmith monk goes on tinkering all through the night to put the runners and other ironwork on the bishop's sledge. In the morning he is so tired that he falls asleep amid the glowing embers of his smithy. Needless to say, his whole workshop burns down with the new sledge in it. The bishop, however, never misses it, because on one of his habitual walks through the snowdrifts in the forest he catches a chill and dies.

As the story proceeds, its framework gradually fills up with all manner of living things from nature. At the very beginning there is mention of abundant wildlife and of "bears who would come to the village on their own, turn over the beehives and disappear into their lairs with honey smeared all over their faces and as merry as if they were a little drunk." But "today's story," the author hastens to assure us, "is not about deer, bears, or moorhens, but about the Most Reverend Bishop Kristupas of

Medininkai and about his sledge." The fully spelled out name and title of the bishop, sandwiched between moorhens and a sledge, somehow becomes almost as much of a playful irrelevancy as the animals that crowd around it, in a manner reminiscent of some of Gogol's puckish fancies. And yet the story is actually about all these things together. A little later one of these irrelevancies, coming from the realm of superstition, strikes an ominous note:

> The Superior of the monastery rejoiced that the good Bishop had come to live with them, and so did all the brothers, including the gatekeeper and the blacksmith, who smote so hard that evening with his hammer that he broke its handle in two, and the sparks, people say, wounded the old witch in her right eye, though she is still good at foretelling the future from the wild grasses, the wind, and the stars.

The marginal things and creatures keep crowding into the story but without impairing the lucidity or simplicity of the style. There are jackdaws "with their craws tilted against the wind," the monks and novices tobogganing all over the monastery yard. And when the bishop goes out walking in the snow-covered forest, it is "to be with God amid the overhanging linden trees and the slender pines." As the carpenter monk begins to build the sledge, his creative fancy runs away with him, opening the gates of nature to all kinds of creatures which then cover the whole sledge, along with the images of saints:

> This sledge was to shine and glitter like the snuffbox of the Provost, and it would be covered with splendid carvings. On one side he would portray the Lithuanian prince, St. Casimir, and the other would display a shaggy bear with a hunter and three hounds. The front of the sledge, he decided, would show the rising sun, with countless rays to dazzle the beholder. Nor would he neglect the runners. There goldfinches and bullfinches would sing, and magpies would dart about in the air, and small squirrels would perch with nuts clasped in their forelegs, while otters dived into the water looking for prey. The Bishop would scarcely need a horse to draw the sledge, for the bears and does, the buntings and the starlings would lift it into the air and bear it to heaven, just as the prophet Elijah was borne into the skies long ago.

The beautiful thought of the bishop being borne aloft to the skies by all these creatures, along with the sledge, turns out to be a prophecy, for indeed the sledge goes up in smoke, and the bishop, too, catches his death of cold in the forest amid all the wildlife, as if they all were messengers from the beyond, come to invite him to ascend into the regions of eternity. The reader is as heartbroken as everyone else in the story to see this magnificent sledge destroyed by fire, but the bishop himself is now safely in heaven, where, again, all the angels and archangels and all the patriarchs of Christendom crowd around him with great joy, and glory be to God.

Stories of this kind seem to quiver on the edge of pure fancy, and in fact some of them, such as "The Pope's Bird" and "The Departure of the Saints," do become legends surrounded by the medieval atmosphere of a morality play. An interesting story in terms of this transition is "Noon at a Country Inn," because its curious intermediate position between a legend and an ordinary anecdote is established not with the help of some supernatural elements but rather by means of describing perfectly realistic settings in images reminiscent of folktales and legends. We have a tavern in the woods, a hungry traveler, an innkeeper, and a friar—nothing fantastic about them. Yet there is something about the very solitude of that country inn, standing in the woods all by itself, which calls to mind the little cottages we have all read about in Grimms' fairy tales. The traveler wears enormous (seven-league?) boots and is dressed in velvet, the way some of the fairyland princes dress when they set out on their journeys. The tavern keeper has an enormous black beard (might he be Bluebeard?), and the friar sits in a corner next to a "tame fox tied by a chain," inviting the reader's fancy to see some mysterious association between the two. He could be the guardian of this fox, which, in turn, could be some enchanted princess. Or this fierce and clever captive animal might symbolize the friar's own sharp wits and possible earthly appetites bound by the laws of his order. The friar also reads some mysterious book, as if he were not a friar at all but a magician of some sort. Yet these curious people and objects which seem ready to cross into the realm of fantasy at one touch of the author's magic wand, remain on the level of ordinary reality. What the author has achieved is the depiction of one category of existence in terms of another.

This, of course, is what actually happens in authentic fairy tales, and it is not surprising that Vaičiulaitis should turn to this particular genre. The second half of *Where the Thatched Cottage Is* consists of fairy tales (perhaps they should be called fables, because the actors in most of them are animals), and two other books, *Auksinė kurpelė* (*The Golden Slipper*) and *Gluosnių daina* (*The Song of the Willows*), belong almost entirely to this genre. In his tales Vaičiulaitis retains the basic artistic devices used in his novel and short stories. The aim is still lucidity of style, balance, proportion, and a skillful compositional pattern capable of containing a hint of sadness, a touch of humor, and a deep, warm sympathy extending from humanity to all forms of life and all the elements making up the world we live in. Often the plots of the fables are based on a ludicrous contrast between an enormously powerful beast and some tiny creature. The point then is to demonstrate the victory of the weak against the great ones of the animal (and, by implication, human) world. There might be, for instance, an enormous bear furious with a squirrel for dropping a nut on his head. All his might avails him nothing when it comes to catching the fleet-footed creature high among the tallest pines. At other times the small living things are so minute that they cannot be reached by the huge forces bent on their destruction. In one tale a gnat is sentenced to be beheaded by the king. The only problem is where to find the gnat's head. When the ax swings, there is no target. Gradually the moral emerges that in the world of fairy tales—the looking-glass world where all realities are reversed—the small and humble creatures emerge victorious, a fact that pleases both the reader and the Good Lord who made them small.

In the composition itself there are interesting experiments in the development of a structural principle that would hold its validity in the transitions from fantasy to reality and back again, following the same logic of cause and effect, embodying the same patterns of experience. This is especially noticeable in *The Song of the Willows*, in which most pieces represent an intermediate genre between short story and a legend or fairy tale. In "The Lamb of God" the central image uniting both idea and structure is the figure of the lamb. We see it at first in human form. A gentle old beggar, Daubrys, comes to a farmer's homestead on

Christmas Eve to ask for food and a place to sleep. He is very clean, helpless, and kind—not at all the standard figure of the ragged tramp. One is reminded of the Lithuanian folktales in which the Lord Jesus Himself wanders on earth, incognito, among the poor. A soft, clean snow is falling, and the hired hand comes in with a newborn lamb in his arms. It is a cold winter night, and both the lamb and the beggar Daubrys are given a place to sleep on the kitchen floor, on freshly spread straw. The idea of the manger, the Christmas symbol, is now embodied in human and animal forms, pointing clearly to the inevitability of the divine dimension as a unifying factor. This is provided by a picture on the wall: Saint John the Baptist carrying a lamb. As the old man Daubrys looks at it, he remembers the legend of the Christmas lamb, brought to the manger by shepherds, which never grew old. It continued to live until the day Christ was crucified, and was later resurrected together with Christ, to go on living in our hearts. Thus the lamb in the room, in the picture, and in the legend acts as a unifying device establishing the continuity of the central theme.

In another tale, "Benvenuto di Giovanni Presents His Painting to His Patron," the unifying element is expressed more in the structure itself than in a single central figure. The theme is again Christmas—the adoration of the Magi painted by the artist—but the content is essentially of an intellectual nature. In presenting his work, the painter describes his artistic credo. The subject of the painting itself helps explain the nature of his beliefs as an artist, since it depicts man's wisdom paying homage to the miracle of Christmas. The work has been inspired by the radiant glance of an innocent girl, and it is to be given to a monastery as a contribution ordered by the patron, a rich merchant. In this way we have three people—the girl, the artist, and the merchant—who together have produced a gift to God, thus repeating the act of the Magi and connecting the biblical legend with the reality of the given moment. Such an approach to the structure of the story makes possible other correspondences. A great festival just held in the city of Sienna now repeats itself in the painting, in the procession of the Magi, and the earthly joy of the inhabitants has been transformed into holy ecstasy. In this way the underlying realities of a work of art—the heavenly and the earthly—have been defined. The words of Giovanni himself elucidate this principle of artistic creation. He claims to have given his work "law, order, beauty, love, and truth." Law is the old faith of the classics, that one must follow the example of the great masters of the past, contributing to it the fruits of one's own imagination. Order is in the two basic planes of the painting—manger in the foreground, procession of the Magi in the background—corresponding to the two realities being embodied in art, with the human principle expressing its allegiance to the divine. Beauty lies in "the calm dignity of the painting, the noble modesty of colors, the gracefulness of the lines and proportions, and in the harmony and movement of all these component parts." Love is "love for art, for its eternal longing, its strange and restless call," leading, after all is said and done, to truth—the Holy Child, the Savior.

This description may indeed be applied by the reader to the work of Vaičiulaitis himself. In the lucid and subtle style of his prose, he has followed the laws of all the classical writers who had respect for the written word. The delicate balance and graceful design of his compositions fulfill the requirements of art as an expression of order and discipline in the satisfaction of the creative instinct—requirements often ignored by those timid minds who dare no more than to follow the chaotic impulses of passing fashion. The warm humanity which permeates all of Vaičiulaitis' work gives it a value that transcends the accomplishments of intelligence and skill alone. And this, of course, is the main difference between art as mere artifice and art as an embodiment of deeply felt, personal truth.

4 Aspects of Poetic Imagery in the Work of Jonas Aistis

Jonas Aistis was born July 7, 1904, in central Lithuania. After studying Lithuanian literature in the University of Kaunas, he received a stipend from the Lithuanian Ministry of Education to study French literature in the University of Grenoble, France, between 1936 and 1940. His doctoral thesis dealt with linguistic analysis of Gospel translations into ancient Provençal. Between 1944 and 1946, Aistis worked in the archives of Nice and in the Paris National Library. Emigrating to the United States, he taught high school until 1952, then joined the Free Europe Committee in New York as an assistant editor. At the present time Aistis is working in the Library of Congress.

Aistis has published the following books of his poetry: *Eilėraščiai* (*Poems*), 1932; *Imago mortis* (*The Image of Death*), 1933; *Intymios giesmės* (*Intimate Songs*), 1935; *Užgesę chimeros akys* (*The Dead Eyes of the Chimera*), 1937; *Poezija* (*Poetry*), 1940; *Be tėvynės brangios* (*Without the Beloved Country*), 1942; *Nemuno ilgesys* (*Longing for the Nemunas River*), 1947; *Pilnatis* (*Full Moon*), 1948; and *Sesuo buitis* (*Sister Life*), 1951. Aistis has also written a good deal of literary criticism.

WHEN Jonas Aistis began to write around 1927, his highly original and intense poems generated considerable excitement because his was one of the new voices of truly modern Lithuanian literature, speaking an old language in twentieth-century idiom. The appearance of these new writers was one of the logical consequences of the re-establishment of political independence in 1918. In the short period of freedom between the two world wars, Lithuania found itself in the paradoxical position of being an old country with a rich historical heritage faced with the task of developing a new, indigenous civilization and a new literature, for in centuries past Lithuanian culture was almost exclusively Polish in character. The young writers were trying to emancipate themselves from the traditions of patriotic romanticism, oriented toward the legend of the past, which had dominated Lithuanian letters several decades earlier, when the new national consciousness was being formed. The commanding presence of long and glorious history had guided the inspiration of such talented poets as the "bard of national resurgence," Jonas Maironis (1862–1932), who created significant poetry by echoing strong and vibrant patriotic emotions in sonorous, rhetorical, yet profoundly lyrical cadences of his own. Except for the much older poet Kristijonas Donelaitis (1714–80), who wrote epic verse on rustic themes, Maironis was the important and influential Lithuanian poet at the turn of the century.

With the coming of independence, however, Maironis, although still very popular among his readers, was unable to consolidate his achievement in a new literary school. The reason was that the most talented young poets, such as Aistis, could find no meaningful way to continue in his footsteps. Maironis had forged into poetry the language of ideas and aspirations which in themselves were not essentially concerned with art. His gift of intensifying and crystallizing mass emotions by expressing them in noble statements of deep conviction did not require an intimate confrontation with a reality not defined in ideological terms. For Aistis and the other poets, however, the world was new and mysterious because it represented the realities of the moment rather than the hopes of the past, and consisted of things rather than ideas. The dream country of which Maironis spoke was now real; it entered into and blended with the most ordinary manifestations of daily life. There it was—Lithuania—trees, meadows, rivers, clouds moving across the sky. The magic inherent in this landscape could now only become manifest in an entirely different dimension of experience—one in which the presence of art itself was the dominant factor. A new poetic language had to be developed, and this was a challenge that not only promised but also required a new freedom of expression.

It is precisely this freedom, this new way of looking at the world, which characterizes the daring and unorthodox imagery we find in Aistis' poems from the very beginning. He declared his independence from the traditional ways of translating reality into art. The old emotional logic of images, developed in the romantic tradition, did not correspond to his perception of reality any longer, and Aistis sought to discover new metaphorical relationships among words with long-established meanings. The color of the sky at sunrise, for example, did not evoke in him any of the stock responses taken from the traditional poetic vocabulary but produced instead unexpected images composed of terms previously thought to belong to entirely separate categories of poetic associations. There is an early poem in which the sky at dawn seems made of "blood and wax." This image is more than a certain way of seeing the colors in early dawn. The poem is about love disgraced by physical passion. It implies a deep wound in the heart of the beloved, and the blood from that wound spills over into the morning sky. The image of wax then begins to carry implications of death, at least in the moral sense, and we can visualize the horizon as a funeral altar where wax candles are crowned by the burning sun. As the poem develops, other images appear, reinforcing the disgrace of passion by allusions to trampled rues and black pitch—customary symbols of punishment of the adulterous woman among the Lithuanian peasantry:

> When the blackness of the night
> Paints with tar the strands of day,
> Then we will the garden rues,
> Then we will the lilies . . .

At the end of the poem, the images of wax and blood and wounds are ironically contrasted with the brightness of the new day:

> Morning flowers were bespattered
> With a brilliant diamond spray,
> Wax and blood was in the sky,
> Also wounds and scabs . . .

Once this basic image is born, Aistis goes on cultivating and developing it in other poems, in a variety of different contexts, thus constantly adding new facets to his original artistic experience. The juxtaposition of blood and sky becomes for him one of the more frequent means of poetic expression. We meet it again, for instance, in the tragic and blood-colored sunsets which seem to symbolize important aspects of Aistis' poetic outlook upon the world. The slow death of light in the evening reveals to him his own passionate, even fanatic, love for brightness and life, for everything touched by the sun, and creates a painfully intense desire to explain how terrible it is that the night must come. For this reason a sunset acquires cosmic proportions, becomes the tragic metaphor of crucifixion, and the earth opens like an enormous metaphysical wound. Sunsets have a theatrical quality, of course, but so does the mystery of the death of Christ, and the opening lines of the poem "As in a Shakespearean Tragedy" combine them both into a single image: "The heavy, bloody, satin curtain of the evening is lifted, / And sun is sweating blood, like Christ in Gethsemane."

In another poem, "The Seven Psalms," the setting of the sun over the sea transforms itself into a legend—the ancient theme of doing battle with darkness for the fairy princess of immemorial dreams. The evening, again, is a wound:

> There are the silken cobweb threads,
> And evening there is open like a wound,
> And swords are sharp, stuck deeply in the sun,
> The seven agonies, the seven psalms!

The basic image of mythical battle is then constructed around the swordlike rays of the sun as it goes down in the sea:

> A host of heroes rides across the sea,
> They crack the golden helmets with their swords . . .
> I know, they come to save you, oh my love—
> The seven agonies, the seven psalms.

Then, as darkness comes, the swords of sun are extinguished one by one:

> Oh, Lord, their ranks are thinning, strength is lost,
> And they are swallowed up by fierce abyss.
> I know my love will never reach the shore—
> The seven agonies, the seven psalms.

In the poem the central metaphor of legend is enriched by the poetic substance of romantic love (that is, the theme of love as an artistic device) and is surrounded by religious connotations not in their metaphysical aspect but as vehicles of lyrical emotion. Love and faith are again used figuratively in the poem "Saint Francis" to suggest the inexplicable human yearning which seems to penetrate the soul, together with the strange and melancholy colors of the evening:

> Such an ascetic image of the evening.
> My Lord, the sadness of my silent joy!
> Around the sun St. Francis' wounds,
> The lilac trees—a cloud of "l'Origan."
> And I stand up—a fierce paleolithic man,
> A string of flying cranes in autumn . . .
> Beyond the sea, beyond the evening, far away,
> St. Francis' wounds of fragrant jasmine.
>
> Why is my suffering wooden? Christ,
> A lunatic love you taught me!
> With dove in hand, unrecognized,
> I'll go now, mocked by love and by the earth.
>
> Oh, pain—the wounds in arms and legs and in my chest,
> Black drops of blood under the thorns—my head . . .
> Oh, love—the evening drawn in lines of sorrow,
> The fragrant dreams of lilacs in the night of May!

The device of placing the color of the sky and the blood of wounds in the same semantic category invites the imagination of the reader to discover the special emotion which alone can establish a common bond of meaning between such disparate phenomena. This emotion, in turn, although it bears the names of love and of sorrow and yearning, is not actually fulfilled by the implications of any of these, but points instead to the mystery of creative experience itself, the understanding and description of which is the ultimate aim of Aistis' poetry.

Aistis himself has called this experience "the enchanted mystery of sorrow" and has pursued it along several lines of imagery, some of which meet in the poem above. The lonely figure of Saint Francis, for instance, reappears under different names in other contexts but always signifying some higher value condemned by the world. In the poem "The Royal Hound" it is the clown who dares to mock the hypocritical expressions of mourning upon the death of the king's dog and is himself hanged for it. Clowns, as we know, have always been sad and wise, but the martyred clown of Aistis' poem is also intimately related to persecuted innocence and beauty because he performs the same metaphorical function as the king's daughter in another poem who is chained for life to a millstone because such is her evil stepmother's will. Saint Francis and the clown and the suffering princess are all confronted with a cruel outside force in such a way as to suggest the polarity between the creative impulse and the deadness of things.

This would define the poetic experience essentially as suffering and sacrifice, but it can also be perceived as a deep primeval hunger, reaching, perhaps, all the way to the original chaos from which man's consciousness was born. The "fierce paleolithic man" in "Saint Francis" is possessed by the same inexplicable urge that makes the cranes fly south. In a poem entitled "At Some Time" the image is different, but the underlying context is the same. Here poetic word emerges like lava from dark, unknown depths:

> As if a thunder, hoarse and far away,
> The unclear call of the primeval word,
> And then, like lava, love and deep desire
> Break out, like sun, in cadences of verse.

The imagery is now that of a persistent and fiery striving. In solitude, in pain, and in chaotic darkness the mystery of art aspires to light through the poet's consciousness. The hard intensity of such images is offset by other sets of metaphors in which the same mystery assumes the gentle and lyrical aspect of beauty. The fragrant blossoms in "Saint Francis," for instance, are only one variation of the many references to flowers and blossoms scattered throughout the poems of Aistis, always in a context that allows the expansion of lyrical feeling to the point where it begins to function as a mode of transformation from reality to art. Sometimes the opening of a flower describes the birth of the poet's vision, calling forth a landscape from tender memory:

> Now again the landscape's covered up with mist
> And I so much wanted to embrace it all,

For the blue had opened: silken eyes of flax
Saw the golden vision of my longing born.

In another poem, entitled "The Snowflake," the beauty of a snowflake in the sun is compared with the eyes of the beloved as they open like apple blossoms in the spring:

The eyes were like the blooming apple trees of May,
It was a day so full of sun.
Solveig! is coming on her skis
Through snowdrifts straight at me!

The imagery of blossoms and of sparkling snow is tied in with specific literary references to Ibsen's *Peer Gynt* and also to poetry of the Russian symbolist Alexander Blok, echoing Blok's poem "Solveig" which begins with the lines: "Solveig! You came on your skis to me, / With a smile at the spring which had come." There is a special melancholy in both *Peer Gynt* and the poetry of Blok, consisting of a strangely helpless, pained sensitivity to beauty and of the desire to dream one's life away in poetic visions evoked by the touch of the beautiful. Such feelings strike an answering chord in Aistis and contribute a great deal to his conception of art. One must be careful, however, not to go too far in comparing Aistis with Blok, because the latter had worked out a definite system of symbols centering around his vision of the Beautiful Lady, while Aistis stops just short of assigning a systematic set of symbolic values to his metaphors. The resemblance between the two poets lies not in symbolism but in an inner tension, manifest as lyrical sorrow, which precedes Blok's symbolic conceptions and is indeed their prerequisite.

Another characteristic of Aistis' poetic language is a deliberate confrontation of two different idioms—one usually taken from the common fund of lyrical expressions known to most romantic poets, and the other from an urban vocabulary, at times witty, at times prosaic, spotted here and there with foreign terms, especially French. From "Saint Francis" the line "The lilac trees—a cloud of 'l'Origan' " would be one example of such a juxtaposition, combining, as it does, a conventional reference to lilacs with the name of a French perfume. There are other poems with

French or English or German phrases interwoven in the over-all texture of the language.

A variation of this approach can be found in the poem "August Night," in which, instead of foreign phrases, the awe and wonder at the sight of thousands of falling stars is conveyed in a prosaic idiom which then itself acquires a lyrical quality because of the intensity of feeling:

> Quiet down, my heart, be still, you silly fool,
> No need to get excited and to pound so—
> None of your business what goes on in heavens,
> Goes on in heavens on an August night!
> Oh, but the stars so sorrowful and falling,
> And just the forest looming, quiet as ever—
> It makes me want to cry. Oh, devil take it!
> A night like this deserves the pen of Flammarion.

The effect of such language is to shock us into poetic awareness, which begins at the simplest level of emotion and constitutes a precondition for the birth of imagery. The images themselves, when they appear, often seem to draw their strength from the poetic relevance of unrelated concepts, producing such lines as "The silk-textured longing of the cranes" or the sun which "fell apart and spilled all over, / Bit off the sea in red." We see landscapes in which leaves and rivers are so sensitive to pain that they feel raw to the touch, or tall grass emits cries of shock in the night. Words in Aistis' poems often acquire meanings that are, as he says, "like cobbler's happiness, just barely possible."

In contrast to images deriving their complexity from the extension of one semantic category to another, Aistis also writes extremely simple verse in which words are placed next to one another in ordinary logical sequence and in a single emotional context. Such poems always seem to quiver on the verge of song:

> Field and road and meadow. Crosses.
> And the grove—a ribbon blue,
> Rich design of clouds in heaven,
> Sadness of the song. And you.

The single word signifying feeling, "sadness," casts a spell over the rest of the quatrain and unifies it into an effective statement of mood. It is a mood both pensive and melodious because there is a hidden music in the lilting trochaic lines. Poetry of this kind contains in it something of the spirit of Lithuanian folk songs, and it comes as no surprise to feel the constant presence of folklore heritage in Aistis' otherwise urbane and sophisticated verse. Aistis is not really interested in continuing and expanding the folk genre in written poetry but searches instead for ways to re-create the mood, the general flavor, and to use it as a stylistic device for his own artistic purposes. For example, the poem "A Young Lad" is an essentially modern story of an ill-fated romance. A young man writes a love letter to his girl who nevertheless forsakes him and chooses another. The unhappy fellow then wonders if she might not have left him because of something he wrote in that letter. His sad thoughts are conveyed in a manner which resembles the style of folk songs, with their constant repetition of phrases, with diminutives, direct address, and with the same restrained lyricism of feeling:

Why did you, my words,
So come out together
That my little girl
Had no faith in you?

That my little girl
Chose herself another,
Why did you, my words,
So come out together?

In most of such poems Aistis combines the folk elements with his own style to create verse which is intimately personal and yet related to the historical continuum of poetic feeling among the simple people.

Aistis' deep attachment to his country is not limited to the profound interest in folk heritage. There are many poems in which the central theme is simply the native soil and its people and in which the whole artistic purpose is to express his devotion to them. The moving poem "Lithuanian Women" recounts the hard lives and humble patience of the peasant women in the claws of sorrow and of time and ends in a kind of tragic apotheosis:

Thus turn gray the faces, thus the wood is weathered,
And no sign is left of suffering so great,
Only the sharp swords which penetrate the heart,
And the Holy Mother's pain under the cross.

Who then can your sorrow? Who the deeply hidden?
Who can see in you Antigone of old?
Wide and tragic spaces open like a wound,
Bend your head in sorrow, peasant-made Madonna!

The reference is to wooden statuettes of the Madonna of the Seven Sorrows, carved by country craftsmen, which can be found in wayside chapels throughout Lithuania. In echoing the images of swords and of the wounded sky in "The Seven Psalms" as well as the "wooden suffering" of Saint Francis, this poem underlines one of the most characteristic traits of Aistis' verse, namely the underlying unity of all of its imagery, whatever the specific topic or purpose of a given poem may be.

In all he does, Aistis continues to seek some unattainable dimension of experience, and the realm of art and the beloved homeland are only different names of one and the same vision, the dream country, where poets always wish to dwell. And it is not only the vision of the poets—it is the common human longing, expressed so well in many fairy tales. Quite naturally, therefore, we find that there is an aura of the legendary permeating the poetry of Aistis. He often chooses a fairy tale to be the embodiment of his experience, although we must remember that these are not real tales but only situations invented by the author to serve his design. Like the motifs of folk songs, they are artistic devices, akin in their nature and function to the metaphorical constructions of poetic imagery. We have already seen that in the poem "The Seven Psalms" the sunset is also a legend, a battle for the imprisoned princess under the sea. There are also poems describing caravans, as if from the *Arabian Nights*, trailing off to nowhere across the desert in search of happiness. Others center around the legend of Lorelei and of Parsifal, searching for love and the Holy Grail in a way which suggests Aistis' own search for the mystery of poetic experience. Perhaps the poem entitled "Fairy Tale" comes closest to being a direct statement of the meaning of legend in his poetry. Legend is simply reality enchanted, that is, reality transfigured by art, to which the poet must always return:

> Again we meet, reality enchanted.
> And I have yearned so much for you!
> There, on the shores, by the sea,
> The amber towers are standing.
>
> The amber towers, reaching for the sky—
> In them she lives;
> The ancient lindens whisper to her quietly,
> To princess mine.

So the poems turn and turn continuously around the same central core, the "amber tower" of the poet's dreams, and all the images are but so many names for something that cannot be explained. The basic images and metaphors appear again and again, constantly acquiring new meanings in their metamorphosis, until the reader begins to feel the same underlying design echoing back and forth in the words and cadences of each poem, uniting them all in a single musical statement of meaning and emotion. Aistis is organic and indivisible in one concentrated image, just as he is in all his poems. He speaks to the reader with all his being.

Yet, in all this unity of purpose, in the organic continuum of execution, there is a lurking doubt about the possibility of communication by means of art. In one of his poems Aistis wrote: "But do not judge from words and fields and forests / About myself—they are not me, but only my disguise." One might say that it is precisely the disguise, the mask an artist wears, which constitutes the essence of his craft, his main interest for the reader. But Aistis seems to feel that unless his real self somehow comes through in his work, he might fail as an artist. The processes of artistic creation, his very skill, seem a mystery to him—something he does not fully trust because they might be just so many lies, just ink and not the blood of his heart. Among the Lithuanian poets Aistis is especially remarkable for his constant, torturous interest in the very process of writing, and many of his poems are in fact meditations about his own verse. He feels that a poet is a slave to his words, and perhaps even, as he says in "Narcissus," the poet *is* the word:

Just so the greedy hearts of poets
Forget themselves while looking at the words,
And imperceptibly they turn to words themselves.

A verbal universe is in its essence not factual but conceptual, and therefore it may well consist of nothing but illusions. In one of his poems Aistis portrays the ambivalence of art. While, on the one hand, an artist merely deceives himself and his readers by playing God, there is, on the other, something genuine in the fictional universe of his words:

The frowning, black-browed evening came
As if a murderer, with bloody hands,
And in my thought I trod the ancient path of love,
I had the power to pronounce "So be it!" and it was.
Alas, there was no evening with black brows,
'Twas not a real evening, just one of my creation,
But you will walk along my ancient path of love
When you pick up my book from the dusty shelf.

The path itself, of course, is only an illusion, but the feeling that gives it birth will remain and make its inroads in the reader's heart. At least, this is the poet's hope, and hopes, as we well know, have a way of not being fulfilled. Most likely there will be no communication; the reader may obtain some pleasure, but not from what the poet has tried to say. The story of literary criticism is to a considerable extent a tale of such misunderstandings, and Aistis knows it as well as any poet. However, there is a peculiar twist in his reactions to his critics. Aistis does not seem so much to resent their obtuseness and lack of response to beauty as, on the contrary, their readiness to believe that the web of illusions created by the poet does actually represent reality:

But I said, my dear, that this was only verse,
Nothing but black ink, and these black thoughts of mine.
They discovered you there, found in them my love,
Found your cruel heart, and painful wounds in me.

The point is, probably, that the theme of romantic love, always present in his poems, must be understood for what it is, an artistic device, no different in essence from the elements of folklore or legend or from the contrast of two opposed idioms in his poetic language. The same is true of the images of beauty; as artistic devices, they amount to a mask hiding a tragic awareness of life. In a poem entitled "Erratum," Aistis takes off the mask for a moment and explains the dichotomy between image and reality in terms of age insisting upon the illusions of youth:

> Now the waves are different, and the sea has changed.
> Yes, too much of ink here, and too little blood!
> I would like to dash the page proofs to the flame
> And to start all over, everything anew.
>
> When the storm was howling, when the autumn wailed,
> And the forests groaned, and the branches broke,
> I was putting down a strange, unreal evening,
> May adorned with cherries, apple trees in bloom.
>
> How could I of blossoms in the winter's prison!
> And of sunny summer, when its echo's gone . . .
> So I beg you kindly: do omit these verses,
> 'Twas a human error, malice unforeseen.
>
> Winds and cherry blossoms whirled in their dance,
> Says the printed text, but the truth is this:
> Storms have bent the tree, years have crippled man—
> On page eight, line nine, reading from the top.

Yet the question of communication between the poet and his readers remains unanswered, for the poet's confession, rhymed and organized in images, becomes another mask. If on invented evenings unreal suns go down in seas of ink, what then is truth? If truth is art itself, then we are faced with a paradox which mocks the artist—truth can only be told by lying, reality does not exist except as fiction. There is no mystery to the creative experience—it is all just words. When an entire lifetime has been devoted to the creation of verbal universes that turn out to have no meaning, the end result is tragic beyond endurance. This is why Aistis sometimes breaks out in pure despair:

Sometime I saw in lies a hidden truth of sorts—
I lived this truth in agony and faith.
Now I am sick of truth and lies! And myriad stars
Have blossomed forth on heavy eyelids. . . .

The despair, of course, is not entirely pure, for there is art in the measure of lines in which it is conveyed and in the elaborate figure of speech describing tears. A poet simply cannot speak to us except through the mask of fiction, unless he abandons art altogether, in which case what he has to say might not be very interesting. We all have known sorrow and despair; we turn to poets for something of value found in the mask itself, in the art of speaking well of human tragedy. Aistis knows that he cannot help being a prisoner of his own creative gift, even if he thinks of it at times as of an evil stepmother who chained the princess to the mill. Disappointed in himself and in his readers, he keeps returning to his art.

I'm coming back to you; where to, my love,
Can I return now, all the bridges burned,
The ships all sunk,
And nobody expecting me?

It does not matter, though, that bridges have been burned and there is no one waiting for the poet. Ulysses and Penelope are no more real than a myth can be; that is, myth can only be a paradox—the perception of truth by means of an illusion. The poet, this "sailor from so many sunken ships," as Aistis put it, cannot help setting out to sea over and over again. Poetry is not a vocation that is chosen; rather, it is, in Aistis' words, "a fairy tale which comes and happens."

In this surrender there is also victory, like immortality in death. The poem "Saint Sebastian" (translated here by Demie Jonaitis) describes with force and beauty the moment of agonized waiting for the arrow of death to strike, for the fatal transition into the unknown which in itself is the exceptional condition of the artist, his agony as well as his apotheosis:

I trembled; eyes uplifted, I deplored
That agony might break my will at last—

One arrow here, the first to strike, O Lord,
And all that dread anxiety has passed.

I feel the fall of warmth and gentleness,
Drop after drop on me; my joints melt, while
Upon my vigil falls the far-off smile
Of my Redeemer coming, luminous.

Almighty, gloried be! I thought, so long,
This moment I would need a will that's strong.
Instead, You come towards me . . . O Lord, your light—
I cannot look, I'm blinded like the dead.
The vaults ring, jubilant with gentle might.
—I cannot lift my sinking, leaden head.

We have already spoken of Aistis' deep attachment to his native country. It remains to note his experience of exile. Exile left a deep mark, perhaps a scar, on his poetry, as it did in the work of all the other Lithuanian writers struggling with the problem of artistic identity in a world not of their making. Aistis' experience is exceptional because he left Lithuania long before there were any clear signs of the impending tragedy. He went to France in 1937 and has thus remained in exile longer than any other writer. A glance through his poems written in France before and during the war reveals a striking similarity of mood with the poetry produced much later, poetry of Kazys Bradūnas or Bernardas Brazdžionis written at the time when they had to leave their country, toward the end of the war. We find in them the same desperate and painful longing for just a handful of native soil, just a flower, a sweep of landscape, which betrays the perfectly natural homesickness and solitude of a man in an alien environment, where nothing he sees or touches relates to his inner world. Yet we must remember that the situation of the other writers was vastly different because they had to work in the context of great and tragic events which changed or destroyed the meaning of everything a man lives by, while Aistis in these early days still had the old frame of reference to rely upon. Lithuania was free, Europe had not yet gone mad, and he was just a traveler in foreign parts. The lack of any significant difference in thought and feeling between the work of Aistis and that of the other writers, produced in entirely different circumstances, seems to show that for most poets of the older generation exile did not really happen—all they experienced was simply dispossession, the physical removal from the country of their birth. Today, after twenty years, this is still the prevalent feeling in the Lithuanian community abroad. People still respond most deeply to the words Aistis wrote as far back as 1937:

> I remain alone . . . not the faintest echo . . .
> And you may be hurt, mistreated there by all?!
> Evening went away—a visage veiled in sorrow.
> We were left: the longing, night, and I.

When the Soviets came for the second time in 1944 and the final tragedy of exile did actually take place, Aistis responded immediately with great emotional intensity, but now it was his turn to misunderstand the true nature and dimensions of the catastrophe. The younger writers, Antanas Škėma, Henrikas Nagys, Alfonsas Nyka-Niliūnas, lived through the agony not only on a national but also on a universal plane. Their exile was for them just one manifestation of the general destruction of all the familiar humanistic values of pre-war Europe. They knew that they were now aliens in a world which had lost its sense of reality and become itself an exile from everything that life had once meant. Aistis, on the other hand, perceived the tragedy within the old familiar framework of suffering Lithuania, a country which had fought for its life throughout history and now had to do it again. There was nothing new for him in the Soviet occupation; his fatherland had become occupied before and had survived, and so, in the historical perspective, one has to keep faith in still another resurrection. The wheel seemed to have turned full circle, and Aistis now found himself in the same position Maironis had been in—a passionate, suffering prophet calling on his people to presevere in adversity, to struggle and to prevail in the end. Lithuania was again just a shining vision, and again it could be spoken of in the language of patriotic dreams:

> Just believe, my country, just stay true in faith,
> Proudly raise your face, marked by sorrow's hand—

Not just from today you had your gardens plundered,
Not just now you entered paths of agony.

Many generations have traversed this road,
Many more will flow like rivers to their fate—
Never having failed in steady hope before,
You will strive for freedom, you will keep your faith.

It took a long time for Aistis to realize that the significance of events this time went much deeper than ever before, so deep, in fact, that the very basis for faith in his country was shaken and exposed for what it was—a beautiful illusion. He began to meditate darkly on whether or not there was something in the Lithuanian national character itself which contained the seeds of self-destruction. Aistis had written patriotic poems before, praising the legend of ancient Lithuania with its great heroes, its conquests and self-sacrifice. Now he took another searching look at all this history, and it began to seem that there might have been less heroism than predatory drive, less sacrifice than grim, though petty, bickering. While Lithuanians went all the way to the Black Sea, they failed to notice that others were slowly taking over their own native hearth. His vision now turned to darkness, and he wrote poems asking some of the most bitter and honest questions that any writer had asked of his own people. For the most part he was answered by silence—there was little to say.

The silence continues. The Lithuanians in exile go on trying to build the best possible illusions from their lives. The poetry of Aistis remains with them enshrined in the glittering prison of general respect and recognition, as a cultural possession belonging less to him than to all the people. His heartache, however, is all his own.

5 Antanas Škėma—the Tragedy of Creative Consciousness

Antanas Škėma was born in Lódz, Poland, November 29, 1911, and died in an automobile accident in Pennsylvania, September 11, 1961.

Škėma returned with his parents to Lithuania in 1921. He studied medicine, then law, in the University of Kaunas. In 1935 he began to study drama. From 1936 to 1940 he was an actor with the Lithuanian State Theater in Kaunas, then moved to Vilnius in 1940 to become an actor and director in the Vilnius State Theater, where he remained until 1944.

In Germany he continued his work as an actor in several Lithuanian theaters in the displaced persons camps until 1949, when he came to the United States and became an elevator operator. While in the United States he was elected to membership in the PEN International Writers' Club.

Škėma's published works are *Nuodėguliai ir kibirkštys* (*Charred Stumps and Sparks*), 1947, a collection of short stories, including a one-act play, *Vieną vakarą* (*One Evening*); *Šventoji Inga* (*Saint Inga*), 1952, short stories; *Čelesta* (*Celeste*), 1960, a series of sketches written in the "stream of consciousness" manner; *Balta drobulė* (*The White Shroud*), 1958, a novel; and the plays *Pabudimas* (*The Awakening*), 1956, *Žvakidė* (*The Candlestick*), 1957, and *Kalėdų vaizdelis* (*The Christmas Play*), printed in *Metmenys*, (*Pattern Sketches*), a Lithuanian cultural magazine of the younger generation, in 1961. Several stories, an unfinished novel, and plays remain in manuscript. A new edition of Škėma's complete works has been undertaken recently; the first volume came out in 1967.

THE death of Antanas Škėma in a highway accident in 1961 brings to mind the fatal crash which took the life of Albert Camus. Death came to both men unexpectedly, although long awaited with a terrible, clear-eyed knowledge. Such an absurd way to die was cruelly, ironically appropriate for these men who understood absurdity so well.

By his death Antanas Škėma also vindicated his belief that the universe is governed by absurd and pitiless laws which require that vengeance be exacted upon those who disturb its dead, inhuman order by exercising their gift of imagination. In his works, the main protagonists usually perish at the highest point of their creative consciousness, when they become rebels against the inherent meaninglessness of the universe. It does not matter that they challenge the world not as a conqueror would but in the effort of love, asking only that reality should assent to transfiguration by the spirit of poetry living in the heart of man. If there is God, as we hope there is, and if He is good, as we must believe, the creative effort of man should bring him the reward of fulfillment. What happens instead is that man is obliterated forever in the bottomless void. Škėma's work, therefore, leaves the impression of a tense and worried attempt to puzzle out this impossible state of things. It resembles a tortuous and prolonged dialogue with an incomprehensible, silent God whose presence reveals itself only in the suffering and destruction of man.

Back in the era of romanticism Victor Hugo could pray to God like this:

> Je viens à Vous, Seigneur, Père qu'il faut croire,
> Je Vous porte à peser
> Les morceaux de cet coeur, plein de Votre gloire,
> Que Vous avez brisé.

Škėma's prayer is very different indeed. The people we meet in his works for the most part carry within themselves pieces of their broken hearts; they search for their Father in whom they must believe—some because they are mere childen, too young to countenance the possibility of nonbelief and others because they had been so cruelly punished for the creative and questioning spark they possess that they have become nothing but fearful, obsequious slaves of the nameless power which struck them. Such a slave is Antanas Garšva in the novel *Balta drobulė* (*The White Shroud*), when he prays feeling the vault of madness—the equivalent of death for the poet—closing inexorably over his head:

> Lord, You see how unhappy I am.
> I know I come too late, but save me.
> I promise

> I will tear up my notes, my poems,
> I will not think the way You do not wish.
> I will pray,
> I will enter a monastery.
> Lord, help me at least in my death.
> I believe You forgive at the last moment
> For all of one's life.
> Lord, Lord, into your hands . . .
> Oh, no, I'm just a miserable human being, Lord.
> Looooord!

Victor Hugo wrote his prayer at a time when people believed in impressive turns of phrase, in beautiful, dramatic gestures which, they knew, would not bring the pillars of the world crashing down about their ears. They thought it possible to tease a little the good God who holds the key to the mysteries of the universe. "*Je viens à Vous, Seigneur*," sounds like a noble, even elegant, rebellion against the God who, in His infinite mercy, will surely restrain His wrath. Good and evil will still remain clearly recognizable, and it will be possible to play the Prince of Darkness without jeopardizing one's rights to the kingdom of heaven. The people in Škėma's works, on the other hand, live in our time, when the pillars of the world have become so shaky that one or two atomic bombs will knock them down altogether. In such a world, games with God are no longer possible—unless played by madmen—and the last prayer of Garšva is a scream of terror coming from a heart that is humble and faithful yet filled with total despair. We can listen to this scream again in Škėma's play *Pabudimas* (*The Awakening*). There is a woman being led to execution by the Soviet secret police; we do not see her on stage, but only hear her voice:

> I won't go, I don't want to any more. Let go of my hand—there's a nice fellow—just for a moment. All right, I'll rest for a minute, all right, all right. Don't, you're hurting me, I won't go I said, I won't go. All right, don't drag me, I don't want to, I don't. Please don't drag me, I don't want to, I don't want to, all right. I don't want to, I don't, I don't, all right . . . (*The words turn into a scream, the steps conquer, they drag the woman on. The scream vanishes behind the door.*)

The Communist god here is quite different from that in *The White Shroud*, but in both instances the essence of the prayer is the same—helpless terror. Both powers are equally immovable. Adam committed the original sin and was punished, but he, at least, tasted of the fruit of paradise and could know good and evil. Today this fruit is already rotten—we don't know even this much any more—and yet the punishment goes on.

Such is the first impression upon reading Škėma. A rebellion, we are told, is an effort to assert one's human dignity. The mighty creative fire of the Renaissance was lit when the long-suffering medieval slave of God stood up and proclaimed his desire to be human. In *The Awakening*, Kazys, a Lithuanian rebel against the Soviet rule put to terrible and revolting torture, also cries that he wants to be human, but in the middle of his cry, "his face becomes all wrinkles, tears spurt from his eyes, animal groans issue from his throat."

If we listen well, we can hear this horrible scream in every critical experience undergone by Škėma's protagonists, as if this were the ultimate wisdom, the last word of the philosophers, the final "amen" after the prayer of an innocent child.

Paradoxically, at times Škėma seems capable of hearing a note of triumph in his human cry of despair. This would seem to go against all logic, but Škėma knew, as did Dostoevsky's Underground Man before him, that logic is the province of limited minds—minds that dwell safely inside the walls of what they call reality and therefore cannot begin to understand the quality of a creative act. The finger writes two and two makes four. Who does not believe in happiness is a pessimist. Who tortures and kills is a soulless monster. Who betrays his own people to the enemy is a despicable traitor. In Škėma's work, however, two and two may well add up to infinity. His ideas are not abstracted from human experience and cut to manageable size on the writer's desk. They remain as organic parts of a living man, and therefore their nature and validity is subject not as much to logic as to the infinite variety of unpredictable human responses to life in which passion, fear, desire, and inspiration may well play the dominant part.

In *The Awakening*, for instance, the Soviet secret police investigator,

Pijus, attempts to force Kazys, his former friend, successful rival, and now an underground hero, to betray resistance secrets by torturing Elena, the woman they both love but Kazys has married, before Kazys' eyes. Pijus continues to love both his captives and also secretly hates them both with the fury of the defeated. Now he wants to win his victory by means of the power given him by an ideology which, as he thinks, stands for the immutable laws of history. Pijus has accepted this ideology not for its intrinsic values but for the hypnotic force of its perfect logical design, from which he hopes to derive his own personal perfection and invincibility. "The sun," says Pijus, "makes the fragile flower grow; the sun also burns out deserts. Water has the same quality, and so does fire, so does earth itself. In our system man shall acquire his greatest possession: absolute objectivity." As it turns out, however, it is precisely this objectivity that Pijus lacks in the performance of what he thinks is his duty but what actually amounts to a desperate and tortured effort to resolve his own endlessly complex dilemma which he himself cannot begin to comprehend. And so he loses again. Having set up the inhuman torture of Kazys and Elena, he cannot bear their suffering and shoots Kazys, without having learned his secrets, on a sudden impulse of pity. Pity has destroyed the invincible force to which Pijus had committed himself. Loving both Kazys and Elena, he has tortured them both, and while torturing them he has understood that he possesses no right to do so in the name of his truth because he does love them in human terms. His truth forsakes him, and he himself falls into the hands of the Communist police. In his last hour he prays again, striving to believe in a different God, repeating the Lord's Prayer after the priest Antanas, another of his victims. Thus the protagonists all perish, but what remains is stronger than the darkness enveloping them. It is man's love for freedom, in the name of which Kazys and Elena die and remain victorious, and man's love for man, which constitutes the tragedy and the glory of Pijus. In this way, the noble qualities of man remain triumphant, and in their agony Škėma's heroes receive a priceless gift—the same tragic dimension in which resounds the terrible voice of Christ: "My God, my God, why hast thou forsaken me!"

For this reason, the experience of tragedy in Škėma's works can never be described in human terms alone. His protagonists possess the paradoxical ability to function as symbolic representations of the many-faceted relationship between man and God, without themselves becoming larger than life. They do not fit the definition of a tragic hero as someone whose qualities elevate him far above his fellow men, and yet their lives, their passions and sufferings, are comprehensible only in relation to an all-encompassing moral and metaphysical idea. In *The Awakening*, as in other works, we meet a number of individuals who seem to be struggling with nothing more than their personal problems, but the outcome of the struggle always implies something about the nature of good, of evil, and of eternity. The priest Antanas, for instance, waits in fear and trembling for his inevitable death, but over and above his anguish there is the much greater agony of constant thought about his sister who committed suicide because Antanas would not allow her to leave the monastery even though she could no longer live the life of the nun without perverting her own humanity. The terrible question that this priest must face in his hour of death is this: Is it really true that absolute faith demands an absolute commitment? By insisting that his sister must remain in the monastery, has Antanas perhaps committed a blasphemy by transforming the suffering God into a granite idol, born of man's perverse imagination, no different in essence from the "absolute objectivity" which Pijus professed to believe? His moral principles, turned monstrous without the human quality of mercy, come to haunt him in the revolting nightmare of a toothless, idiotically grinning Madonna. Both Pijus and Antanas are forsaken by their respective gods, the priest because he did not know pity and the secret police interrogator because he did. It is quite appropriate, therefore, that they should both kneel down to pray at the end of the play, searching together for still another God.

A curious facet of Škėma's art is his handling of characters. While acting out their lives on the purely human plane, they seem to be aware somehow that what they do has no reality except in terms of the symbolic. They take a strangely impersonal attitude toward their very personal conflicts and very genuine death, as if they know that all the world is indeed a stage and that they are only acting out their parts in some metaphysical mystery. Kazys and Pijus, for instance, locked in desperate combat, show no personal hatred toward each other but rather the solidarity of two actors performing a terrible ritual. Similarly Elena, after unspeakable tortures and after the death of Kazys, can speak to Pijus with an unearthly calm, explaining to him the issues of their struggle and the reasons for her ultimate victory.

Not only are Škėma's heroes symbolic of ideas and forces greater than themselves but they also gradually blend in the reader's mind into a single hero—an embodiment of the spirit of poetry in man. We meet this man-poet in various guises in all of Škėma's works. He comes to us as a little child in the story "Sunny Days," from a cycle called *Šventoji Inga* (*Saint Inga*). The time is the Russian Revolution, and young Martynukas, with his father and mother, is on the way to Lithuania to escape the terrors of Bolshevism. They do not succeed; the Soviet authorities catch up with them and execute all three on the spot. This is the outer framework, the story line. The inner action, however, consists of a giant leap by Martynukas into the arms of God. The leap begins in an old orchard, from a rickety stepladder. Martynukas has a friend, Vaska, who wants to play a practical joke on "the dreamer" and tells him that if he would climb on the ladder, shout three times as loud as he can, "God, my God, please show yourself," and then jump down, he would not fall on the ground but rise up to heaven, to the bosom of the Lord. Martynukas is a poet because he understands words literally, because he assumes that everyone else understands them the same way, and because in his consciousness there is no dividing line between miracle and reality. And so, he jumps:

> And he runs to the ladder, he climbs, he shouts hoarsely, "God, my God, please show yourself!" and he jumps and falls, and rises again and climbs once more. His white shirt is dirty, his hair disheveled, his pants are torn, blood is pounding in his temples, he falls, he rises, he climbs. Ha, ha, ha, chee, chee, laughs Vaska, all doubled up. His laughter grows, expands, laughter inundates all the wide open spaces of the earth, the whole world is laughing, choking with laughter.

While the world is laughing, Martynukas comes to realize that one must die before he can rise up to God. He remembers the hanged White Guard officers, with their tongues sticking out, suspended from the lampposts halfway up to heaven. He does not remember, but the reader does, Jesus Christ hanging on the cross. Soon it is Martynukas' turn. Stood up against the wall, he screams:

> . . . and in his scream he understands that his mother is lying on the ground and that he, too, will soon lie there, and that to heaven one must rise, fly and fly, that one cannot lie on the ground if he wishes to see the good Lord. And he clambers up, holding on to his father's shoulder, and the military commissar Vasilevsky pulls out his pistol and squeezes the trigger four times.

Thus for little Martynukas the ultimate poetic experience is death. Škėma offers no opinion about whether Martynukas rises up to heaven or disappears into the void. Being himself a poet, he keeps his glance directed to the earth. On the earth we see a good man, Medvedenko, who loved the mother of Martynukas and who now is taking his dead love, as poets do, to be buried on a high hill in the steppe, where there is a grove of acacia trees and a cool spring runs over green stones:

> A sweet and sticky smell emanates from the poorly made coffin, the horse can no longer stand the smell, gives the cart a sudden pull and starts running. Medvedenko falls down, a green lizard flashes before his eyes, stiff grass cuts his face, he cries out, stands up, runs after the cart. Small horse, small cart, small man, the hills come nearer and nearer. Oh how terribly burns the sun, we will not get there by evening, we will not get anywhere at all.

In *Saint Inga* there is another cycle of stories called "Three About a Train." Here the image of the poet is embodied in a young man, Ignas, whose life is suspended between two catastrophes—the two world wars of our century. The stories might be said to have an epic dimension of their own, but it is an internal epic, not concerned with the enormous number and complexity of external events but, rather, concerned only with their terrible meaning on the symbolic plane. The meaning, as Škėma sees it, is betrayal and destruction of all supreme human values. Ignas is a poet at heart because he thinks that love is holy, a communion of saints. Knowing his human limitations, he is therefore afraid of it. Thinking painfully, worshipfully of love, he becomes obsessed with the self-created image of his mother. Because of his poetic turn of mind, his mother must, for him, be the ideal of motherhood, must be the Madonna. So, he worships her and is afraid of her, too, and the ideas of love for a woman and love for his mother blend into a single image of sainthood and fear.

It is then that the blow falls. What he sees one night in the orchard might be shocking enough for any man, but for the poetic soul of Ignas it is the ultimate catastrophe and the end of the world. His mother, Madonna, and the high school chaplain are standing there in an embrace, lustfully "rubbing their bellies together." The holy light of sainthood fades like an immaterial mask from his own hidden desires and fears, and everything turns into a foul and evil caricature. Ignas was a dreamer; now his world is a nightmare. In this nightmare he sees himself lying on a bench, naked, with his own mother. The poet's vision had lighted the heaven full of stars; now he walks through swamps with ugly, misshapen stars reflected in the muddy waters.

The tragic irony of the situation is that Ignas, the poet, should have understood that this catastrophic evening in the orchard was really an affirmation of man's basic humanity against the murderous spirit of law wearing the mask of sainthood. His mother, after all, had but two alternatives—be human or turn into an impossible idol of purity, bound tight in the strait jacket of false holiness. As for the priest, he, too, is but a man who, if he were to obey the iron dictates of his calling, would betray humanity in himself as did Antanas when he forbade his sister to leave the monastery.

The defeat of Ignas goes even deeper. Perhaps he could understand this catastrophe but refuses to from an animal fear that his own incestuous desire for his mother would then stand revealed in all its ugly nakedness. In any case, Ignas, like the whole world around him, is left in ruins after the First World War. Then the wheel of time turns, the second global catastrophe comes, it is war again. Ignas is now in love with a beautiful girl, Inga (the symbolic nature of the protagonists is already evident in their names, Ignas and Inga, like Caius and Caia in ecclesiastical terminology, signifying lovers in general). He still does not know how to be human, because Inga for him is again a figure of sainthood—Saint Inga—and she remains unapproachable, a living symbol of the impossibility of happiness. Life itself, as if in cruel and ironic pity, makes Inga literally unreachable for him; she dies in a train wreck. Ignas wanders through the ruins of the war, looking for her grave in cemeteries, where the green frogs of hope are jumping about in vain. His longing grows and takes him beyond, to the metaphysical dimension, where there is a train and Inga, waiting for him and dying forever. Ignas comes to her, but he cannot free her from death because he is still alive and the love of the living is a temporary thing; it weakens with time and loses the power of resurrection.

Thus the image of the poet in Škėma's works always emerges from the tension between love and death. Death and love appear in many guises, evoke a multitude of emotions, ideas, actions, create and destroy many answers to the riddles of the universe. Škėma demonstrates this with special dramatic clarity in his plays, in which his man-poet, burdened with a multitude of complex and contradictory private emotions, is confronted with an enormous and tragic reality requiring radical action and fatal decisions. In *The Awakening*, the extreme situation of the torture room in the Soviet prison forces the actors to destroy one another and themselves, almost as if in some nightmarish dance, with Kazys, Pijus, and Elena going round and round, holding hands with love and death.

In another play, *Žvakidė* (*The Candlestick*), similar complex and tortured poetic personalities try to work out their destinies and fulfill their private desires while the reality of the given moment is crashing down over their heads like a giant wave about to engulf them all. The scene is Lithuania in 1941, in the last few days of the first Soviet occupation, just before the German attack. The last Lithuanian victims of Communism are going to their deaths, often betrayed by their own people. One such traitor is Kostas, a bitter and complex figure. As a child he yearned for music and love but was rejected by his family, and his love turned to hatred or, rather, put on the mask of hatred without ceasing to be love, however perverted. Similarly, his music rises up like a fierce dark stream entering and distorting the Bach toccatas he plays on the organ of an abandoned church. The church is empty because Kostas has betrayed its parson, his father's brother, to death.

Kostas has a brother, Antanas, who, like Abel in the Bible, represents the figure of light. Noble and humble, radiant with love, he nevertheless remains guilty of the fact that their parents loved him and not Kostas. As the German advance turns the sky blood red, Kostas, tortured by the growing awareness that he became what he is out of jealousy, decides to cut through his tangled inner conflicts by taking a resolute step toward damnation. He kills his brother with a huge candlestick before the altar in the church. The Cain and Abel theme thus introduced removes the conflict from the context of a specific time and place and makes it a recurring theme from the very beginnings of human history, translated again by Škėma into the framework of love and death. Kostas brings death to Antanas (and himself) in revenge for the love he was refused in childhood. Antanas, through his love and trust, achieves his fulfillment, which is death.

In these two plays there is a determined effort by Škėma to discern the principles of good and evil through the tangled web of contradictions, ironies, and fears in the shadow of catastrophe. In his next piece, called *Kalėdų vaizdelis* (*A Christmas Play*), Škėma seems at first to give up this effort altogether. We can no longer point our finger to the supposed villains and heroes. All are only sufferers, and through their sins they search for self-fulfillment, half-blinded with alcohol, fear, and pain. The whore Magdalena, for instance, has always wanted to be a dancer and to strew flowers under the feet of priests in processions. Now she sleeps with many men, but "even so, every time I was in bed with a man, I imagined that I was dancing, dancing very beautifully and elegantly." Panašus (his name translates as "he who resembles," i.e., Christ, although he is, perhaps, a madman and an impostor) kisses her gently on her maidenly lips as one would kiss an innocent. Two other people, Skaidra and Danguolė his wife, seem to be in an irrevocable conflict, but from their mutual heart-rending explanations the reader understands that the issue is not hatred or guilt but simply suffering; they have been so created that they cannot help hurting each other.

Panašus invites them both to join his feast of joy, to taste water turned into wine.

The way Panašus-Christ gathers everyone in to the shelter of his love creates a feeling that *A Christmas Play*, far from being a story of crime and punishment, is an apotheosis of universal forgiveness or, possibly, of universal agony in the name of One who has given meaning to all human suffering through his own Calvary. This feeling is present in the dialogues, in the quarrels; everything is permeated with the expectation of some great love which would embrace everyone, sorrows, sins, revolting vulgarity, and all. What we see is the face of humanity covered with dirt, sores, and pus—a face waiting to be kissed by the Redeemer. Quite logically, therefore, the action is set on Christmas Eve. This is the time of expectation. Ironically, also, the place is a mental hospital, described in such a way as to suggest that the whole world might really be nothing but a madhouse, waiting insanely for something that never did happen and never could.

The character of Skaidra in *A Christmas Play* absorbs, supersedes, and transfigures the characters of Pijus and Kostas in the two previous plays. As if he feels himself to be the actor called upon to portray the greatest human sin, Skaidra raises his hand not against other people but directly against Panašus-Christ. And Panašus tells him quite clearly that this is his task. "Do your work, Skaidra," he says, almost as if this were the eleventh commandment of God. Because of this, the role of Skaidra-Judas acquires a special kind of nobility. His task is terrifying, but because it must be done, we are almost thankful to Skaidra for having taken upon himself this sin. We all murder God in many ways in our hearts, but it is Skaidra who literally performs the deed, thus taking up the burden of all our sins. In this way he paradoxically begins to resemble Christ, because His cross, too, is made of all our sins. If we were now to assume that Judas represents the principle of death, and Christ the principle of love, we can see how, in a final paradox, their roles in the fate of mankind blend into one. Death and love are one, together forever in an eternal waiting, like the unending moment of dying in *Saint Inga*, the most unbearable and the most significant reality.

We have previously said that Škėma's heroes seem to challenge the world in an effort of love. The world responds to this effort by completely obliterating the challenger in the end, but the first step toward destruction is to make man realize that he is not wanted on earth. The whole world is ruled by logical inevitabilities which, in their dead clarity, are entirely incomprehensible to the living imagination. The blind laws of the universe do not admit the possibility of its poetic transfiguration, and for this reason the universe remains unreal for Škėma's man-poet. He is doomed to be a stranger, an exile.

Such understanding of the fact of exile separates Škėma rather sharply from some other Lithuanian writers for whom exile is merely physical—the loss of the homeland, its meadows, brooks, native villages, and of people dear to them. In Škėma's works exile is a general human condition, insofar as "human" specifically means imagination, creativity, and a yearning for immortality in an organic fusion with the very sources of being. A man is an exile because his spark of divinity alienates him from the earth, his mother. The only way back to the native soil is over the threshold of death.

This deep-seated conflict between the imperative need to belong to the world (or, rather, with the world to ultimate reality; Škėma has stated that "both worlds are unreal, the actual and the one created by me. In a real world they would blend into one") and the unavoidable necessity of remaining a stranger is reflected in all facets of Škėma's fiction, first of all, perhaps, in his style. We find tender, warm descriptions of man's response to life in himself and around him, descriptions that seem to weave together man's own consciousness and the throbbing vitality of nature into a rich and colorful tapestry of being. In contrast, we also find bitterly ironical statements, juxtapositions of highest exultation and lowest animal needs, as if Škėma, burdened by the foreknowledge of his heroes' doom, wanted to expose the cruel mockery of their situation in a kind of tortured revenge for the indignity inherent in man's bondage to nature's laws. A typical example is the picture of a man with diarrhea, sitting in the outhouse and contemplating the blueness of the sky through a heart-shaped hole in the door. Torn by such contrasts, the narrative often resembles a confused mosaic of accidental sights and inner visions, of masks and living faces, of past and present, and of distant places continuing the landscape directly before one's eyes. It does seem to represent a recognizable picture even on the surface, but its real meaning lies in the symbolic relationship of one piece of mosaic to another. Here is a picture of a man walking down Broadway from a collection of sketches entitled *Čelesta* (*Celeste*):

> Golgotha is the falling of a burning airplane into the abyss, the cry of a four-year-old over the mother's corpse, the steps of a pregnant girl, the agony of a man under interrogation in a jail cell, the silence of the paralyzed in bed. A little song about love lost is quivering on Broadway, there are many beggars on Broadway, the sailors are squeezing the girls' hands, my cross is higher than the highest skyscraper; it is an advertisement for a fragrant soap.

A walk on Broadway thus becomes the road to Calvary, and every fact of existence contributes to the final agony of the Crucifixion.

Škėma's longest work, the novel *The White Shroud*, is concerned with the same issues that exist in his other works. The main hero, Antanas Garšva, is again a poet, trying to create, to feel life as profoundly as he can. The deeper his feeling is, the greater the suffering. While still in high school, Garšva learned the precepts of Schopenhauer: "optimism is a bitter mockery of human sorrow; life is evil because life is struggle; the more perfect an organism, the more perfect is its suffering." The novel is full of life, but it begins with Garšva attempting suicide and ends with him becoming insane.

From one point of view the novel is mainly about the defeat of the poet. Garšva possesses the two essential poetic gifts—the ability to have a completely original, profoundly personal view of life and the ability to describe what he sees. The task of the poet, for him, is to accomplish a miracle—to speak such language that from his words, as from the touch of a divine hand, the blind would see and darkness would change into a world rich with color and form. But Garšva does not succeed, and the hand of darkness closes his own eyes. The causes of his defeat are several, none of them accidental, all connected intimately with the innate qualities of the poet himself. Thus, in a way, his being a poet is also his own undoing. With the same gesture with which he challenged the powers of darkness he delivers a mortal blow to himself.

First of all, a poet is a kind of distortion of the laws of nature. By conceiving a special dimension of being, he breaks the general course of life; for this reason he is a miracle and a monstrosity at the same time. At the very beginning of the novel we can see that Garšva knows it:

> Many geniuses were sick. Be glad you're neurotic. The book was written by Louis E. Bisch, M.D., Ph.D. Two doctors in one. The double Louis E. Bisch affirms Alexander the Great, Caesar, Napoleon, Michelangelo, Pascal, Pope, Poe, O. Henry, Walt Whitman, Molière, Stevenson were all neurotics. It is a convincing list. At the end: Dr. Louis E. Bisch and Antanas Garšva.

Garšva is sick, and his illness is inherited from his mother. His mother liked fairy tales about handsome princes and knights dying in battle. The fairy tales were sad. The mother's hair was black, she was beautiful, and she wore clothes of black satin. She carried in herself the seed of mental aberration which rose to the surface because of her husband's vulgar jealousy. Under emotional stress she wasted away, became insane, turned into an ugly monster. Thus the gift of poetry becomes intimately connected with the heritage of madness.

Secondly, every word of the poet crashes against the wall of reality and, because this wall is much stronger, it is the poet who gets crushed and not reality. In the case of Garšva, this happens during the first Soviet occupation of Lithuania. By this time Garšva has advanced his poetic development to the point where he is able to grasp the genuine ancient spirit of poetry in Lithuanian folklore and songs. He understands that the oldest Lithuanian songs were based on play with words, on groups of sounds with purely musical and emotional but nonverbal meanings, stemming from the slow and continuous blending of man with nature. As for the contemporary romantic notions about the Lithuanian national character, manifest in the work of poets who wanted to write "like the people," Garšva has this to say:

> He remembered the old Lithuanian harmonies his father used to sing, true in their lyrical atonality. Then came the serfdom, and later the

> liberated slaves could do no better than to imitate their former masters—to harmonize the songs, to transport to the north the creaky old Mount Olympus. Perkūnas, Pykuolis, Patrimpas, the high priests, the vestal virgins—all were but imported southern gods and their servants, now hastily putting on Lithuanian names and national costumes.

And here is the true national spirit, as it seems to Garšva:

> *Lole palo eglelo,*
> *Lepo leputėli,*

> sang the nightingale. All that was needed was to stand in the forest and to watch the snakes hugging the ground with their long bodies, see the toads observing the universe with their concave eyes. One had to meditate without cogitating. Words were nothing but magic formulas. Incomprehensible and significant, like the formation of fog. . . .
>
> Honeycombs, sheaves of grain, rues, tulips, and lilies. Lazy and sweets-loving bears. The sap of pine trees—golden amber. The foam of the Baltic Sea, sucked in slowly by the amber sand. . . . Ancient Balt, musical Balt, show me the tree to which you prayed. Does it command? No. Does it comfort? Yes. Look at the smoke rising into the sky, at the will-o'-the-wisp, at the bird in flight. At the cherry leaf. You may.

The Bolsheviks do not understand this and tell Garšva to write a truly "proletarian" poem, presumably one that will meet the demands of "socialist realism." Garšva cannot force himself, and is so severely beaten by the secret police that his innate tendency toward psychological disorders turns into a steadily growing, irrepressible threat of madness. Ironically, the hand that beats Garšva belongs to a true Lithuanian of the ancient cast, a village lad who is personally rather fond of the "unacceptable poems" by Garšva.

The third defeat of the poet is due to the fact that he always sacrifices too much to poetry. Religion and poetry have at least this much in common—that they demand from the elect their full devotion, a renunciation not only of the world but also of themselves. Generally speaking, love may be said to increase the measure of perfection in man, to deepen his capacity for feeling, to bring him nearer the poetic consciousness. But to a poet love is a hindrance, for it provides a shelter, a home, protection from reality, whereas a poet should always remain vulnerable to reality, since poetry is pain. Garšva meets Elena and falls in love and then deliberately renounces his love, cuts the thread of human ties and remains alone. This refusal then destroys his heart. Reality is the organic and irresistible urge to love and be loved. Refused, this urge turns into still another fury driving Garšva into madness. Nevertheless, the very process by which a poet is defeated in this life brings a rich treasure of new thoughts, new experiences, new understanding. And this is the meaning of the creative life. In his defeat, Garšva remains victorious for our sake, just as Kazys and Elena are victorious in *The Awakening.*

After all the human agony revealed by Škėma, the lasting effect of his work is one of a mysterious elevation of the soul, as though it were a priceless, though painful, gift. We might return to the ideas of Schopenhauer, which Garšva pondered so carefully: the more perfect an organism, the more perfect the suffering. There is an exquisitely poetic depiction of such suffering in the cycle called "Apocalyptic Variations" in *Saint Inga.* The motto for this cycle is from the Book of Revelation (21:18–21): "And the building of the wall it was *of* jasper: and the city *was* pure gold, like unto clear glass. And the foundations of the wall of the city *were* garnished with all manner of precious stones. The first foundation *was* jasper; the second, sapphire; the third, a chalcedony; the fourth, an emerald; the fifth, sardonyx; the sixth, sardius; the seventh, chrysolite; the eighth, beryl; the ninth, a topaz; the tenth, a chrysoprasus; the eleventh, a jacinth; the twelfth, an amethyst." Such is the kingdom of heaven. As for the earth, one episode in the "Variations" describes a collision between a trolley and a truck carrying gasoline in Chicago. This is how the people on the trolley perish:

> A great fire stabs through the walls of the trolley. It is too late to jump out. Pure gold splashes on the hair of the boy, and the hair bursts into emerald. The mother grasps her son's head, sapphire and chalcedony, and chrysolite and sardonyx tear her stomach to pieces. Fists beat against the windows, the glass shatters in sardius and beryl. Jasper, topaz, and chrysoprasus shoot forth from between the twisted fingers. Then comes the darkness, because fire licks out the eyes and the people can no longer see jacinth and amethyst.

Perfect suffering is pain beyond enduring, made from the same rare jewels that went into the making of the kingdom of heaven. This may well be the essence of Škėma's perception of the world. When spiritualized, this suffering is the goal toward which man strives in Škėma's works. This is why death is needed, for it is the ecstasy which raises man to his highest degree of perfection.

6 Kostas Ostrauskas and the Theater of Death

Kostas Ostrauskas belongs to the younger generation of Lithuanian writers in exile, having been born April 5, 1926, in southern Lithuania. While still in high school in Kaunas, he became a member of the Lithuanian Young People's Theater. High school education was completed in Luebeck, Germany, in 1946. Ostrauskas then attended the Baltic University in Hamburg, Germany, until 1949, when he came to the United States. He studied Baltic and Slavic languages in the University of Pennsylvania and in 1958 received his Ph.D. in Lithuanian language and literature, having written his doctoral dissertation on the late nineteenth-century Lithuanian novelist Jonas Biliūnas. At the present time Ostrauskas is a member of the Institute of Lithuanian Studies. He writes plays and since 1958 has been head of the music library in the University of Pennsylvania.

His published plays are *Pypkė* (*The Pipe*), written in 1951, published in 1954; *Kanarėlė* (*The Canary*), written in 1951, published in 1958; *Žaliojoj lankelėj* (*In the Green Meadow*), 1963; *Gyveno kartą senelis ir senelė* (*Once Upon a Time There was an Old Man and an Old Woman*), 1963; and *Duobkasiai* (*The Gravediggers*), first published in English translation in the Lithuanian student magazine *Lituanus* in 1967. *The Pipe* was published in English in *Arena,* the quarterly of the PEN International Writers' Club, in 1963.

Ostrauskas has been active in Lithuanian cultural organizations in exile, as member of the cultural council of the World Lithuanian Community Organization and as member and head of the literary section of the Institute of Lithuanian Studies.

KOSTAS Ostrauskas is generally thought to represent the "theater of the absurd" on the Lithuanian stage in exile. His short plays produce a strange and haunting effect while distorting our conventional notions of life, unlike the traditional theater, which usually mimics or reinforces them. What we see on the stage at times does not seem to make any sense at all, and yet some compelling power reaches out from the plays to make us go on exploring them for profundities that we feel the author must have hidden somewhere between the lines. It is a difficult game, however, since we do not really know what the ground rules are. Nothing in our usual conception of stage reality, developed through the long collaboration between tradition and art, seems to correspond to the spectacle set before us. In one play, for instance, an actor rises from the audience and demands our attention because, as he says, he is "bringing the pipe." Then he gets up on the stage, turns out all the lights, and laughs uproariously in total darkness. In another play, a decrepit ancient kills a young man with a hammer, then puts the hammer to his lips like a flute, and out come the sweet strains from *Orpheus and Euridice*. The guilty conscience of the contemporary playgoer, so often browbeaten and accused of insensitivity, will prompt him to nod his head wisely in appreciation of the fine point undoubtedly just made; as he does so, he becomes perhaps the most absurd figure in the whole theater.

We may use this ludicrous figure of the spectator as a starting point in our discussion of Ostrauskas' work, since a spectator *is* reality, and reality, when looked at in a certain way, can appear more irrational than the wildest fancy. The word absurdity should thus be used with some hesitation in describing this kind of theater, because sense or nonsense often depends on the relative angle of vision. A square peg seems absurd when we try to fit it into a round hole, but otherwise it is a perfectly sensible, very square peg. In reading Ostrauskas, we are struck first of all by this ability to see the potential strangeness in the very simplest things in life and to manipulate the shifting points of view to produce a significant commentary on the human condition.

Ostrauskas' longest play, *Kanarėlė* (*The Canary*), is especially remarkable for its deceptive ordinariness, concealing a rather special vision. On the surface the play seems quite conventional, obeying, as it does, most precepts of the traditional theater. The setting imitates a clearly recognizable reality—an old, broken-down hut in Lithuania, inhabited by professional beggars. There is a plot in which the ordinary human passions of envy and hatred provide the motive for action. The play also observes the three classical unities and even has something reminiscent of the Greek chorus—loud and piercing voices of children—providing a counterpoint to the deep inner silence of the main character, a beggar named Juozupas who is blind and later becomes deaf as well. The story itself is fairly simple. Juozupas is a good man whose inborn nobility arouses sympathy in people and makes him successful in obtaining alms. Jokūbas, his fellow beggar, envies both the success and the nobility, which he knows he cannot achieve. He would like somehow to destroy and humiliate Juozupas so that there would no longer be any reason for him to feel inferior. The opportunity presents itself when Juozupas brings home a caged canary which he, for reasons not immediately apparent, simply took off somebody's window sill. Jokūbas then induces the two other people in the play, a beggar named Rokas and a half-insane girl, Aneliukė, to collaborate with him in substituting a sparrow for the canary, the idea being that the next morning, when Juozupas wakes up and hears the rasping voice of the sparrow instead of the beautiful song of the canary, he will be shocked into recognizing his own unworthiness. Actually, the spiteful and childish Jokūbas does not understand his motives as clearly as that; all he knows he wants is to make Juozupas look ridiculous for a moment. During the night, however, something terrible happens; Juozupas becomes completely deaf. In the morning he hears nothing, and thus has no way of knowing that a sparrow has been substituted. What he does know is that God, for some reason, has punished him beyond all measure. He is not conscious of having stolen the canary in the way that a true thief would; the beauty of the bird's song simply overwhelmed him and made all rational and responsible thinking irrelevant. The play ends with Jokūbas and Rokas being crushed by their deed, the cruel consequences of which they did not foresee, while Juozupas, having decided that he must have been guilty after all, goes back to the town to return what he still thinks is the canary, as if hoping that once the restitution is made he will be able to hear again.

The complexities of the play begin to emerge as we look closer at its texture. We notice things which make no sense within the simple realistic context, and their very absurdity then suggests the presence of another level of meaning. It seems peculiar, for instance, that the three paupers should actually own a house, poor though it is. Some realistic explanation for this could, perhaps, be devised, but the point is that none is needed. The house provides its justification as a symbolic reflection of the beggars' own inner world within the confines of their decrepit imaginations. What we really see on the stage are people with a confused inner striving, held prisoner by their human nature, embodied many times over in the rotting, broken, miserable things surrounding them in the room. The canary in its cage—a bright yellow, singing dot in this gray mass—becomes a thing of beauty beyond description, a bird of paradise imprisoned on the earth. This symbolism is then repeated in the human dimension. Aneliukė, the half-wit, is inwardly full of song and light, but only confused, disjointed words and snatches of melody come through the fog of madness enveloping her. In this context, the ridiculous and nasty prank of Jokūbas acquires a terrible significance, for it snuffs out the brightness of these human hearts, turning them into gray sparrows, still imprisoned, still frightened, but no longer beautiful. The fact that Jokūbas cannot possibly understand such implications makes his own situation, and the logic of his deed, unbearably absurd and ironical.

The sudden deafness of Juozupas, so pointless at first glance, now also acquires its place in the hidden logic of things. His whole nobility is based on the absence of hatred in his soul and on the conviction that everyone else is also good. The little canary has been like a guiding light in his dark world, a symbol of all his dreams ever since childhood, before he went blind, when he saw one in a rich man's room. At that moment he understood something inexpressible except through tears, and this wordless mystery of beauty remained with him all his life as the only thing worth possessing. We might even say that he therefore became a beggar out of the richness of his heart, like a poor wandering monk who has nothing to offer in return for alms except God's own glory. If Juozupas had heard the sparrow in the cage, he would have understood that there were people who hated him enough to aim straight at the center of his universe, at this shining light of heaven. It is better, then, to become deaf and hear nothing. What happens to him is thus not misfortune but salvation, the terrible grace of God.

The so-called absurd theater has come into existence in our contemporary world which knows (or at least claims) that God is dead. If so, then salvation in itself becomes the greatest absurdity, and it would seem so also in Ostrauskas' play were it not for the fact that he deals with a world where the presence of God is overwhelming, whether it be true faith or just a mechanical repetition of His name during the prayers that beggars chant for hours on end. A beggar lives constantly with God, even if he does not believe in Him, and therefore he gets accustomed to measuring his life according to the precepts of religion. There is a religious aura in the play which transforms Juozupas from a pitiful figure to one of tragic dignity. On the other hand, it augments the small nasty thing Jokūbas does into an act of boundless evil, crushing this man under a moral burden out of all proportion with his puny soul. At this point we may begin to understand something of the peculiar contribution that modern theater has made to our consciousness of moral values in life. In the traditional plays the outstanding heroes were people of tremendous spiritual dimensions, and the great villainies were performed by men of corresponding evil strength, but here we see no such relation between the characters and the significance of their acts. We may call such theater absurd, but it is also true that it has brought imaginary human experience much closer to our own reality and made real-life villains much more comprehensible and therefore terrifying. Ostrauskas belongs among those playwrights of our time who know that in a world gone mad, truth can only be made apparent by means of a distortion.

The stylistic devices in *The Canary* also have the quality of becoming more complicated as we take a closer look at them. What at first seems like a continuous flow of nondescript language breaks up into several layers characterized by distinct features. Rokas and Jokūbas speak the rude idiom of the beggars, full of barbarisms, snatches of proverbs, and stock phrases which, through constant repetition, produce a kind of hypnotic effect, so that we sometimes even fail to notice how deliberately inappropriate they are to a given situation. Juozupas, on the other hand, is apt to mix the untutored beggarly speech with sudden turns to great unconscious lyrical beauty when he talks about something dear to his heart. Describing the first and only time he saw a canary in his childhood, Juozupas says:

> I still remember when I used to run about the estate, still too small to have any pants on. Once the master called me—a good man he was—took me, runny nose and all, to his chambers, and he says to me: "Look, kid." Oh, lordy! Sings and pecks at little white grains as if barley. "That's a canary," says he. "Did you ever see one?" It took all my breath away . . . I stand there, mute like a fence post and just keep swallowing my tears . . . Yellow, tiny, and light as a feather, and the song so sweet like honey from the meadows. "Never did see one, eh?" says the master. "Well, you won't ever see it again." And he laughed.

Juozupas' language at such times acquires a certain musical rhythm, thus building a bridge between words and music in the play. We hear music when the canary sings and also in the strange, haunting snatches of song coming out of Aneliukė when she is particularly disturbed or enchanted by something in her misty madness, as if she were a crude peasant Ophelia. The presence of music interwoven with ideas, emotions, and the general texture of life is always felt in Ostrauskas' plays, manifesting itself either in direct references to musical works or, more often, in the rhythmic patterns of language spoken by his characters. The counterpoint to music in this play is sharp, merciless noise—the chirping of the sparrow, the loud, mocking voices of children in the yard outside, flooding the room just at the point when Juozupas begins to understand he has become deaf.

The separate layers of stylistic texture prefigure one of the basic principles of construction in the other plays, where the stage reality seems composed of a number of separate elements producing the effect of verbal collage. The play *Pypkė* (*The Pipe*) has several component parts. The most metaphysical as well as the most ordinary, inanimate categories of reality are represented by the pipe itself. In the hands of one of the actors it is simply a thing. Behind him, speaking to him, it is a woman, coming from an immaterial dimension unknown to any faiths or superstitions of man, constructed by the author himself for the purposes of the play. The actor, called simply A as if he were just a supposition, a point in some geometrical design, exists on three levels at once: in the theater, where he is aware of and speaks to the audience; in the grave, because he is already dead; and in the past, in his memories of the day he died, played out for us on the stage. On that day he was killed by Z, another actor. As his name (or, rather, designation) suggests, Z stands at the other end of the alphabet, and thus between themselves A and Z presumably comprise the whole range of human experience. We don't know if Z is also dead—he may lack one of the levels on which A exists—but he, too, can speak to the audience, and, moreover, he is aware of his creator, the author, who pushed him onstage to explain himself.

Like *The Canary*, this play also contains several levels of language. There are the melancholy-philosophical ruminations of A, who describes for us the life in (or beyond) the grave: "The coffin falls apart, the shroud rots. What's the difference? All of us get muddy water dripping into our eyeholes—you call it rain or melting snow. But for us it's the same: muddy water." The Pipe also speaks in the same idiom. At the same time, both the Pipe and A can be very sardonic, especially when they mock and tease poor Z, who is really a simple soul, perhaps a bit cynical, but no match for the playful, biting wit of A. Beyond the philosophical and the sardonic, there is also the biblical level, consisting of direct quotations from the Gospel, about the evil spirit driven out from man and walking alone in dry places. The arid atmosphere of the play seems to suggest the desert for the evil spirit to wander in. The Gospel language is also used by the Pipe to produce mordant, mock-sententious commentary on the events by means of combining biblical phrases with plain popular proverbs: "Verily, verily I say unto you: there is more than one spotted dog."

A curious stylistic device is the exact repetition, in one passage, of every word said by A in the stage directions given in parentheses. This results in a kind of echo-dialogue between the character and the author, the effect of which is to create a verbal stage, superimposed upon the physical one seen by the audience, resembling it exactly, but giving it a special emotional coloring. Both the author and A seem to be addressing Z, describing for him the joys of smoking the pipe which Z has come to buy from A and for which he is ready (although he doesn't quite realize it yet) to kill A if necessary. There is tension in the air, hovering somewhere around the words of A, the stage directions, and the actual room we see. Suddenly this tension breaks into the open for a moment and then becomes veiled again as the scene goes on:

A (*musing*): Imagine. Late evening. Wind. Sleet running down the window panes. Too much light in the room.

I get up and dim the light.

(*Gets up and dims the light.*)

Only one lamp is left.

(*Only one lamp is left.*)

I sit down again.

(*Sits down again.*)

Next to the fireplace.

(*Next to the fireplace.*)

I take the pipe from my pocket, and . . .

(*Takes the pipe from his pocket, and . . .*)

Do you have a match?

(*Both stare at each other. A pause.*)

(*Finally* Z *lights a match and hesitates.* A *smiles and takes the burning match from him. . .*)

A: Thank you.

. . . and light up.

(*And lights up.*)

And stretch out my legs.

(*And stretches out his legs.*)

And puff on my pipe.

(*And puffs on his pipe.*)

Clouds of smoke.

(*Clouds of smoke.*)

The clock is ticking.

(*The clock is ticking.*)

Can you imagine it?—

A fireplace, a soft chair, legs stretched out, pipe smoke in the semidarkness, the clock ticking . . .

(*A fireplace, a soft chair, legs stretched out, pipe smoke in the semidarkness, the clock ticking . . .*)

Warm and cozy.

(*Warm and cozy.*)

The play tells a simple but strange story. A rich uncle of Z died without leaving him anything. Before his uncle's death, however, Z found out that there was a pipe in his possession, with a large diamond concealed in it. This pipe was left to the maid who, not knowing its worth, sold it to an antique dealer. Z ran to the shop in search of the pipe, but A, who happened to be there at the time, bought it first. Z then made an appointment to see A and buy the pipe back without, of course, telling him what is in it. After a long and tortuous conversation, A definitely refuses to sell the pipe. Losing all patience, Z grabs him by the throat and—perhaps unwittingly—strangles him. Picking up the pipe, he sees that it is the wrong one; it has no diamond in it. The play ends in darkness, with retribution standing behind the slowly opening door. We realize at this point that the play also carries overtones of a crime story as an additional dimension. Whatever Z's rights to the pipe might have been, it seems that too passionate insistence on anything in life inevitably becomes to a degree criminal.

The plot, absurd in itself, becomes even more so when all the complexities of style and levels of language are woven into it. An effort to look for deep symbolic meanings brings no reward; we find no such diamonds in *The Pipe*. Groping for at least some common sense (as we ordinarily understand it), we are mocked at every turn by the author and his characters alike. There seems to be no logic at all in much of the dialogue and in a good deal of the action. Why, for instance, didn't the uncle tell his maid that there was a diamond in the pipe? Why did he put it there in the first place? For what reasons does A refuse to sell the pipe to Z? To provoke him into killing? Why?

Then the dialogue. The first thing we hear is an explosive burst of laughter. The Pipe, voicing our sentiments, asks A why he is laughing. "I don't know," says A. This, the Pipe agrees, is sincere laughter. But was his laughter "then" sincere? "Only my end was sincere," answers A. This can only mean that A died sincerely—an absurd thing to say since death, even in suicide, is something that happens to us rather than something we do, whether sincerely or not. Soon thereafter A contradicts himself and claims that he knows why he is laughing, namely, out of pity. This again is a direct denial of the ordinary emotional logic, for usually pity is a matter of tears, not laughter. So A both does and does not know why he is laughing, and his pity provokes merriment, and this laughter is sincere, and in this it is exactly like death. On top of this A adds that it is not laughter at all but memories of days past (that is, of the day he died—to remember means to laugh, means to relive death once more). Obviously, the words "laughter," "death," "sincerity," "pity," and "memories" do not depend on their dictionary meanings and are connected not by logic but by something else. In order to grasp what that "something else" may be, we must first be thoroughly convinced of the absurdity of all linear, conceptual thinking about the play. We are made to feel like a Zen disciple who cannot achieve enlightenment until he hears the sound of one hand clapping, except Ostrauskas presents us a different *koan*, one that might be expressed in the question, what is the silence of two hands clapping? A syllogism works like two hands; we say "all men are mortal," then "Caius is a man," and then we hear the clap, "Caius is mortal." But if words do not possess the meanings we expect of them, there is no clap but only silence. In a way, the play is about the eloquence of this silence, because it teaches us several things.

One important thing is that action, the achievement of some purpose, is an impossibility within the terms of the play, since ordinary logic there always runs into incomprehensible blind alleys. It seems logical to Z that A should sell the pipe for a hundred dollars, since he does not know the true value of it. He is sure the business can be settled very quickly. Yet A tells him it is going to be a very long and tiresome evening, at the end of which he refuses to sell, explaining himself simply by saying, "I don't know." Z keeps trying harder and harder and is led further and further astray until he ends up doing what he did not intend (that is, assuming he did not intend), namely, murdering the man. The existence of Z's aim is in itself an illusion. There is no diamond in the pipe. Consequently, when Z introduces himself to the audience by saying, "I am he who knows what he wants," the Pipe just giggles in reply, "Dear me, how wrong he is."

Even the existence of reality itself is called into question. First of all, if the meaning of words can undergo unpredictable changes, we can never be certain that our image of life represents anything. Furthermore, since the present moment is too infinitesimal to be captured entire in our consciousness, what we call reality is actually the sum total of past moments, reconstructed in memory. Memory, however, is a constantly changing thing, and therefore we can never truly relive a single day from our past. We will remember only some of it, and even that will change each time we return to it in our mind. This is demonstrated in the play when A tries to reconstruct the room in which he dies, to "dig this day out of the grave," as he says. He cannot do it right, because things have already changed. Suddenly there is a piano in the room or a chair is missing (at this point the connection between the audience and A's fading memory is made by the Pipe's suggestion that he pick up a chair from the floor) or the roses have moved away from the window sill to the table. The particular things that change, and the reasons why they do, are, of course, determined by the author, thus giving him the opportunity to suggest certain clues to the character of A. There is something very absurd about A; he is color blind, yet he objects to the color of the roses because he always liked yellow ones. The roses are actually yellow; hence, what A objects to is the change that has occurred in his memory, although even then he could only imagine the color. At the same time, he is touchingly vain, like everyone else; he cannot play the piano, but his memory puts one in for him. A is obviously trying to play with Z as if on a musical instrument and gets murdered for his pains. This might suggest, however remotely, Hamlet's comment to Guildenstern that a man's mind cannot be played on like a flute. In this sense, then, A's death is also a retribution for presuming to possess an inner superiority that allows him to treat other people like toys. The missing chair might signify A's distaste for the impending visit of Z whom he will have to invite to sit down.

The most appalling thing about all these changes, however, is that we know A is already dead. Therefore his memory has decayed with the gradual disintegration of his brain, thus also destroying the past, that is, reality. In the sense that the living, too, die with each passing moment, there is no difference between A and us. Our reality is also in the constant process of disintegration. The strange words of A at the beginning of the play, "Do not fear me if you don't want to be afraid of yourselves," suddenly acquire a frightening meaning. They suggest that we are all dead already and therefore the only unchanging, unalterable reality is death itself. Death is the force that warps the meaning of words and destroys all illusions of logic and order and time and space. The presence of death makes everything we call existence an absurdity. The play is thus a confrontation with death; what it depicts is the destruction of our consciousness. The door that opens in darkness at the end leads to the grave. Possibly it is also the theater door, opening into the night after the performance.

It remains to add that absurdity, being grotesque, contains in it the element of humor. This explains A's uproarious laughter at the beginning and throws a certain light on the play's motto, from Aristophanes: "I laughed fit to cry."

Žaliojoj lankelėj (*In the Green Meadow*) is a play constructed on the principle of mirror images or musical counterpoints. Almost everything in it is a reflection of something else within the play, although not necessarily a very accurate reflection or one with quite the same meaning. First of all, the play has two texts, one written entirely in Lithuanian (with English phrases creeping in here and there). In the other, everyone speaks Lithuanian except Gus, the tavern keeper, who speaks English. Occasionally Gus sticks in a Lithuanian word, especially toward the end when all his pretenses break down and he must increasingly see himself for what he really is.

The name of his tavern, In the Green Meadow, written in green neon lights, has its opposite across the street, in blood red—Sam the Crab Man. The tavern is located in an out-of-the-way, slummy section of a great city, a place which seems to crawl with T. S. Eliot's ragged claws. The green colors of the countryside have no reality in them other than hopeless longing. The tavern's name was suggested to Gus by a poet, a regular customer, who did not think it up himself but took it from a Lithuanian song. The song is about a hundred girls raking hay in a green meadow, only "my beloved one is not there among them." This reflects the situation of Gus, who is American born but lived in Lithuania and left his wife and children there when the war came and he had to escape. Gus is a tough guy. He has a sign saying "Let's live it up" hanging over the bar; he clangs the cash register with aggressive glee and pretends to himself with all his might that he is a perfectly happy fellow. He even invents a girl whom he supposedly sleeps with so that the bed will not be so cold at night.

For this reason Gus absolutely refuses to recognize his double in a bedraggled creature, a Man Without a Home, who, attracted by the green sign, walks in one hopeless evening. He also left his wife and children in Lithuania, only he makes no attempt to put on a happy mask but abandons himself to his murky gloom. Gus, like a good bartender, insists on cheering him up, hearing out all his troubles, but the man resists. There is a growing verbal conflict during which Gus, as in O'Neill's play, *Hughey,* is forced to admit more and more of the truth about himself until he cannot bear it any longer and pushes the man out into the street and under the wheels of a passing trolley.

The play is thus about a murder that is also a suicide, because Gus kills that in himself which was truth and unhappiness. There is nothing else in Gus, however, so he also becomes just a dead shell. We are left in effect with two mangled corpses, one in the tavern, crying out for his absent wife, and the other in the street, saying nothing.

This whole situation has its reflection in the supernatural dimension, in the form of two absolutely identical chess players dressed in funereal black who have been playing one game for several months now. They sit in the tavern, facing each other, *very* quiet on this particular evening because it is the last time; in one hour the game will be over. They almost give the illusion that there is only one chess player, playing against himself in front of a mirror. When he wins, he will, of course, also lose, checkmating himself. This is exactly what happens. The game ends when the Man Without a Home is killed, with both players losing to each other, since Gus has also become not much more than a living corpse.

The only person in the tavern to whom the chess players react is the poet, because he has the gift of prophecy. He drinks more and more as the evening wears on; his inspiration grows and with it the dark forebodings of catastrophe. He understands that someone's life is at stake in this game of chess and says so. The players turn and look at him. He utters a prophecy in verse—"In this stuffy attic of life / Someone will die tonight"—and the players look at him again. We begin to suspect that the poet must also die, albeit figuratively, which he does—as a poet. At the end of the play he tears up his poems in an act of facing the truth about himself, which in his case turns out to be an act of liberation from the burden of creativity. The game is over for him as well. In fact, the relationship between him and the chess players can also be described in terms of mirror and counterpoint. The poet has been writing a few lines of verse for a very long time, at least as long as the chess game has been going on. His last achievement (also his first) is a single poem about the death of man in the Black City which, like a raven, croaks out the final hour. Both the chess game and the poem culminate in the double death of Gus and the Man Without a Home. Gus dies the worse death, because physically he must remain alive and continue facing a truth beyond his capacity to endure.

Thus the central core of the play is surrounded by multiple shadows of double images and premonitions, of symbols and fancies, all leading inexorably toward the fulfillment of fate, as in Greek tragedy. Ostrauskas is quite conscious of the Greek theatrical tradition and uses some of its principles, such as the Aristotelian reversal of fortune. A shattering example is Oedipus slowly recognizing the truth about himself as he relentlessly questions the messenger. In Ostrauskas' play Gus the tavern keeper finds out about himself in precisely the same manner. The killing of the Man Without a Home is also accomplished according to the Greek theatrical tradition; it occurs behind the stage, and we only hear his cry. Aside from the Greek elements (which, by the way, might demonstrate just how deep are the roots of the modern "theater of the absurd"), there are also deliberate references to French symbolism, particularly at the end when the poet combines the lyrical tones of Lithuanian folk songs with the haunting music of Verlaine's "L'heure exquise." The poem is well chosen because, like the play, it is full of voices and mirror reflections and speaks of the hour of dreams, which are turned here into the final nightmare of death. "*Revons, c'est l'heure*" is thus echoed in the play with a kind of brutal irony.

The theatrical sounds accompanying the play punctuate its progress toward the tragic conclusion. Every move the chess players make is re-created in the ominous beat of drums. A noisy trolley screeches past the tavern several times, always frightening the Man Without a Home into hysterical panic because on the unconscious level of his soul, where premonitions dwell, he knows already that the trolley will be the instrument of his death. Ostrauskas has created here a literary counterpoint to Tennessee Williams' streetcar named Desire by creating one whose name is Terror. The first time the trolley passes is synchronized with the entrance of one of the chess players. The last time, the man dies under its wheels. At this moment Gus suddenly turns on loud and raucous music on the juke box, creating the effect of both a Greek chorus and a gangster movie. All these multiple echoes, in a sense, destroy the play's reality, because we can no longer recognize with certainty which is the ultimate level of meaning. Again, as in *The Pipe*, one thing remains real beyond any doubt, and that is death. The substance of death in the play would be naked without the shadow-play of art. Ostrauskas' theater reminds us of a magic lantern in which unsubstantial shadows come to life in the light of illusions. We watch this with fascination, and when the light goes out, we know the truth.

The fairy tale, one of the oldest forms of art known to man, is also among the most modern because it presents a deeply felt truth in the envelope of absurdity. Therefore, its symbolic devices, such as metamorphosis can be utilized in the modern theater. In a tale a prince may be turned into a frog; in Ionesco a man becomes a rhinoceros. Kostas Ostrauskas is perfectly aware of the connection and gives it a satirical turn in his play *Gyveno kartą senelis ir senelė* (*Once Upon a Time There Was an Old Man and an Old Woman*). He achieves his irony not by direct aping of fairy-tale devices—no one is turned into anything—but by violating the internal laws of fairy tales, by matter-of-fact statements that would be quite absurd without a fable. The phrase "once upon a time," for instance, is really a very strict formula demanding that the events described should take place in some indefinite past, in fact, that they should be removed from the context of real time altogether. Ostrauskas, however, puts his fable-play squarely into the present moment, introducing automobiles, college students, and the latest newspapers, but within a framework of logic that is comprehensible only in terms of unreal stories of nonexistent time, that is, fairy tales. His old man and woman, for instance, could well have survived from the days of Methuselah or perhaps Snow White and the seven dwarfs. Sitting in their rocking chairs in the middle of an empty room, they are a living example of what it means, literally, to "live happily ever after." But they are not really happy; their only son, "who could have been eighty years old by now," was killed by a passing car in the very flower of his youth.

It is their son's death which keeps them alive, for they must now complete an earnest task, to kill twelve young college students who must be living images of their dear departed Jonukas at the time when he was crushed under the wheels. It is a sort of revenge by them against life for mocking them with so many likenesses of their son without, however, resurrecting him. Their method is to rent out a room to a student and then, after proper preparations, to kill him and put him in their son's room.

When the play opens, the two old people have already dispatched ten young men and are about to do in the eleventh. The situation admittedly seems reminiscent of *Arsenic and Old Lace*, but in it the old ladies are a bit daft, while Ostrauskas' two people are perfectly normal in every respect, except, in the world where they live, everything happens in exact reverse to ordinary logic. For instance, the preparation necessary for killing the students consists of knitting a sweater. Normally, an expectant mother will knit something for her coming baby, but in this play the woman knits in expectation of death. Jonukas had just put on a new red sweater when he was killed, and so she must make one exactly like it for each of the prospective victims. When the sweater is finished, the old people very kindly invite their roomer to put it on as a parting gift. The student thinks he is going home on vacation, but the oldsters know exactly where he is going. They tell him where, but, of course, the thought is too absurd even to register with the student. So he goes to his room to catch a nap before the journey, and the old man comes in and prolongs his sleep into all eternity by means of a well-aimed blow with a hammer. Huffing and puffing, the old couple then drag his heavy, lifeless body to their son's room, the man makes an appropriate mark on the wall, and they sit down again in their rocking chairs. There is a gleam in the man's eye; the woman answers with a shy, blushing, happy smile. She is about to begin on a new sweater.

Underlying the action of the play is a world of symbols and the even deeper realm of sheer, playful nonsense. The old man plays some music on his hammer—a passage from *Orpheus and Euridice.* This piece is heard intermittently through the whole play, giving it the dimension of a myth which says that in order to recover our dear departed we must come down to Hades and be among the dead. The old couple, of course, live among the dead, the students they have killed, whereas in the realm of spirits their Jonukas presumably enjoys the company of his peers, who have died as absurdly as he did. The general tone of the play and the direction in which its logic must go is indicated by what Jonukas did when he was still a small child. It was then he wrote "3-2=5" on the wall, as if it were a new mathematical principle of anti-logic, in its way as shattering as Einstein's relativity formula.

Lest we become too serious about all these implications, however, the author takes care to make us understand that everything in this play is really just a game. He does it by means of an exquisitely silly passage from a Lithuanian newspaper, read by the old man at the end:

> THE OLD MAN (*reading*): "The concept of 'plays' includes light movement, without sharp ripples of irritations, as, for example, the play of sunrise, of its rays in the dewdrops; the play of the mermaid, with the lapping waves of the river Nemunas in a ballet; the pastoral play, when the shepherds in a grove, on a quiet day, whistle on the instruments they have made, etc."
>
> THE OLD WOMAN (*dreamily*): Ahhhh . . .
>
> *The Old Man pulls the hammer from his pocket, gracefully puts it to his lips, like a flute, and begins to "blow"; a gentle pastoral melody comes out.*
>
> *The Old Woman is knitting.*

There are more quotations from the press, some actual, some invented. They all constitute a part of the collage of fact and fancy, reality and fairy tale, from which the play is made. Some of the fictitious "excerpts," in their turn, point to a legend which may add another level of meaning —the Arabian tales of the thousand and one nights: "When the one-thousand-and-first East-West disarmament conference began, the chairman of the Western delegation said 'yes.' The East answered 'no'—or could it have been the reverse?—and the meeting ended." As we know, Scheherazade tells her tales in the hope of postponing her hour of doom. The world situation thus understood enters the play's proceedings in which the old people postpone their own death by killing others until the time has fulfilled its measure of twelve. "Then," says the old man, "we shall rest."

The dialogue supports this mood of gentle, frightening nonsense. It is disjointed and fragmentary; the sentences (actually, odd words most often) fall like cryptic pronouncements, mysterious and absurd in their extreme simplicity. They contain echoes of ancient folk songs, the ritual dirges which give the play itself the feeling of a completely insane but stately and dignified ceremony celebrating the human condition. Such idiom completely destroys any idea of personality or genuine emotion in the characters. Sometimes in their conversation the old man and the old woman even get a bit mixed up about who is who between them and cackle rhythmically at each other, driven by the emotion (if that is the word) of remembrance:

THE OLD WOMAN: Then Jonukas was only a student.
THE OLD MAN: Oh! What a man!
THE OLD WOMAN: Straight as a reed . . .
THE OLD MAN: . . . strong as an oak . . .
THE OLD WOMAN: . . . blue eyes . . .
THE OLD MAN: . . . alert . . .
THE OLD WOMAN: . . . brainy . . . Just like me.
THE OLD MAN: Like you? Like me.
THE OLD WOMAN: Like you? Like me.
THE OLD MAN: Like who?
THE OLD WOMAN: Like me.
THE OLD MAN: Like you.

Occasionally the old woman bursts out crying suddenly, not without reason (her son is dead), but mechanically, like one of those new dolls, with the ironical finger of the author pressing the button. In fact, both the old people look like dolls, wrinkled, very sweet and dead, as they happily go about their business of killing.

Those who think of death as "anti-life" will find this play very clear and logical. The machine of time and logic, of cause and effect, has been put into reverse gear, and it moves backwards just as blindly as it moved forward, frightening Dostoevsky with its inexorable dumb power. One might add that it moves in reverse just as happily, for the play is especially amusing when we discover that, under its influence, we have started thinking backwards.

Death, whose pervasive presence changes the texture of reality and alters the notions of sense and nonsense in all of Ostrauskas' plays, finally enters upon the stage as one of the characters in the play *Duobkasiai* (*The Gravediggers*). Its role in the play is defined by the motto, from Michel de Ghelderode, "*La mort, quoi, cette Providence des dramaturges.*" In *The Pipe* there is a passage in which A describes the various ways by which the dead arrived at their destination—the grave: "Some were nailed in the coffin, others wrapped in a shroud, others again have fallen and buried themselves—without coffin and without a grave." To say that one has buried himself is meaningless, except on a symbolic plane. The medium of the theater, however, demands that verbal symbols become representations, that they be acted out on the stage. Ostrauskas devised a situation in *The Gravediggers* in which the act of burying oneself becomes literally true and visible to the audience, and he established a direct connection between this play and *The Pipe* by quoting from it in the text. Two gravediggers are mysteriously commissioned to dig two graves. As they proceed, it begins to dawn on them that these graves might be their own. At this point, death itself enters in the guise of a sexy-looking wench in tight pants and sweater. After amusing herself for a while with the gravediggers' fears and their courage, she confirms their awful suspicions and makes them bury each other in the graves they have prepared.

If the perspective of death can make life grotesque, it will also make it to some extent humorous as well. Shakespeare knew this when he wrote the gravedigger scene in *Hamlet* as one of his passages of comic relief. This passage figures prominently in Ostrauskas' play; it is quoted at length and forms an important part of the conversation. One of the gravediggers is a former actor, forced into his present occupation by the exigencies of exile. He despises his new job and will not admit that he has sunk to such a low station in life. To protect himself, he continues to act. He quotes abundantly from *Hamlet* at every opportunity; he also pretends that digging graves is just another role he is playing, albeit unwillingly. In fact, it becomes evident that in his insistence on illusions, his stubborn play-acting, he has completely lost the substance of his own life. This, then, is what falling down and burying oneself may mean.

The second gravedigger, also an exile, had been a farmer. Consequently, there is no need for him to pretend; he has always been digging up the earth, he knows it is honest work, and so he can be true to himself and face reality wherever his fate may take him. The trouble is that death comes equally to the false and the true, for those who spend their lives burrowing in the ground must eventually rest in it forever.

The presence of quotations from Shakespeare shifts the framework to a supranational context, or even to the province of art itself, while continuing the basic idea. Hamlet in the courtyard is, after all, also an exile who has clandestinely returned to Denmark. A further effect of the abstraction is that the characters, released from their compulsory allegorical trappings, become interesting in themselves as objects of artistic design. In this respect the figure of death, in particular, attracts attention by its unconventionality. Death has often been a woman in both literature and painting but here is made sexually attractive in a slightly vulgar way, like a cover girl on a cheap magazine. Her curvaceous figure moves nonchalantly between the grave pits, exuding the curious and teasing atmosphere of vulgarity and elegance, threat and flirtation, of great and ancient knowledge and the dark, silent chill of total oblivion. She responds to the first gravedigger's Shakespearean eloquence with the humble words of Ophelia, to which she adds matter-of-fact expressions that seem somewhat vulgar only because of their naïve realism. It is the passage from *Hamlet* in which the melancholy prince offers to lie in Ophelia's lap. Full of cruel and humiliating sexual innuendoes, this conversation, transplanted to the graveside in Ostrauskas' play, acquires forceful irony because this time death itself, speaking the language of the victim to a man fond of illusions, consummates the terrible union. To jump into Ophelia's grave, to lie between the legs of a maiden—a beautiful thought, as Hamlet said, except that now the embrace will last forever and will be very real indeed, and our false Hamlet will truly guard his silence. As we watch him squirming under the growing realization of where his eloquence is taking him, we realize that, in the words of another Elizabethan playwright, "there is nothing of so infinite vexation as man's own thoughts," especially when they concern his end.

The relationship between death and the second gravedigger also has sexual overtones but of a different kind. Death is all things to all men, and here it plays the role of an absolute and, to the mind of the second gravedigger, evil power that is irresistible but must be fought to the very end if man is to maintain his dignity. In the image of a woman, death becomes a special kind of evil as she toys with the gravediggers—a sadistic-masochistic figure of sorts, mimicking the perverse feelings that can arise in people when they deal with the opposite sex as a helpless victim. She plays a little, becomes interested, even sympathetic as time goes on; then her very sympathy turns imperceptibly to cruel amusement, and then she begins to feel the urge to be "punished" in her own turn. The second gravedigger fulfills this function. He curses her, spits on her, and even whacks her bottom with his shovel, sending her sprawling in the dirt. Eventually, death covers both gravediggers' heads with earth and disappears, but not before she undergoes her own paroxysm of weariness and despair, enacted before the audience first in a sensual, almost obscene, *danse macabre*, and then in a heart-rending cry for her own old age, her own death. It seems as if when we die, our death itself must pass with us into the unknown dimension of nonbeing. The difference, of course, is that we never return from it, but death does, and starts again, mysterious, incomprehensible as ever. We remember Ophelia again. We may flirt with death or hate it, we may fight or worship it, or think that we have argued it out of existence, but there will never be a real dialogue between us and the unimaginable; death will only respond in Ophelia's words: "I think nothing, my lord."

Albert Camus's definition of the absurd as a confrontation of man, asking questions, with the universe, which is silent against all reason, has sometimes been applied to the modern "theater of the absurd." This theater has been understood as a symbolic ceremony in which the audience asks questions and the stage either says nothing or gives absurd answers that can only mean there is no answer. Considered from this point of view, the plays of Ostrauskas are not really representations of total absurdity. Perhaps it is true that he does not supply answers to questions concerning the ultimate meaning of existence, but no literature or philosophy has been able to do that.

If, on the other hand, we ask questions about the structure and meaning of the plays themselves, Ostrauskas does answer in terms that offer some insight into the nature of man and how it is expressed in art. That which seems meaningless or incomprehensible at first glance usually turns out to be a modern application of the technique of "making strange," in which our accustomed reality is made to appear different in order to reveal another aspect of meaning within it. Ostrauskas has an eye for such manifestations of reality which, looked at from a certain angle, first strike us with their absurdity and then open exciting avenues of insight. In *The Gravediggers*, for instance, we are shocked by the unimaginable things death can do to the integrity of the human body. After a man's consciousness has been destroyed, a gravedigger can pick up his skull, like some alien and meaningless object, and throw it away, commenting with horrible levity that this individual apparently "yelled his head off." After the shock recedes, what remains is the wonder that this collection of disintegrated bones did indeed once sing and speak and in thought ranged the length and breadth of the whole universe. In other words, the amazing thing is not that, having conceived of immortality, we become things but that, being things, we can be conscious of immortality. Perhaps we can begin to realize the dignity and marvel of man only after we have thoroughly understood how fragile a creature he is, how petty and mean in his relations to others, how confused and how frightened when faced with the great unknown.

The plays in effect describe the indestructibility of man or of the idea of man's divinity when placed in the position of victim of his fellow creatures or of death itself. Sometimes we see a triangular relationship in which two people attempt to destroy a third who seems to transcend their fear or ignorance. Jokūbas and Rokas, who are only beggars, know that Juozupas is more than that and try to reduce him to their own condition. The old man and woman are, over and over again, murdering youth, which is irretrievably lost to them. At other times there are just two antagonists who destroy each other in the vain effort to attain a value which they know exists but cannot find. This is the conflict between A and Z and between Gus and the Man Without a Home. Finally, in *The Gravediggers*, mutual destruction results from the fear of a dark and overwhelming power. Yet the real question always is, what do we have left after the image of man has been divested of all its human misery, including that of his own life? Juozupas in *The Canary* remains in the end a figure made noble and mysterious by suffering; in *The Pipe* the diamond which neither A nor Z could possess does exist somewhere, in somebody's pipe, amid the billowing smoke of illusions. Sam the Crab Man will in the end get us all, but he will never reach the green meadows of our longing, nor will the murders committed by the two old people ever destroy the Elysian fields. At the end of *The Gravediggers* death understands that it has been swallowed up by its own victory. Ostrauskas does not speak of hope but makes visible the knowledge that man, in dying, does fulfill himself in some ultimate dimension corresponding to the marvel that he is.

7 Algirdas Landsbergis—Structure and Meaning

Algirdas Landsbergis was born in 1924 in Kybartai, southern Lithuania. He studied Lithuanian language and literature in the University of Kaunas in 1941–43, then switched to English in 1944 in the University of Mainz, Germany. He also taught German and English in the Lithuanian displaced persons high schools of Wiesbaden and Kassel and participated in the avant-garde *Žvilgsniai* (*Glances*) collective of young Lithuanian writers. In 1949, Landsbergis came to New York, where he continued to study English in Brooklyn College, then received his master's degree in comparative literature from Columbia University in 1957. In 1949–53 he worked in the Brooklyn Public Library, then in the Assembly of Captive European Nations in New York. At the present Landsbergis teaches in Fairleigh Dickinson University and travels with lectures on East European literatures. He is a member of the PEN International Club.

Landsbergis has written short stories, plays, and a novel, in addition to literary criticism. His plays are *Vėjas gluosniuose* (*Wind in the Willows*), 1958; *Penki stulpai turgaus aikštėje* (*Five Posts in the Marketplace*), published in 1966 but performed several years earlier; *Meilės mokykla* (*The School of Love*), 1965; *Barzda* (*The Beard*), 1966; and *Sudiev, mano karaliau* (*Good-bye, My King*), 1967. Most of his short stories are collected in *Ilgoji naktis* (*The Long Night*), 1956. The novel *Kelionė* (*The Journey*) was published in 1954.

Of the English-language versions of Landsbergis' plays, prepared by the author himself, *Five Posts* (Voyages Press, 1967) was produced in the United States and Canada. He has translated Lithuanian written verse and folk songs into English for the collections *The Green Oak* (Voyages Press, 1962) and *The Green Linden* (Voyages Press, 1964) for both of which he was co-editor with Clark Mills. His own short story "The Wind of Greece" has been published in English in *Selected Lithuanian Short Stories* (Voyages Press, 1959), and "Words, Beautiful Words" in *Lithuanian Quartet* (Manyland Books, 1962).

Perfection of Exile

THE highly developed self-consciousness of the modern writer no longer permits him to equate such things as intensity of feeling, profundity of thought, and even the presence of beauty, with the essence of art. Clearly aware of all the techniques and devices of his craft, he knows that art is not primarily an object but rather a process, a manner in which the artist's awareness of various aspects of being is organized and controlled by his imagination. Such knowledge requires an artist to be relatively free of commitment to any limited ideology, that is, any closed conception of reality, because it would tend to determine the nature and function of his devices and direct his imagination along channels not native to art iself.

Among the Lithuanian prose writers working in exile, Algirdas Landsbergis is perhaps the most self-conscious and analytical, the most "modern" in the sense described above. As an individual, he believes in man, but not necessarily in any of the ideological systems that man devises to protect himself from the consciousness of his own infinitude. As an artist, he understands that art is first of all a display of complex relationships among idea, structure, and reality, and only then, if at all, a confession of faith. His work, therefore, provides one more example of a break with the Lithuanian literary tradition—a break so typical of younger people who first started to write abroad, in the violent circumstances of war and exile, when the voice of Europe in agony was much louder than that of any faith they may have inherited from their adolescence at home.

To the established Lithuanian writers before the war, reality seemed solid enough to be regarded as something given, as a reliable framework within which to depict imaginary people whose lives would embody the author's ideas. The problems of structure seldom extended beyond the requirements of plot; the only important question was how best to arrange the thoughts and actions of characters according to generally understood and accepted notions of reality. Algirdas Landsbergis, however, could no longer depend upon the world to furnish him with a logical pattern of meaning because it was shattered beyond recognition by the pressure of enormous and tumultuous events. We know what we believe only as long as the image of life seems clear to us; when this image is destroyed, all we have left is a heap of fragments which the artist may look at as an embodiment of his despair but not as a foundation for any coherent idea to be expressed in art.

Some writers were so outraged by this collapse of reality that they could speak of nothing but the despair itself; in their works the howl of terror and protest seems to represent the ultimate wisdom of man. Landsbergis was too much of an intellectual to surrender so completely to the bitter flood of emotion that he would give up any effort to understand the universe, in whatever form it might present itself. The driving force in art was, for him, still the search for some rational insight into the nature of experience, for an idea which would satisfy the demands of a free creative intelligence. He did not exactly "shore up the fragments against the tide," as T. S. Eliot did in "The Wasteland," but picked up and studied these fragments, trying to reconstitute from them some new structure of meaning. The relationship between reality and idea in his art expresses itself essentially as an effort to reconstruct the image of man in general and, specifically, the image of one's own self in such a way that it would continue to sustain the will to live and to hope for the future of civilization. Landsbergis' heroes ask themselves who, or what, they are; they cannot find an answer until they know what anything is. Thus, in search of selfhood they must try to puzzle out the broken pieces of the world around them, and it is this process which constitutes the action, and therefore the structure, of his novels and short stories. The traditional notion of plot is discarded; people no longer engage in conflict by following their passions, meaningful to them because they live in a world they can understand. The only real conflict is now inside the individual himself, and it arises from his desire to make some sense of things.

The novel *Kelionė* (*The Journey*) recounts the experiences of Julius Laikūnas, a young novice in a monastery who, unable to bear the thought of impending death, escapes to Germany just ahead of the advancing Soviet armies in 1944. Completely lost in a nameless German town, he is picked up by the authorities and made to work in a weapons factory. There he meets a motley collection of slave laborers, homeless souls like himself, gathered up by the Germans from all corners of Europe. Most important, he meets his foreman, Weiss, a former Wehrmacht officer who has lost one half of his face, burned to a crisp near Leningrad when he had to save his life by lying very close to the flaming trunk of an uprooted tree. Having become half human, half monster, both outwardly and in his soul, Weiss is a terrible example of what the demon of war can do to the image of man. A strong and proud person of superior intellect, he is, on the one hand, intensely devoted to the vision of beauty and harmony he sees in Renaissance art, in particular the angels of Fra Angelico, and, on the other, bitterly contemptuous of and cruel to the shabby crowd of foreigners working under him. What he desires most is to become whole and beautiful again, which is not possible because unity with himself means for him a number of irreconcilable things, broken pieces of his personality: the victory of the German idea, the vision of superior beauty in art, the satisfaction of revenge for his ugliness, and an intimate communion of minds with the chosen few who can understand his magnificent dreams. His wife, Hilde, a petty German bourgeois, is not among these few, since she is blind to the mystical beauty of Fra Angelico, hates and despises her husband's ravaged face, and deceives him with anyone who comes along. In his twisted mind Weiss conceives a fantastic plan of revenge upon his wife. He will select the best physical specimens among the "subhuman" slaves and send them to work for extra food in his garden, where they will meet Hilde, seduce her, and thus defile her by their animal lust.

This is where Laikūnas comes in. He is young and handsome, so that presumably Hilde will not be able to resist him, but he is also a foreigner and therefore scum. Several such men have already shared her bed, after which Weiss, to complete his morbid pleasure, beat them cruelly with an iron wrench, supposedly for having dared to put their hands on a German woman, his wife. Yet Laikūnas is also different, because he alone in this gray mass of foreigners, "animals in human form," can understand and share Weiss' vision of paradise among the angels of Fra Angelico, pure and dignified in their colorful harmony. Therefore it seems to Weiss that between him and Laikūnas exists that bond of superiority over all the rest which Weiss always sought. This makes his revenge upon Hilde even more perfect. Weiss is sure that Laikūnas, as one of the angels, will resist his wife's advances and thus inflict upon her the ultimate humiliation of being rejected by a foreign laborer, supposedly unworthy to crawl in the dirt under her feet.

Laikūnas, however, is a fallen angel. One day he brings an apple to Hilde's room, and they both taste of it—Adam and Eve in hell. Feeling himself doubly defiled—by the moral violence done to him by Weiss and by physical relations with his wife who has no love to offer and only takes Laikūnas to revenge, in her turn, upon her husband—he rises up in revolt. The opportunity arises at the very end of the war, when several of the slave laborers barricade themselves inside a tower to resist German attempts to execute them before the American troops can reach the town. Laikūnas joins them, not so much to fight the Germans as to say "no" for once to everything around him and thus cleanse his soul. The tower is destroyed, and Laikūnas, the only survivor, spends several days in a hospital, delirious, dreaming mystical dreams.

These dreams actually constitute another plane of reality, containing the meaning of surface events: exile, war, his relations with Hilde and Weiss, and the fate of his fellow workers, several of whom had been very close to him in a special way. Here Landsbergis reveals to us his usual method of treating the broken pieces of life as symbols pointing to an underlying unity in which the image of man is reconstituted on the level of paradise, where the six Fra Angelico angels dwell, each representing one of the basic characters in the novel. The first is Father Gailėnas, back in the Lithuanian monastery, who shares with Laikūnas his ugly fear of death but insists nevertheless that they should both do the unnatural thing and accept the crown of martyrdom, becoming like the clay statues of saints in the church that will be smashed to pieces by the Soviet soldiers. Laikūnas rejects the sacrifice and runs away, feeling guilty but also somehow justified in his desire to save himself for some other destiny in which he would achieve a more human self-fulfillment than is possible in terms of a narrow idea, such as martyrdom for faith.

Weiss is the second angel; Laikūnas shares with him the vision but not the murky hatred. He must free himself from that in Weiss which is not human but resembles a gargoyle; this is only possible by means of revolt.

Then there is the Russian Grigorij—a perfect opposite of Weiss, a figure of endless, mournful love and mercy, ready to feed the infinite procession of the poor and hungry of the world from the inexhaustible depths of his insipid heart. Grigorij and Weiss, representatives of the two warring nations, are actually the perfect complements of each other. In his mystical dream Laikūnas sees Grigorij lying on the ground in the shape of a tree and understands that Weiss could regain the other half of his face by pressing its burned remains against Grigorij, the healing stump. In the world, however, Grigorij's love is meaningless, since love and hate have both been hopelessly twisted and confused in the ruins of what had seemed a logical universe. Laikūnas hears him out but does not follow him because his own path leads to some as yet indefinite future vision, while Grigorij, like a discarded Dostoevskian ideal, can only go to the past, where there is more suffering, that is, back to the Soviet Union with the other repatriated Russians.

The fourth angel, Aram, is a handsome, vain, and boastful Armenian, exuding the luxuriant profligacy of the Orient, with its lavish, orgiastic appetites for color, fantasy, and the flesh. He had been one of the workers chosen by Weiss to seduce his wife and had been marked by him with a deep scar on the head. He is a living denial of the possibility of pure spiritual love or, rather, an affirmation of glorious earthly joy. Yet there has been so much greedy flesh among the agonies of war, in this cauldron of unholy loves, this Carthage which Europe had become, that it is impossible not to recognize flesh as an illusion. Aram best serves Laikūnas by his death in the crumbling tower, shielding him from falling debris with his own huge, mortally wounded body.

The fifth and last angel, except for Laikūnas himself, is Lorenzo, a Communist, a seeker of perfect justice and order, who had once, during the Spanish Civil War, killed a man looking exactly like Laikūnas. That was the ideal of communism—the beauty killed by its devotees at its very inception. Now Lorenzo, as if still hoping to resurrect the dead vision of his faith, protects Laikūnas with all his might and yet must in the end decide whether to kill him all over again by betraying him to the Soviets or to die by suicide himself. He dies and thus becomes one of the angels, meaningful only in withdrawing from the world he had wanted to rebuild.

The relationship between Laikūnas and all these people is postulated on the concept of authority. All of them, from Father Gailėnas to Lorenzo, treat him in some sense as a son. They protect him, feed him, teach and punish him; they all embody attitudes which had seemed valid in the context of the past, before the holocaust, and on these attitudes they base their authority over Laikūnas in the chaotic present, when all foundations of their special faiths have already collapsed. In this sense, Laikūnas fights the most important battle with the memory of his own father, killed by the Soviets, a figure of free and noble vision and also of personal weakness and misery, an inadequate receptacle for the holy idea of fatherhood and therefore broken by the tragic course of events.

In the end, all the main characters surrounding Laikūnas, all his fellow angels placed in the position of fatherhood to him, with the figure of his own father dominating the background, fulfill their function in the novel by transferring from the physical to the spiritual plane of existence. Gailėnas, Aram, and Lorenzo are dead. Weiss will be tried as a war criminal and presumably executed, and Grigorij will also undoubtedly perish somewhere in Siberia. Their relationship to Laikūnas is now the same as that of idea to reality in art.

Structurally, the chronological order of events in the book is broken up and reorganized in accordance with the inner action—the continuous line of significant spiritual experiences by Laikūnas. Thus, he may understand the meaning of what happened between him and his father at some time in the past only after he lives through another event, with other characters, in the present. Laikūnas therefore exists in a fragmented world, composed by the author on the principle of the mosaic—not, however, from virgin stones but from pieces which had formed another, now defunct, pattern of meaning in the past. As an example, we may take the description of how Laikūnas escapes from Lithuania. His departure is prepared by a series of images conveying the imminent breakup of his Lithuanian world, in which he thought he had found his place. First, there is the conversation with Father Gailėnas, a solidly built, powerful man whose voice breaks with fear, opening a crack in this thick clay vessel containing the glory of God. This is followed by the image of Saint Sebastian in a painting, with a huge gaping wound in his side, trickling clay-colored blood. We know Laikūnas will not accept martyrdom when, looking at Saint Sebastian, he cannot understand how it is possible to smile with such a wound. Then we see Saint Veronica holding up her scarf with the image of Christ—a face shattered by agony. Later Laikūnas enters the monastery for the last time:

> Blood sacrifice, blood sacrifice. Julius let his glance slip across the marble statues of saints, as if in farewell. Good-by unfortunates. An earthly power is coming to conquer you. Good-by, and with every heartbeat he saw their heads falling and shattering on the floor. His father was lying with his hands tied, blood clotted around the mouth. Saint Sebastian raised his meek eyes to the heavens, so he would not see the clay-colored blood seeping from his side. Good-by, good-by.

Everything which had once had substance and purpose has now become only a representation which loses all meaning as it breaks up before Laikūnas' eyes. His soul filled with these fragments, Laikūnas climbs into the railroad carriage filled with escapees like himself. They also have ceased to be individuals with separate identities. Their faces made exactly alike by fear, they are now meaningless pieces from which a new mosaic will be built. As the train proceeds to Germany, Laikūnas remains suspended among various possible planes of existence, amid memories of childhood, confrontations with his father and with Father Gailėnas, dreams and immediate impressions of the new life before him, all passing through his mind like a surrealist picture of no particular content while the train, in its own rhythm, keeps clanging out the fundamental questions: "Who am I? Where did I come from? Where am I going?"

The difficulty with such an approach to structure is that these multiple fragments of shattered reality contain many more legitimate possibilities of reconstitution into some new image than the author can control or even comprehend. How many new combinations can be made from a set of a thousand digits? Where is the law, or principle, which would limit the choice by establishing the validity of some possibilities, rejecting others? In other words, what can art contribute to the search for meaning in life? In his later works Landsbergis continues to pursue this question, seeking out new ways of handling the relationships among reality, structure, and idea. The need is, obviously, to simplify the situations. The whole chaos of wartime Europe cannot be meaningfully contained within a restricted circle of characters without either embracing a deliberately limited point of view or undertaking a sweeping work of epic proportions. Landsbergis chose to set aside the genre of the novel, concentrating instead on limited, identifiable issues which can be resolved in a short story. His next book, *Ilgoji naktis* (*The Long Night*), contains several stories, each amounting to a confrontation with a single question of crucial importance to the characters. In the first and longest story, bearing the same title as the book, we see a young girl, Rima Dauvydaitė, locked in a cellar, her hands tied behind her back. She has been captured as a Lithuanian anti-Soviet guerrilla, and she knows very well that her fate is sealed. In the morning she will die, but right now there is one question that must be decided. Did her commitment to fight the invaders have any meaning? As the night drags on, she examines her young life and the choices made along the way to the present doom. We are made aware of two levels of being. One represents the past; it does not exist any more, except as an idea, a memory of former hopes and love and suffering, and of a search for some compelling faith. The other level is the reality of the given moment: damp cellar, hunger, solitude, pain in the bound, twisted arms, and the knowledge of certain death.

On the floor above her are two young members of the Soviet security forces assigned to guard her. One of them, Vasilij, feels strongly that his life has reached a crossroads, that he must also decide whether it is possible to maintain a separate identity, to perform an individually meaningful act of courage and at the same time to belong to history as part of the homogeneous Soviet mass. Here again we have two categories of existence. On the one hand there is the realm of idea—Vasilij's past convictions, his search for meaning—and on the other, reality, the smell of sweat and gun grease in the room, a captive girl in the cellar, and a mysterious alien country which seems to know some secret of strength inaccessible to his understanding. The action of the novel thus moves along these four separate planes, visually reinforced by their "stage setting." The relationship between the two sets of levels is complicated because Vasilij feels that Rima's inner world must be somewhere far above his own; this is what puzzles and angers him, for as a Communist he should be her spiritual superior. It does not help him much to know that physically he is standing over her, in the position of the conqueror.

Beyond this confrontation there is still another dimension containing, in its turn, a symbolic physical representation of dark and tragic significance; in the marketplace lie the bodies of murdered guerrillas, among them Rima's husband. When morning comes, Rima will be taken to view the corpses in the hope that she might break down upon seeing her dead husband and betray the resistance secrets. Vasilij knows about this and understands the cruelty of such an act. This is what makes it imperative for him to come to some decision. He must either renounce communism and all it stands for as a terrible illusion or deliberately close his eyes to everything, forget all questions, and murder his own soul in the name of an idea that has already betrayed itself.

Thus both these people move along the planes of their own lives inwardly toward the point of decision and outwardly toward each other. Vasilij came to this little Lithuanian town from Leningrad, across the battlefields of the war and those of his own soul, on which he fought a losing struggle to be himself and also a Communist. Rima arrived from Kaunas, the capital city, through the forests where the guerrillas fought and also through several encounters with people who meant the most in her life. If they should now meet on both levels, their issues would be resolved. There is such a possibility in the story. If Vasilij should decide for humanity instead of abstractions, he could perform a concrete human act that would also amount to the great heroic deed he always dreamed of; he could go down to the cellar and release Rima. She, for her part, would then know that the human principle had won, and this knowledge would make her fight meaningful. The only remaining question, of course, would be where in this Communist-occupied territory could they go?

There is nowhere to go, and there is also no possibility of their meeting at the point of decision, because on the ideological level they had actually been moving in two opposite directions. Rima had proceeded from confusion to clarity, and Vasilij from clarity to confusion. At first Rima did not know where the true values of life were, whether in her family, or in personal love, or in art, or, finally, in what includes them all—her country. Gradually, through her life and through that lonely night, she comes to understand that the simple facts of the rising sun, of little stones at the bottom of the creek, of all the familiar shapes and sounds of her native land amount to the overwhelming truth that this land must follow its own destiny, not the one which the occupiers are trying to foist upon it, and that it is worthwhile to fight and die in order to contribute to the fulfillment of it. Vasilij, on the other hand, at first thought he knew what communism was and what his own purposes should be, but as life goes on, he sees that people around him do not live by the official ideology but by something else, that they even suffer and perish for that undefined something, and that here, in this strange country, the very earth seems to deny any validity to the concepts he is trying to embrace. This dichotomy becomes too difficult for him to comprehend, and he runs back to the shelter of the red flags, committing himself to something he knows he can no longer value as an ideal.

The geometrical principle of construction in this story is carried through not only in the main outlines but also in a number of details. At all levels we perceive intersecting planes of objective reality and inner experience; all issues are seen by the author in terms of actual or figurative special relationships. We observe this method at work in the descriptions of a given situation such as the siege of Leningrad, which is conveyed by the image of a solid vault of noise from the firing guns clamped over the town, cracking and crumbling underneath. Similarly, a party arranged to celebrate Rima's high school diploma can be visualized as a space crisscrossed by several planes of reality, a meeting point of separate lines representing the different lives and circumstances of each person. The first and underlying plane is the fact of German occupation. It has caused the people to live as isolated spheres of consciousness, across which communication has become difficult. Kęstutis, Rima's future husband, comes to the party with the experience of a battle against the Germans behind him. This battle has made him different from anyone else; it has crystallized his decision to become an armed fighter from now on, against any occupying power. He meets another man, Liudas, a competitor for Rima's affections, who brings his own world of esthetic values, of disengagement from the course of history, in the name of art. Rima's father also embodies in himself a world unknown to others. He is a bureaucrat who plays it safe, thinks and speaks officialese even in his family, although with them it is vitally important to know the truth. Yet he, too, shuffles the papers inside his soul to find a letter from a relative in Siberia—a desperate cry from still another, tragic dimension of existence. Rima's mother is oppressed by the reality of a housewife in wartime. She has arranged the banquet by the slow and painful process of selling odds and ends from her possessions (each, in turn, representing different emotional associations with past levels of life) in order to buy scarce items of food on the black market. The real price of all these things was her fear of being caught, and it is this fear which she contributes to the supposedly happy occasion.

Such writing becomes essentially symbolic in nature. Nothing really exists any more, everything signifies. Gradually all the people in the story begin to lose their organic presence, becoming not so much individuals as representations of issues. In trying to explain to us the workings of their hearts and minds, Landsbergis transforms them into sets of symbolic, geometrical patterns. This effect is also visible in the other stories in the book in which the central characters, if real, possess only the reality of an idea and, if imaginary, consist only of a deep desire that an ultimate idea should exist. In the short sketch called "A Face with Sharp Cheekbones" the main issues are arranged according to a vertical pattern—a staircase. A drunken man climbs the stairs with a nameless loose woman to her room. At each turning of the stairs, as in T. S. Eliot's "Ash Wednesday," he is repeatedly confronted with his own spiritual crisis, materialized here in the figures of priests to whom the man feels he must confess and from whom he must receive justification for all the terrible cruelty and absurdity of the world he has seen during the war. The man's inner reality thus acquires shape and identity in two outer realities, one factual (the stairs) and the other fictional (the priests). In this framework the main issue becomes one of human communication, achievable only if the imagined priests can explain to him why "if there is meaning, should I be tortured by the fear of meaninglessness" and if they can prove that the cross men must carry "is really a cross and not just a piece of stone"—in other words, that our life is indeed an *imitatio Christi* and not the labors of Sisyphus. Of the three priests, only one is able to communicate and restore him to faith, because all he has to give is his own uncertainty, from which emerges the deep, eternal waiting for the ultimate resolution of all issues—for Christ.

This intense waiting, this striving for some remote, unidentifiable and yet ultimate source of light in Landsbergis' work, provides the center of gravity around which the different planes of reality arrange themselves, forming a kind of symbolic guiding star in the reader's mind. Its unseen presence is felt in the story "The Procession," in which a selfish man who has always stayed out of trouble by reading French classics and remaining obedient to the powers that be in this "sufficiently perfect" world, and who has avoided any risk in the name of humanity, finds himself in a group of exiles to Siberia. Dehumanized, he learns humanity; in death he meets eternity, which comes in the shape of an endless procession of spiritual rebels throughout history, walking forever toward the unknown source of eternal justice. They are like the Magi, crossing very real and boundless deserts, following a star that could be imaginary, in search of a Bethlehem that may not exist.

In a story called "The Wind of Greece" we see Landsbergis experimenting with a variety of levels from a number of different perspectives. The plot simply describes three "displaced persons" who go to work at an American base in Germany, eat lunch, try unsuccessfully to steal some food, and then return to their camp. The story is told simultaneously from three points of view representing each of the DP's. One of them is a farmer who contributes the consciousness of basic things in life, of food and of the physical effort necessary to obtain it. The second is a rowdy, a restless fighter who adds the sense of adventure, of plunder and amorous conquest over the pretty Greek girl in the kitchen who is guarded by an enormous monster of a cook. In the mind of the third, an intellectual and a dreamer, the simple sequence of events is elevated to the level of myth, of Theseus and Ariadne in the palace of the Minotaur. The story shifts continuously from one point of view to another, creating ever new avenues of symbolic commentary upon the substance of the myth and its relevance to the course of human history, without reaching any philosophical depth of insight beyond the realization that meaning in art is of itself a mere structural interplay—a labyrinth of possibilities.

In a short story called "Man at the End of the Corridor," from a collection by several young Lithuanian writers under the title *Proza* (*Prose*), 1951, Landsbergis extends the attribution of a visible symbolic shape to an idea into the realm of the fantastic. It is a semi-humorous tale about a little girl in a DP camp who sees in the window a transparent lieutenant of dragoons in nineteenth-century uniform, pleading with her to say that she loves him because only the love of an innocent girl can release him from the evil spell he was put under long ago by a jealous rival. This standard fairy-tale situation receives a new element; the girl is not really very innocent. She is in fact, a perfectly normal child, which means, of course, that she is both greedy and cunning, able to manipulate the unfortunate dragoon into breaking his code of honor to satisfy her childish whims. Corruption, it turns out, is an essential part of being human, and those who embody in themselves nothing but the pure ideal of virtue must become transparent specters like the dragoon.

In recent years Landsbergis has turned more and more to the stage. This was a logical development, issuing from the very nature of his art. He discarded the novel because it was not possible for him to control the countless implications inherent in the relationships among the multiple fragments of reality constituting the new mosaic of life. He found the short story an inadequate instrument for conveying the complex interplay of the various planes of reality because, like a novel, it is a linear genre in the sense that it does not permit the visual simultaneity of impressions, indispensable for a work constructed on several levels at once. A play can simplify this task because the various planes of experience can be made visible by means of stage design, and also the shifts from one reality to another can be dramatized by the arrangement of scenes allowing for abrupt transitions. Of course, this requires that the traditional means of presenting a play as a narrative sequence be abandoned, but Landsbergis was ready to do that even in his prose. His method of delineating a character more as a representation than as a growing organic whole also suits the stage better than it does the narrative technique. In addition to all this, we must remember that Landsbergis always liked to put his people in special situations, frames setting them apart from the ordinary course of life. Rima is spatially fixed in the dark cellar, and even her movements are restricted by the bonds. The man in "A Face with Sharp Cheekbones" must resolve all his problems while climbing a staircase. The lieutenant of the dragoons plays out his destiny framed by the window—an equivalent of the stage. Weiss in *The Journey*, with half his face burned, in effect wears a theatrical mask—a face that signifies something even without any reflection of inner life in it. Placed in such positions and given what amounts to stage costumes, Landsbergis' characters do not so much live as act out their lives, making the theater much more the natural medium for them.

The plays themselves show a steady movement away from realistic presentation toward abstract symbolic designs in which the specific possibilities of the stage are utilized to the fullest extent. The first play, *Vėjas gluosniuose* (*The Wind in the Willows*), effects the separation from reality by means akin to poetry. It creates a special lyrical mood by the use of poetic language dominated by metaphor and symbol. The action takes place in the sixteenth century, a time far enough removed from the present to have an exotic aura of its own. The plot itself is semi-legendary; it deals with the miraculous appearance of Saint Casimir, the patron saint of Lithuania, to lead the outnumbered Lithuanian-Polish troops to victory over the Russians in a crucial battle. Landsbergis removes the action of the play even beyond the limits of legend, to the realm of pure imagination, by shifting the focus from the battle itself to the night just before it and by having Saint Casimir come down to earth incognito to learn something about the people he will lead the next morning.

Having moved the scene away from the battlefield, Landsbergis deprives his play of action in the ordinary sense. All the important things now happen inside the people themselves, as they do also in his prose. On this level of action, Saint Casimir performs the function of a catalyst, initiating important changes in the spiritual condition of the main characters and thus preparing them for the events to come. Within this framework, the play is basically a set of variations on the theme of love, each constructed in such a way that happiness becomes possible only after the resolution of some crucial issue. The issues, however, cannot be solved unless the people learn to accept a fundamental realignment, either of their self-image or in their accustomed systems of values.

Saint Casimir is in this sense a participant in the action on equal terms with all the others. He has transgressed against the ordinary notions of sainthood in that, having already become a metaphysical being, he continues to love the earth and its people with a personal feeling so intense that it obscures the perspective of eternity. He becomes so deeply committed to the people who, in their ignorance, strive for happiness that his supernatural knowledge of their impending doom becomes an unbearable burden, a source of suffering which can be permitted only to those who have not yet reached spiritual perfection. This is precisely the point; Casimir comes to understand that sainthood is not a state of being but a process of becoming, always striving to fulfill oneself, even in the kingdom of heaven.

The metaphysical issues facing Saint Casimir constitute the most exalted plane of action. Just below is the deeply human tragedy of the Lithuanian-Polish king, who has lost the woman he loved above all else in the world and now must continue to go through the motions of being a ruler without caring for anything on earth any more. In his helplessness the king has lost all desire to fight and is ready to withdraw his forces, thus causing untold suffering to his people, who would then fall into the hands of the Russians. Saint Casimir, in his mortal disguise, comes to the king and manages to convince him that royal responsibilities require passing beyond personal sorrow to become the embodiment of the will of the land to fight off the invaders. Having stepped out of the shell of his own tragedy for a moment, the king is also able to take action in settling the lives of several people who had placed their hopes in him.

Among these people is the magnate Kurevičius, who is passionately in love with Aldona, the wife of a man presumed dead or captured by the Russians. There are two obstacles to their happiness. The first is the deep philosophical despair of Kurevičius, who has the gift of understanding that the starry sky, in all its beauty, is nothing but a silent, bottomless void, but lacks the greater gift of knowledge that it is also a perfect poem, like everything else that exists, including the human heart. Such knowledge is, of course, an attribute of sainthood, and Casimir, speaking humbly, succeeds in communicating some of it to Kurevičius, enough, at least, to enable him to respond to the love of Aldona.

The second obstacle stands in the realm of generally accepted moral values. Kurevičius and Aldona cannot be united as long as there is no certainty that her husband is dead, unless they can gather the courage to step over the laws of society in the name of the greater law of love. Here the king is also forced to make a decision that will go against the social and moral structure he is supposed to defend. Catholics cannot be divorced, but it is no good for a king to change the whole framework by embracing the Protestant faith in order to grant Aldona a divorce. Aldona must decide to live with Kurevičius in what, for a Catholic, is a sinful union, and the king must undertake to support them in this. The basic issue, as it was with Saint Casimir, is one of remaining open to infinity. Marriages, like sainthood, are made in heaven, but in heaven, too, they are not crystallized into an absolute and final law. The insight we gain is that nothing definable in finite categories will lead to a true relationship with the infinite God.

Far below Kurevičius in the social structure stands Petras Jasaitis, a simple farmer who is close enough to the earth to feel its beauty in his bones and therefore to perceive also the music of the spheres. Pasternak's words, "poetry will always be in the grass, and it will always be necessary to bend down in order to hear it," apply exactly to Jasaitis as a definition of his personality. He loves Onutė, a little kitchen maid, but cannot marry her as long as he remains a serf. He hopes to be released from serfdom by the king, whose life he saved in an earlier battle, but the king, in his personal despair has forgotten all about him. Only after

Casimir rouses him from the depths of his sorrow back to royal stature can he remember and reward the least of his subjects.

Finally, in the gradual descent from love as a tragic communion with the dead, then as an infinite passion for the living, and as a lyrical song from simple hearts, we meet love as comedy. Vyšniauskas is an impoverished country squire. He would like to be a rich merchant, but that would mean transferring to a lower social class. He loves the cook Kunigunda or, rather, her fried chicken, but cannot marry her unless he gives up his nobility. A braggart and a coward—really an echo of Shakespeare's Falstaff—he does nevertheless have a touch of the divine feeling for beauty, restricted, to be sure, to appreciation of good food and wine, and of healthy cows. In helping him the king also transgresses against what might be called "poetic justice" by rewarding vanity, but what he actually rewards is the gift of imagination in the man, a quality which has in it the intimations of infinity.

The play gains an additional, and tragic, dimension because of Saint Casimir's knowledge that all three men, whose lives now can grow toward happiness, will die in the coming battle. This provides a counterpoint to all human hope and confronts the solution of all issues with another overwhelming question, unanswerable on earth, where everything is temporary. With the understanding that not only himself but all are visitors on earth, Saint Casimir regains the perspective of eternity because it has become relevant to everyone else.

The next play by Landsbergis, *Penki stulpai turgaus aikštėje* (*Five Posts in the Marketplace*), has more surface action. It takes place in a small country occupied by a great power professing a totalitarian ideology. A bloody guerrilla war, which has been going on for seven years, is about to end with the complete destruction of the freedom fighters. Among the last of them is Antanas, a detachment leader who receives orders to kill the chief investigator of the enemy's security forces. The investigator, a native of that country, motivated by complex personal and ideological considerations, has been assiduously putting down all resistance to the occupiers. The orders come supposedly from the central headquarters of the guerrilla movement, but Antanas does not know that the center has already been destroyed and that the instructions were

Henrikas Radauskas

Photograph courtesy of Draugas

Antanas Vaičiulaitis

Photograph by Vytautas Maželis

Jonas Aistis

Photograph by Vytautas Mažėlis

Antanas Škėma

Photograph by Vytautas Mažėlis

Algirdas Landsbergis *Photograph by Gediminas Naujokaitis*

Kostas Ostrauskas

Photograph by A. Vaškelis

Alfonsas Nyka-Niliūnas

Photograph by Vytautas Maželis

Algimantas Mackus

Photograph by L. Kančauskas

Henrikas Nagys

Photograph by Vytautas Maželis

Kazys Bradūnas

Photograph courtesy of Draugas

Albinas Marius Katiliškis

Photograph by Vytautas Maželis

Jonas Mekas

Photograph by Vytautas Maželis

Aloyzas Baronas

Photograph by V. Račkauskas

Bernardas Brazdžionis *Photograph by Vytautas Maželis*

actually written by Albina, the secretary of the investigator and a guerrilla spy. She and Antanas have loved each other in the past, and now she hopes to lure him out of the forests, with her supposed orders so that he will quit the hopeless struggle and survive for her sake. She sets up a situation that might make this possible. The investigator and several other officials are to be invited to her wedding with Antanas, during which he will suddenly pull out his gun and kill the investigator. Actually, of course, Albina is hoping that she can convince Antanas to give up his fight before things reach such a pass and that therefore nothing will happen and the wedding will turn out to be real, rather than just a play to trap the investigator. Due to a number of circumstances, Antanas is on the point of giving up the plan, but the investigator, who has figured out the plan and, for his own reasons, wishes to die, provokes Antanas during the wedding into killing him. Antanas is also killed by the security troops, and so the play ends in tragedy.

This basic line of plot becomes complicated by other interpersonal relationships which contribute new moral and philosophical issues to the play. There are, for one thing, two women in Antanas' life. Genė, a young girl, has been a messenger for the guerrillas ever since her high school days. She has grown up before his eyes, amid constant danger and hardship, and gradually Antanas has come to love her more than his life, but completely without hope, because he knows all the time that he is a man marked for death. Beautiful and innocent and lost to him forever, Genė is a symbol of the country itself—something of infinite value which he can only die defending, never have for his own.

This is why Antanas cannot really accept the chance to survive proffered by Albina. Surviving would mean choosing not only her, whom he no longer loves, but also the principle of surrender, of compromise. The cry, "Give me liberty or give me death!" may sound hollow and rhetorical in a civilization calling itself realistic and sophisticated, but in Landsbergis' play we are not dealing with such a society or with reality in the ordinary sense only. The little country, although not named in the play, is actually Lithuania; on the level where Antanas professes his faith and makes his decisions, however, it is any place that has ever suffered oppression on earth. In this sense it is a symbolic country that exists only in the tragic dreams of poets, and as such it cannot represent any but absolute values. A poem either is or is not. The same is true of the realm of myth, where the dreams of ordinary people walk about like giants in the earth. Albina, by offering compromise, becomes small and real. She lives only in the actual world and can no longer reach Antanas across the barrier separating reality from poetic truth.

When Antanas does vacillate in his purpose, it is for a reason having nothing to do with surrender to the practical realities of the situation. Rather, the opposite is true; the poetic principle is again involved, a recognition of the sacred creative impulse in man. Long ago, when the dead thoughts of the occupiers still had the life of vision in them, because they were then the dreams of rebels, the investigator had written a book called *The Sculpture of the Future* in which he tried to foresee the shape of Utopia in a new stature of man, to be molded according to the laws of logical and perfect justice. This book had once made an impression upon Antanas, who was a sculptor himself before the war began and had also dreamed of the perfect measure of man. At a crucial point in the play Albina brings the two men together even before the wedding is to take place, thus giving Antanas an earlier opportunity to kill the investigator. She hopes that Antanas, once he recognizes in the investigator the author of that book, will not be able to bring himself to shoot him. And indeed, Antanas cannot destroy this man who, however rotten he may now be, had once touched the same wellspring of poetic thought. The investigator, on the other hand, understands precisely at that moment that he must seek death, because Antanas' reluctance to kill shows him once more the true human being he has methodically murdered in himself.

The symbolic and mythical dimension of the play is strongly emphasized by the presence of a narrator—a perfectly rational, even scholarly, man from some future civilization, representing a stage in human development which has passed beyond the point of moral absolutes. The whole play, in fact, is a kind of dramatized lecture by this professorial figure about people in the "relatively recent" past on whom, as he says, "fell the heavenly vault of extreme demands and universal decisions." There is a terrible meaning in these words; they imply that the ideal life of poetic vision ennobles man only as long as it remains unreachable as the firmament. When it descends on men as a categorical imperative demanding immediate fulfillment, it crushes us all.

The plot of the play is thus enmeshed among the symbolic planes of reference which constitute its real structure. Consequently, everything the characters say or do acquires multiple implications of meaning, relating to moral and ideological issues. The task of the playwright then is to recognize and control their interrelationships by means of precisely calculated words and movements of the people on stage. What we have before us is a modern mystery play, differing from its medieval predecessors in that, instead of presenting a simple and straightforward moral message, it leads us deep into complex and often ambivalent questions. This complexity is achieved by means of contrast and irony, paradox and hidden relevance, devices typical of Landsbergis' art in general. The mercilessly hard orders to kill, for instance, present an absolute contrast with the character of Albina who wrote them. "I know the handwriting of her mind," says Antanas; "it is like the gentle lines on an aspen leaf. I keep trying to imagine her composing this plan—and cannot." Still, the possibility that these are not genuine battle orders but only the desperate struggle of a fragile woman's heart causes Antanas to wonder if he should carry them out. His resolution becomes firm only after Genė, the messenger girl, comes with the news that the whole headquarters has already been wiped out. "Nobody can now countermand the orders," says Antanas. This is equivalent to saying that the Ten Commandments must be obeyed now that we know God is dead, but what Antanas means is an absolute imperative independent of incidental catastrophes.

The narrator is present throughout the scene, testing the determination of Antanas and his men by means of an objective symbol, a knife, which he offers to each man in turn as he asks them what they think of the order. It is the same knife Antanas uses to carve little wooden sculptures, pitiful remnants of his creative gift from the earlier times when he was shaping figures of grace and nobility. In this way the knife connects both periods of his life, changing from tool to weapon during the seven years in which Antanas diminishes as a sculptor to the degree that he grows as a guerrilla leader. The painful irony is that he would have never taken up arms except to defend the principle of free creative striving.

This irony becomes especially poignant in the scenes of the play in which Antanas visits his old sculptor's workshop. The figures he created seven years earlier, still in the preliminary clay casts, have decayed with time, remaining frozen in the movement conceived by the artist. They all become symbolic expression, mirror images of Antanas himself. There is the figure of a soldier, weather-worn, returning to the nothing from which it came, and of an athlete, still striving toward his goal with muscles eroded by time. They both represent Antanas, arrested in his noble purpose and eaten up from within by the terrible things he has had to do during the years in order to defend his original conception of truth and of life worth living. His favorite sculpture is called "Girl with a Dying Elk"—a prophecy of his own fate, fulfilled at the end of the play when he lies dead and Genė, his love, looks down on him, saying, "How beautiful is my beloved, like an elk, frozen in his flight."

The motif of Antanas' sculptures is repeated with terrible and tragic force in the picture of the bodies of dead guerrillas tied to the posts in the marketplace. The intent of the occupiers is to frighten the people into submission by showing just what happens to those who dare to revolt against them. At one point in the play the investigator says to Antanas and Albina that these bodies will mark their marriage with a grandiose image of justice, "ants methodically destroying the bodies of those who dared to raise their hand against history."

The action in the play thus crosses three symbolic planes of meaning: the purely human love of Albina, countered by the ideal image of Genė; the creative effort of Antanas, frozen and decayed in the gesture of defiance; and the perspective of the narrator, watching the poetic human madness from a remote point in history. The fourth and final plane consists of snatches of Lithuanian folk songs sung, curiously, by the narrator, in which the whole complex and desperate struggle of Antanas is conveyed with clear lyrical simplicity. These songs have remained immortal in Lithuania through the centuries, always singing of the everlasting death of its warriors, defenders of the land.

The ultimate point of the play is made by Genė, who says that the last remaining important thing is never to forget this time and its tragedy, never through all the changes of history. This, in a way, is why we make statues of past heroes—to remind us forever of greatness which is no longer relevant to our lives. In a sense, this amounts also to a perfect definition of what the play is—a monument.

Landsbergis' next play is a comedy entitled *Meilės mokykla* (*The School of Love*). The keynote for *Five Posts* is given in the motto, from René Char: "*devoirs infernaux.*" *The School of Love* carries the lines from Shakespeare about "the baseless fabric of this vision," the "unsubstantial pageant" from which our dreams, that is, ourselves, are made. One may deduce from this the position of the author; he will weave his thoughts into the unsubstantial fabric of life as seen on the stage. He also explicitly promises to be jocular, to "entertain the reader," in his stage directions. In other words, the unreality of action will rest on the levity of basic structure; the stuff that dreams are made on will be grotesque and comical. If there is any seriousness in the play, it will have to be sought on a plane not subject to the farce pretending to imitate reality on the stage. There is something reminiscent of Chekhov in this attempt to neutralize the circumstances of life so that the requirements of action will not interfere with working out the basic idea. The difference is that Chekhov achieves neutralization by means of a lyrical silence, slightly tinged with mockery, while Landsbergis prefers to hide his vision amid tremendous comical noise. His play is a nonsensical carnival with one or two serious things to say.

The plot, if it is one, concerns a huge, greedy whale of a man named Leviathan who comes to America, via Germany, from a small Lithuanian town, or rather, as the author explains, from the quintessence of all the small towns in the world. He is a living embodiment of the spirit of free enterprise (said to have made America great) blown up to such absurd proportions that finally elements of the poet and the dreamer begin to show in the texture of his soul. Leviathan is surrounded by two ministering angels. One is real; his name is Gabriel and he is a down-at-the-heels DP, his eyes full of dreams and visions, with just the right amount of corrupt knowledge in them—the kind of knowledge possessed by innocent children, as in the story "The Man at the End of the

Corridor." The other angel is actually a devil, intent upon destroying Leviathan in revenge for having scattered his many universes contained in his cherished collection of postage stamps. The two "angels" work together, each for his own purposes, in helping Leviathan develop and promote a huge enterprise called "The School of Love," similar to schools of dancing, cooking, or the like. Success is enormous. All of America and even the "old country" of Europe fall at his feet. Leviathan seriously considers proclaiming himself emperor. At this point Gabriel forsakes him, finally convinced that his dream and Leviathan's never really had anything in common at all. All of Leviathan's enterprises collapse in an enormous multicolored heap of trash, leaving us with a vaguely repulsive feeling, as if one of the Shakespearean "bubbles of the earth" had burst, fouling the air. Gabriel himself goes off with Leviathan's secretary to find the "real" America. The only guidelines they have are the golden leaves of a Pennsylvania autumn, floating in the girl's memories of her childhood, like a vision of Eldorado.

The action of the play is full of fantastic, grotesque events, such as the killing of a malevolent ghost with a spray cleaner (Americans can fix anything) or the mechanical cows mooing in synthetic meadows—a much more efficient means of conveying the basic notions of romance than any actual pastoral landscape with its superfluous sights and smells of organic reality. There are delegations representing various factions of the American public, including a procession of sexual perverts put out of business by Leviathan's school, moaning like the wind-blown, sinful lovers in Dante's *Inferno*. The designers of women's slacks, condemned by Leviathan, have a desperate battle for survival against the manufacturers of pots and pans who are loyal to the new school because it has sent women back to their kitchens. Obviously, the stage cannot hold all these tumultuous throngs, and Landsbergis solves the problem by using both the ancient Greek device of reporting large-scale events going on beyond the stage and the modern process of *laterna magica* in which crowds of people, oil wells, ships, etc., float before us in the background, on a movie screen.

All this grotesque hodgepodge seems at times a bit like Gogol's weird fantasies—for instance, when Khlestakov, in *The Inspector General*, talks of special soups brought, still steaming, by boat from Paris, or of house-sized watermelons, or of 35,000 messengers scurrying all over town. What Landsbergis lacks however, is Gogol's secret self-hatred, which can give his fantasies a sudden ominous turn. *The School of Love* itself *is* actually a school of love; it teaches us to love the impossible creatures that we are. The decision to give the issue a comical aspect frees the author from working out all the complications to an end. Comedy is by definition an oversimplification in which a situation full of symbolic meaning can be hinted at, even scoffed at, and then left for the reader himself to unravel after he has had his laughs. The choice of the comic genre might also signify the author's retreat from the effort to take on the whole mystery of the universe, and that is a kind of saving grace, always implicit in what we call the sense of humor. Unable to reproduce the likeness of God, in which he is made, man sometimes prefers to wear the face of a clown instead.

Among the latest plays, *Barzda* (*The Beard*) is a one-act farce with a tragic meaning. The characters are completely abstract; there is no life in them except as an allegory or a living stage prop. The main figure is Kiekvienis (Everyman). He goes to college, has a father and a mother and girlfriend, Onytė, "a cheerful kid." In addition, there are three sets of military figures: a bearded leader with his bearded soldier, then a corresponding beardless pair, and finally a pair with bifurcated beards. The multileveled reality found in Landsbergis' works is here represented literally, on the stage, where we see three different planes of action. At the bottom lies Onytė on her back; above her, separated by a board, is Everyman, on his stomach. They kiss. Above them, sitting on their chairs, are Father and Mother, with a crib, planning their darling son's future. The military figures arrive from outside this circle and interfere with it, creating the tension of the play.

The plot revolves around the identity of Everyman. No one will allow him to keep his personality as he himself understands it, but instead everyone wishes him to conform to their own idea of him. The girl loves not him but his enormous black beard. To his parents he is the same baby who used to play in the crib and will remain so even after he learns to use Latin words and be a doctor. When Everyman comes home with the beard his girl has made him grow, his parents scream and accuse him of infanticide. The military men represent three different but absolute, mutually exclusive, and totally correct ideologies, limited, to be sure, to principles concerning men's beards. They usurp power in turns and in turns they judge Everyman to be a traitor to truth because he sticks to growing his own type of beard, not corresponding to any of their ideological definitions. In this play all the rest of the characters seem to blend into an Everyone, pressuring Everyman to submit to the ultimate truth, consisting, however, of a multitude of irreconcilable points of view. Naturally, the play ends with Everyman exiled to the Siberian snows, saying "no" a million times over throughout all eternity. Thus we can see a progression in Landsbergis' work, from fragments of shattered lives, through complex interplays of different planes and dimensions of existence, to the ultimate simplicity and solitude of a single man saying "no," the voice of a twentieth-century prophet crying in the wilderness.

It would seem that there is nowhere to go any more. After the Everlasting Nay, what is there to be said? Nothing, if the function of art is to make visible the ideas men must live by. If, on the other hand, art is understood to be a deliberately arranged structure of formal relationships, rather than a mirror to nature or a continuation of human experience in the realm of fiction, the possibilities are inexhaustible, and Landsbergis, perhaps more than most Lithuanian writers in exile, remains open to as many of them as his talent can comprehend. Sensitive to the finest vibrations of existence, somewhat aloof, faintly sardonic, at times a bit sentimental, he is most of all a thoroughly professional and self-conscious artist, concerned with his work, laying no claim to any special knowledge of the mysteries of the universe.

8 Truth and Metaphor in the Poetry of Alfonsas Nyka-Niliūnas

Alfonsas Nyka-Niliūnas was born July 15, 1919, in Utena, eastern Lithuania. In 1938–39 he studied romance languages and literatures and philosophy in the University of Kaunas. His academic education was completed in the University of Vilnius in 1942. From 1946 to 1949, Niliūnas lived in Freiburg and Tuebingen, Germany. While in Freiburg he taught French in the École des Arts et Métiers.

After arriving in the United States in 1949, he was a manual laborer for a considerable length of time until he eventually joined the Library of Congress. In 1949, Niliūnas became a member of the editorial staff of the Lithuanian cultural monthly *Aidai* (*Echoes*). He also was one of the editors of the literary magazine of the younger Lithuanian generation called *Literatūros lankai* (*The Literary Folios*), which first came out in 1952.

The published poetry of Niliūnas is contained in the following volumes: *Praradimo simfonijos* (*The Symphonies of Dispossession*), 1946; *Orfėjaus medis* (*The Tree of Orpheus*), 1954; and *Balandžio vigilijos* (*The Vigils of April*), 1957. An important achievement of Niliūnas is his new Lithuanian translation of Shakespeare's *Hamlet*, published in 1964. Niliūnas has also translated many other poets and is known as one of the most stimulating Lithuanian literary critics.

AMONG the many ways of organizing the perceptions of reality into a personal poetic universe, two seem especially relevant to the poetry of Alfonsas Nyka-Niliūnas. One is to write in close imitation of nature as it presents itself to consciousness intensified by deep emotion, and the other is to treat the objects of reality as a set of hieroglyphics or symbols pointing to the unknown dimension of inner truth, which is felt by the poet as an inexplicable sense of longing. Niliūnas' work, on first acquaintance, seems to belong more to the former category; it has the appearance of being an imitation of life as it is remembered in the dreams of his fellow countrymen, the Lithuanian exiles in the West. In it they find the rainy landscapes full of roaming winds and autumn leaves, melodious with the babbling brooks of spring, which are so much a part of the native landscape that now haunts their memory. They also recognize their present—the cold and gnawing pain of exile, unmitigated by the passage of time or by the hospitality of alien lands, which often reaches the frozen point of black despair. Further on in his work, however, the frame of reference the poet and his fellow exiles share becomes less and less important. Niliūnas has transfigured the objects, colors, and movements of the land they knew in common into another longing and another country, with a reality that depends entirely on the compelling force of these new visions, on the poet's ability to take his readers with him on a different journey—home to their innermost selves or perhaps to a new exile in the frigid void of nowhere.

It is as if Niliūnas undertook to continue by means of his art the search for Eldorado, which lured the conquistadors to death in a land distant from their home. Eldorado not found became a mystery; mystery not revealed grew into a legend and thus transformed itself to poetry, acquiring a meaning quite remote from the original. The poet's Eldorado is as far from and as near to him as his own dreams. It is actually a different dimension of experience which he first became aware of while still in his childhood. It is not a matter of seeing the fundamental realities of the world through the eyes of a child as yet unspoiled by symbolic or intellectual conceptions. On the contrary, the things now recalled from memory are meaningful because of the mystery perceived in them by the child's intense and free imagination. When Niliūnas writes of them from a point in time far removed from his childhood, when the dreams were born, he in effect retraces his steps to the things which surrounded the awakening of his consciousness, carrying with him his life's experience and poetic skill in using the devices of his art to transform those early childhood objects, evocative of dreams, into a system of metaphors and symbols expressive of his present longing. Some of these objects can be seen in the poem "Eldorado" from Niliūnas' first book of verse, *Praradimo simfonijos* (*The Symphonies of Dispossession*):

There is a wondrous world which no one ever finds
Though deep within ourselves its pain resides with us.
For this I turned away from everything on earth,
Desiring, for a spell, to be a wanderer there.

There stands a house with blue storm shutters, by itself;
The toys I left behind in childhood live in it;
My days are sleeping deep within the noonday silence,
Watched over by the wind with broken wings.

Forgotten flowers in a vase, in picture frame old Noah,
And, next to him, in faded window, pigeons carved in wood,
And, with the birds, the noble Spring descends through open spaces
And twilight bells depart to wander in the plain.

'Tis there I take the sunset by the hand
And lead the old man wind beside me, like a dog,
Pick up the ticking clock and hold it, precious doll,
Still promising never to leave them all alone.

There lie enchanted treasures of my visions, endless like the dreams;
My barefoot friends, the girl who came a-running every Spring,
The ancient wind that gathered up the autumn leaves
And now, awaiting my return, like a faithful dog,
He guards the leaves to give them back to me.

This poem touches upon several object-metaphors that occur repeatedly throughout Niliūnas' poetry as central images from which others are developed with increasing intensity and complexity. The wind is an especially important catalyst; it moves through and transforms the texture of the poems into the stuff of dreams, enveloping the consciousness of the individual as a kind of transparent, shifting barrier between the mere presence and the emotional significance of things (their presence, untouched by metaphor, is beyond this barrier; the poet himself is inside, looking out across the wind at a world changed into the image of his longing). The wind itself is also a metaphor expressing the sound and movement of intimate and secret dreams, enveloping the poet with a sense of belonging in his own world of things transfigured. In the poem "Nights," from *Symphonies of Dispossession*, the wind is a father and a pilgrim coming home:

> And when the house was all asleep, there used to come into my room
> The pilgrim wind, grown old, to rock me, his beloved son . . .
> The storm would then subside; the stars would fly in through the window,
> And there was light, as from my mother's eyes.

In the poem "The Return" the poet himself, like a prodigal son, returning inward, is met by father-wind: "Outside the window comes the grim and sad-faced wind, his hair all wet with rain, / And weeps so heavily: 'Where were you, O my son?' " At other times the wind is a dark force, roaring in the trees, reproaching the poet for having left his home, the remembered childhood universe that must pass into nonbeing as soon as the poet forsakes it to meet the challenge of the present day. There is a twofold exile in Niliūnas' poetry. One is physical, and the other, more important, is spiritual, consisting of new horizons in the mind. The pain of this second exile is the pull of previous visions. It could be said that the object-metaphors of the poet's childhood, faced with the threat of oblivion in the river of time, are fighting for their very existence, when they desperately claim a place for themselves in the poet's imagination. This is perhaps why the image of the wind is so often connected with the idea of fatherhood; the poet's early visions acquire a kind of moral authority over him, demanding faith and love in much the same way as, outside the realm of art, one's native land, forsaken by the exile, continues to exert its moral force, as did Jerusalem upon the prophet.

The wind often gives birth to another image—a tree—the two being related by the dynamics of movement, when wind becomes manifest in the swinging, thrashing branches of a roaring giant tree. The poem "Old Tree" combines both tree and wind to overwhelm the poet with powerful, accusing love:

> My childhood still recalls the speech of ancient rustling trees
> When, like a giant, it would drown me in my dreams,
> How grim it thrashes now, not having found me home,
> How comes the wind to take me to the twilight of my youth!

He brings me in his arms, the angry wind,
And, roaring fearfully, he puts me down under the tree,
Like father would. The ancient tree starts weeping as he sees
Me underneath, heartbroken by its voice.

And then he scolds me, like a furious giant:
"Where have you been? Why don't you stay with me?"
The wind, now thin and wasted, echoes the reproach,
And I embrace them, trembling like a leaf in storm.

On the other hand, toward the end of *The Symphonies of Dispossession*, when, with relentless clarity, there comes the understanding that the poet can no longer dwell enchanted in his past, he sees "the martyred winds, still hanging in the churchyard trees." In the context of Lithuanian destiny, this image is reminiscent of the land itself, forsaken by its exiles, forgotten by the world.

The window metaphor is developed in the context of light into an image, at times associated with the idea of motherhood. The window is a means of perceiving reality; in the metaphorical universe of a poet such perception is equivalent to being born into the world of imagination. Furthermore, as a source of light, a window can be related to the eyes, and then the blue eyes of the mother begin to alternate with the image of pale blue storm shutters, as in the first poem quoted, both serving as metaphors of longing. The poem "Winter" develops an interrelationship between these images leading toward a certain cold awareness of death inherent in the vision of childhood sunk into oblivion:

When now the morning wakes me from my sleep,
As if a child returned from deepest dreams,
I see the snow outside the window
And rub my eyes like once, when, as a child,

I saw the snowbound plain the first time through the window:
The floor and walls were drenched in sad and blinding light;
I would get up and, sitting on a bench before the empty plains,
Would cover up my bare and frozen feet
And wait for mother to come in with water buckets
And snow, emitting, like the walls and floor, the bitter winter light.

And even now, with blue, wide-open eyes, I'd cry for joy
And, seeing that we all are home, go gently back to sleep,
But now the field beyond the window stares with empty sorrow
And all the days go by like strangers, mute and grim.

There is a growing realization in *The Symphonies of Dispossession* that it is not possible to return to the dreams of childhood to find the way to Eldorado. We cannot become again the children we once were, not only literally but also in terms of the visions reality had evoked in our childhood imagination. The journey *à la recherche du temps perdu* simply does not lead anywhere at all. The poet reacts to this painful knowledge at first by anxiously protecting such dreams he can still collect. In this context, the image of the window acquires a meaning in direct reverse of its previous function as the organ of perception. Now it is a dreaded opening to reality outside of art, from which we can see the threatening visage of all-destroying time:

The night is ringing like a giant base cello
Forsaken, lonely in reality beyond me, grim.
It fills with heavy chords my room
To which I brought my restless visions, wondrous dreams.
I'm watching now the frozen glitter of the city in the dark
As if these were the lights of some mysterious autumn orchestra.
Out there is Time, a cruel phantom who can't touch my dreams
And watches me, as does the night, outside the window, with a baleful eye.

Ultimately, the bleak awareness, understanding, that both the spiritual and physical exile are irreversible develops into an existentialist statement of calm and total despair, as in the poem "First Elegy":

I have no mother, father, or idea.
My life, a burned-out campfire, holds no flame.
The wondrous lands to which I promised then to lead you
Are sleeping now with frozen dreams in icebergs of the past.
And furious giant stars are looking down upon me,
Encased, like me, in treacherous infinity of space.

. . . .

Today my God will soon be frozen in my blood,
For He is dying in convulsions as my body turns to stone;

The mighty streams of time and of reality have covered me,
And there is nothing left outside me, all's within:
The bleak expanses, noble cities, kingdoms born of pain,
And trees that murmur, filled with wind to very roots.
But who will fill the emptiness now left on earth
And resurrect the visions and the dreams?

Thus the development of object-metaphors in *The Symphonies of Dispossession*, through which the inner universe of the poet's childhood is revealed, proceeds with the reversed movement of feeling which destroys this world just when its component images achieve their own perfection.

Niliūnas' imagery extends to the dimension of fairy tale, and quite logically so because the fantasies and fables we read as children contain for us the essence of reality. There are references in particular to Snow White and her seven dwarfs, hovering forever around the glass coffin, where their queen, trapped in the poet's visions, where God Himself will freeze to death, has no hope of resurrection. A similar fate befalls another world produced by the imagination—Arcadia, the ancient dream of poets, filled with blazing sun, now exuding death. To be sure, this mythical country fills Niliūnas' verse with colors and forms and with the aroma of intoxicating fruit, quite different from his other cold and rainy northern metaphors of sorrow, but all this festival is like an ancient fresco, crumbling to the dust in futile waiting for its creator to return. One such landscape occurs in the second collection of poems, entitled *Orfėjaus medis* (*The Tree of Orpheus*). In the poem "The Summer" we see:

Cart of the drunken Silenus, filled with steaming red wine,
Drawn through the village by slow oxen all covered with garlands;
Steaming cup of joy in the hands of the dark-skinned beauties
Brought to their wet ruby lips; cupids have gathered like bees
Into the blossoms of cherries, rocking in peace of the gardens.
Street and house, and the path, and the bird grown gray in the wind,
Drown in the fire; in the fields not a sound, on the road not a shadow;
Only the threshold is weeping, only the doorway is sobbing,

Waiting for measured steps of the youngest prodigal son.
(This is where I was born and grew up from the radiant earth.)

On the whole, the texture of poetic reality in *The Tree of Orpheus* often seems different from that in *The Symphonies of Dispossession*. The poet's field of vision now expands from the lonely room of childhood to a much larger frame of reference which includes, first of all, landscapes and seasons sunnier and calmer than the turbulent, rainy, and desperate spring and autumn of the *Symphonies*, and, secondly, metaphors and symbols which derive not only from the dreams of a lonely child but also from the visions of other artists in other times, especially those of ancient Greece and of the Renaissance. The creation of one's own particular world is now connected with the universal and immemorial urge of man to make myths and to relate them through the centuries to other contexts of experience. The previous world of object-metaphors now consists not only of things remembered on the threshold of conscious poetic creation but also of experiences which left their mark upon the poet later in the course of life. Niliūnas now seems to be trying to express himself in relation to the words, colors, and images of others. Hence such lines as, "The wind of summer was Watteau; the coolness of the room, Vermeer," and "Her voice, so high and clear / In picture galleries of spring is shouting: Veronese!" And another: "Strange shadows of fantastic rocks / Which had Madonna with the child / Who's lost in Middle Ages and in the solitude of visions by Piero di Cosimo." In the poet's own childhood there are new playmates: "There play with me the gold-haired Ghirlandaio / And, of the burning eyes, Giordano Bruno." The previous bleak, direct visions of the night now alternate with the images of reality reflected in sumptuous and baroque mirrors of art: "In front of a mirror, huge and richly framed, / The autumn night reclined like the Venus of Velásquez." The very sound of these foreign names has a curious, evocative, musical effect, enriching the texture of the Lithuanian syllables, which sing a different melody.

When Niliūnas does return in *The Tree of Orpheus* to the imagery of the *Symphonies*, the images themselves become richer and more complex as a result of new meanings and symbols gathered from other contexts of experience. The title itself may be an illustration; previously the metaphorical concept of a tree was not connected with any specific mythological allusions, but now the tree is the tree of Orpheus, the most ancient maker of myths and, moreover, one who, like the poet, has visited the land of the dead in search of his love—his vision—and who, again like the poet, lost it as soon as he turned back to look at it.

Some images which in the first book did not develop much beyond their original conception are now expanded to contain entire new metaphorical worlds. One example of this increased complexity is the image of a vase. In "Eldorado," from *The Symphonies of Dispossession*, there is a vase with some "forgotten flowers"—a microcosm within the house of memory, dreaming in its own solitude. In *The Tree of Orpheus* this microcosm expands to circumscribe the wide horizons of the earth, as in the poem "The Vase," in which it encompasses the whole autumn sky: "The autumn day is like a blue-colored crystal vase," containing the mountains, the wind, gardens with red birds, and by nightfall the galaxies, all transformed to melody in a song of love. In the next poem, "Silver," the image of the vase becomes as large, and as small, as a pair of cupped hands containing silver cities—the poet scooping up the first snow in homage to his love. In "Fairy Tale to a Woman Never Seen" the vase is Snow White's crystal coffin, and in the "Seventh Elegy" a city street is conveyed in terms of a vase and a painting, the two images converging to remind the reader of stained glass, which in turn presents the world as still another vessel—the church:

Intoxicated by the autumn spaces, I was walking
On Church Street, with its pavement warm and stripped to nakedness.
The midday was like the transparent wall of a giant vase, with drawings on
the glass;
Stern oaks were murmuring in the town square, itself so picture-like;
The light and birds were falling in the golden vessel shaped by the horizon.

With the changing texture and increasing complexity of the poems in *The Tree of Orpheus*, as well as in the third book of Niliūnas' verse, *Balandžio vigilijos* (*The Vigils of April*), the objects depicted tend to become more symbols than metaphors; that is, their presence signifies more an intellectual conception of life than a direct emotional response to it. One such symbol present in both the later books is the mirror. It may, in a sense, be related to the images of windows and of eyes because it also functions as a means of perception. The mirror is a kind of receptacle that circumscribes the poet's world, transfigured and remembered. The symbolic event connected with the mirror in Niliūnas' poems is the breaking or covering of it, signifying the death of memories. In *The Vigils of April* there is a whole section entitled "Legend of the Mirror" which elaborates this aspect of the mirror's significance. One poem, "The Dirge," connects a blinded window with the mirror and the eye in metaphors of death:

> Your window has been blinded long ago with trees in bloom
> And only Nothing, treacherous and frightful, looks through it.
> The mirror on the wall that saw you doing battle with the Angel,
> Fell down and died, so suddenly and blinded, in the dark.
> The voice died down in forest; Spring is walking through the house,
> Snow is not melting in the yard—the eye of God, now dead.

In "To Mother" the mirror is mother's love, turned away from the poet in death:

> Death is the parting word, one which we never
> Could pronounce; your mirror now
> Will turn once more, to light.
> But it will never speak again
> What our longing wished to say.

The final poem of this cycle, "The Legend of the Mirror," contains a statement of the poet's basic relationship to the objective reality; he escapes its interfering threat by looking at the mirror of his own imagination:

> The objects—curious, angry gods—had wanted
> To live by my existence, but I waited
> For wind to bloom under the window.
>
> And so, in fighting them, I fell
> In love with mirror, who came in

On tiptoes to my room to show
The lines of silence, radiance, and joy
In face that was his own, unseen by gods.

The general impression produced upon the reader is that the reality we see in the poems of Niliūnas is all his own and that the objects, colors, and movements of the "outside" world are used by him as hieroglyphics by means of which to write down the story of his soul. For this purpose the poet handles his images in such a way that they conform not to the logic inherited by objects from reality before they became metaphors but to that of author's own experience. We can see this shift of logic in some of the details, for instance, in the line "My books, read by the solitude and light, both leaning on their elbows." There is a special quality in the solitude perceived as light silently falling on these dead objects, books, containing many lives, fables, and dreams. It is a quality that characterizes the poet meditating upon his remembered room rather than the room as such. Solitude and light are therefore not things but the poet himself, transformed into his images. There are more anthropomorphic images of this kind. The wind and the trees, as we saw earlier, can speak to the persona of the poems, can weep and scold him, not because they are used in terms of the pathetic fallacy but because they constitute the poet's alter ego embodied in object-metaphors.

Once we learn to enter into this reality distorted toward the symbolic the way a hieroglyphic is, we can accept as logical such series of events in nature as might appear implausible in the kind of poetry which aims at imitating phenomena instead of using them for its own purposes. We are then also prepared to perceive a basic unity of feeling in a number of disparate images composing a single poem, such as "April Night," from *The Symphonies of Dispossession*:

On April night the longing starts to hum
Like a singer in the street, his back against moist willows on the river shore;
The yellow buds, just born that night, start climbing up the branches,
The earth is burning from the visions and the dreams.

And moisture, shouting in the walls, flows like the blood;
The struggling veins break out to make their bond with earth.

At midnight I wake up, because my eyes, in flood, have left their shores
And now rush down the body's sleeping depths.

The door, enticing me and wounding me, is open;
The clear-eyed wind engulfs me, shakes me as a friend;
Deep purling of the Spring, like vagabond guitar,
Has poisoned all the fields with sleeplessness and pain.
And this is why I follow where the river of my body whispers
And where the willow, green, embraces me with joy.

The familiar references to the wind and the eyes are blended here with street singers and vagabond guitars—things belonging to an entirely different type and flavor of imagery. Similarly, the springtime moisture that penetrates the wall is placed in a context where it can "shout." What unites the poem, however, is the all-pervading flow of water, blood, and longing, which shapes the outlines of emotion and not those of objective reality.

Among "logical impossibilities" that crystallize the crux of the experience, instead of obscuring it, are such expressions as "the table, eaten up by light and by the days," or the sound of "your nonbeing rustling in the grass," or again the image of the wind, bent down by heavy blossoms. We can also grasp the emotional logic of such lines as "A tree has grown up in your face, / The roots have torn the holy ground" even if they seem to explode the fabric of reality as we ordinarily know it. All these images point to a free transposition by the poet of one category of reality into another, producing an effect not unlike that achieved by some of the French symbolists or perhaps by the cubist painters. From this context Niliūnas proceeds to poems in which the strands of symbol, metaphor, and realities transposed are woven together into a rich and extremely complex pattern of images. Such is the poem "Body and Voice," from *The Vigils of April*, quoted here in part:

The voice was born beyond me; it is a tree tied to a book,
A chained anemone that grows and spreads
With yellow cries of birds. The earth
Was voice; it also was a glance; large crowds of eyes
Throughout your skin and hair. Golgotha,

In bloom of olives buried in the symbolism of time,
Golgotha.
Between the body and the voice there is a strange resemblance.
The voice gets moist in Spring from branches in the plain,
The body becomes mucous in the breathing of the winds and of the insects;
The voice, unheard, takes root within the emptiness of time,
The body, if not touched, will vanish in the time's deep dust
And only voice remains: lips in the rain,
Cannibal tree and shriek of Oedipus
To that hand that can't be torn away from woman's breast.

The voice of human passion from which both creativity and tragedy are born can be perceived here through the elaborate play of metaphors. Such poems try for more than the description of inner worlds; in them the effort is made to understand the instinct for creation and for death, both equally characteristic of man. In an important sense Niliūnas is a poet of the fatal conflict of opposing drives that not only inhabit man's soul but in fact define the human being as a creature born of tension between irreconcilabilities. This tension is responsible for the dynamics of his verse; there is a movement of passion across the structure of his images which gives it a meaning best understood in terms of the tragic ambiguity of the human condition.

We can distinguish several aspects of this ambiguity in Niliūnas' work. Perhaps the most important of these presents the experience of exile, so frequently found in contemporary Lithuanian literature written in Western countries. Usually the theme of exile conveys a movement in only one direction—either a desperate striving to be back home among one's own, found in the poetry of Kazys Bradūnas, or a resolute turning outward, a renunciation of any and all possible shelters for the heart, seen in the work of Algimantas Mackus. Niliūnas depicts the agonizing coexistence of both strivings at once, not in the context of actual events in the nation's history, but on the plane of art itself. "Home" in this dimension is the place where dreams were born, a childhood house transformed in memory into a complex of artistic images; the point at issue here is not the actual exile but an alienation, by means of image, from reality. When the poet reaches out for home, hoping, as he puts it, "to return into myself," he is actually searching for that point in time when the metaphors produced by his imagination seemed to make the world around him personally meaningful, truly his own, where he belonged. The visions themselves, however, describe the yearning to depart, to wander far away in the lands of the imagination. The poet is then torn between the two desires, which are in fact two different aspects of the same inner need. To yearn for the horizon is to yearn for something inside; people go out to find the inner world of dreams. The poem "Happy People," from *The Symphonies of Dispossession*, speaks of this:

How happy, strange, and childish are the people,
So restless in their lives for something they can't find.
They cry, awakened children, back from wondrous voyages of dreams;
Like children, they go out to seek these fabled lands.

How happy are they when they're home again,
Back from their youth, past midday, when the evening's near.
They sit around the fire to warm again their childhood vision,
To bring it back to life, and to be near again.

And when the veins once more soak up the childhood wind,
Increasing the already heavy burden with enchanted song of home,
They leave again in search of something, even though their feet are bleeding.
They go because their journey lasts forever.

Sometimes this charmed, or accursed, journey takes the traveler across the measure of time, bringing together past and present moments without, however, blending them into a new dimension of eternity. So the poet remains in pain, suspended without hope between "then" and "now." In *The Tree of Orpheus* this experience is conveyed in terms of a cradle and a ship, both vessels carrying the same dreams—of an infant trying to set foot upon the endless spaces of a just-born world and of an old conquistador in search of Eldorado:

> I still remember when, before this bleak expanse
> With falling leaves and full of wind,
> I, little baby—pair of faded eyes,

Pale hair, like stubble in the fields—
Held on to ropes from which my cradle was hanging,
Like an elderly conquistador, departing on an epoch-making journey,
And looked into the distance.

Now evening's here again,
And with the turning leaves
Go 'round my days, and autumn, suffering, the world;
And only I can never hope for my return.

Perhaps the greatest irony results from the poet's efforts to step outside this magic circle, the metaphorical universe of his own creation, by making a commitment to reality, to the simple facts of everyday life. "Everyday Poem," from *The Tree of Orpheus,* is a record of this attempt and of the understanding that the only perfect liberation is death. The poet sets the scene, consisting of a vision of his beloved dead in the ancestral earth, over whom the native village sleeps. The village is the "home" of his imagination; the effort now is to construct reality from it—to build a bridge between plain fact and metaphor:

Today I am no more the sickly wanderer who listens to his memories in sorrow.
I firmly take an ax, a saw, and go a-clattering across the yard,
Because my sorrow is no longer meaningless—
I am the hero of the ordinary, calm and strong.

This bridge would be the recognition that his dreams are but the realization of ancestral bonds with earth and with the dead in it, as well as with the living, throughout the generations. The village folk have had their fairy tales and sorrows, as the poet has, and both have found no liberation from the eternal cycle of life and death. This cycle in itself, then, is profoundly meaningful because it is the only real thing that man can know:

Along the street, toward the blue and icy well,
Will come, all covered up with snow, in threadbare sheepskins,
The old Uršulė, like a worn-out copper coin,
To dip her buckets in the heavy, heavy water.

> And she will be for me the grandest symbol, signifying meaning
> In patient waiting of the cherry trees, now chained to earth,
> And in the rising of the trampled roadside grass,
> And in the falling of each tree, past many summers, to its death,
> To endless joy of nature which had raised them up.

Yet even this bond is nothing but a concept and a feeling, the fruit of man's own imagination. The ancestral home in which we can enjoy communion, through simple labor, with all the living and the dead is in itself no longer fact but meaning—the significance we have ascribed to life to save us from despair. Tied to this vision, we realize that, having made slaves of us, the vision cannot be Eldorado because in ultimate reality man should be both at home and free. The poet, an experienced traveler across the endless landscape of illusions which is our life, then begins to wonder if Eldorado might not be found in the only land he has so far not visited—in the alien dimension of death. Death, however, obliterates both image and reality. We can speak profoundly of it this side of the barrier, but once we cross, there is only silence. In the end, the poet has no choice but to remain committed to the world of fiction he has made and to the suffering it has brought him:

> And thus my body will be suffering forever, the painful pull of every day,
> Because I am the giant god of this reality—a death-bound man.
> I made a universe. I freed the things and dreams in it from sorrow and from death,
> But I became their lowly slave.
> When in my slow defeat the freeing fire engulfs me, like the earth's engulfed by Spring,
> And when it burns forever that which forces me to seek adventure, fall and rise, and then collapse forever,
> Then, to my liberated spirit—
> Will then eternity be the wondrous Eldorado of my dreams?
>
> So this is why I fear this perfect liberation.
> (Death is like any other empty sheet in our calendar.)
> And this is why I am a slave of poverty and pain, of new-born sorrows of the passing day which press on us,

And for this reason only I have taken in my hand the ax and saw (oh, wondrous smell of earth!)
And feel my blood uniting with the blood of coming troubled day.

When the world is conceived essentially as metaphor, as a poetic image, it becomes inevitable that the human consciousness confronting it should also be presented symbolically. In Niliūnas' poetry the main images representing man have been chosen so that in their confrontation with the world of things, of object-metaphors, they themselves stand in opposition to each other, expressing two radically different attempts to come to terms with their reality. One figure is that of an alchemist, a tragic symbol of the desperate human need to transform stones into gold, the deadness of things that merely exist into the noble iridescence of meaning, purpose, dream. There is, of course, a close parallel between the poet and the alchemist. Both proceed with great care and method, taking into account the laws of nature as well as the inexplicable promptings of mystery, to accomplish an impossibility. Both must know that their undertaking is absurd, yet both insist upon their faith that nature can be moved by magic and that there is a key to the logic of miracle. Tragic, pitiful figures, the poet and the alchemist answer, nevertheless, to the noblest possible definition of man as an exception from the dead inevitabilities of nature, an error in the universe, an absurdity of inconceivably large, perhaps infinite, magnitude which may yet prove itself to be a reflection of the ultimate face of truth.

A conception of man which seems directly opposite to the poet-alchemist and yet, in the end, attempts to reach the same absolute source of meaning is formulated by Niliūnas in terms of what he calls the "man-landscape." It represents a desperate human commitment to the poetry of earth, to the realities of home and of physical existence. It is also a refusal to accept the thought that living things and the human heart are mere metaphors of heaven, that is, of an ultimate metaphysical dimension of being.

Both definitions of the poet, as alchemist transforming nature and as man-landscape who blends with it, are in their turn confronted with yet another figure of man—the God-man, Christ, who must, while sharing the exceptional, yet limited, condition of man in the universe, transcend it on His own terms. He is no longer the seeker, for He knows, in fact He is, the mystery. Becoming human as well, He would be the comforter, the fulfillment of the poet's dreams, the answer to his questions, or, as the Gospel has it, the way, the truth, and the life. This might justify the hopes of the alchemist but would destroy the poet as man-landscape by rendering him superfluous and meaningless. The relationship to Christ therefore becomes ambiguous—a sad rebellion—for the poet knows that he can gain Christ's eternity only by betraying the here and now which constitutes his human essence.

The figure of the poet as alchemist is developed in *The Symphonies of Dispossession*. At first the conception resides not in the poetic "I" but in the surrounding space; nature is given those attributes which define the poet's own emotional and mental anguish. So in the poem "The Hymn of Autumn" we read:

I feel the heavy steps of Autumn, as if it were a gloomy Alchemist,
Who comes and brings enormous burdens made of gold and sorrow, and of
  the cry of the unknown,
And in heart-rending bleakness of the landscape there are the sobbing shutters
Which, in the evenings of my childhood, could never solve the timeless puzzle
  of pain.

The basic elements of the autumn landscape typical of Niliūnas' poems—the golden leaves and the cloud-laden, murky spaces—provide the point of departure from which the symbol and its context are developed. Later the alchemist becomes the poet himself, quite conscious of his task of transforming darkness into meaning and also aware that such transformation has no reality, is only an illusion:

I came to tell you that the lights are going out over the world,
So sadly, for some reason, like hoarse and wind-blown song of Autumn.
That sorrow: Don Juan, now growing old, is wandering in the streets,
And rain, for all eternity, is falling from the sky.
The sun is gone. . . . In dying, it gave birth to restlessness!
And you will have to light the endless depths of heaven with your heart,

You will be forced to conjure up a sun from your illusions, Alchemist
condemned by fate,
And spread the eyes of your beloved across the sky, like new-made stars.

A sun of man's own making is a dangerous idea, for it may turn out to be the most terrible of all illusions—madness. In *The Symphonies of Dispossession*, Niliūnas writes with special empathy of the Lithuanian painter Čiurlionis who at the turn of the century conceived a semi-abstract world of his own with mystical suns and relentless darkness and who ended his life in insanity. The final tragedy of the poet as alchemist is conceived in terms of the dread spirit of Čiurlionis' paintings:

But I beheld above the mountains and the suns a radiant Madness,
Which lights the last few days of greatest alchemists with searing pain,
And giant Christ, raised up upon the cross by smiling man,
Who looked at me with limpid eyes and dreadful sorrow,
While in the storm there flew on broken wings, the human spirit,
uncontrollable by gods,
And Night was coming, like a queen, in all of her ambiguous grandeur.

Finally, *The Symphonies* ends with the confrontation between the poet-alchemist and Christ in a poem entitled "The Sixth Elegy." The deeply troubled and intense thoughts of the poet distend the verse lines almost beyond any measurement by feet, turning them into involved and tightly packed clusters of emotion trying to become philosophy but not resolving any issues, in spite of assertions that a resolution has been found:

> For now I know there is a Wall of China standing in between our painful life and the Reality we search for, and that ideas are a burden, meaningless to us who float along the stream of life.
>
> For no one ever will be able to enter unto us; for our daily lives (perhaps because of this we do defend our homes to death) are but the nailing on the cross.
>
> And for intoxicating thought of Truth, brought to us once, now poisoning with the illusions of Rebellion and of Truth, we do in wrath (believing!) murder Christ, thus killing ourselves.

> And this is why I cry to God: "O, Lord! do save my daily life, wipe out the perilous mirage of Your eternity,
>
> Because I am an alchemist who has created in himself whole mountains of illusionary gold of dreams and also sun for millions of my nights of living death!
>
> The urge, beyond control, to realize myself in this life here will be the only joy of living, the creator of Reality immortal, to Man for whom the night ambiguous (perhaps it will revive?) is waiting, treacherous, when days of painful life will come to end.
>
> And when You'll open wide the cages of existence to bid us go to Your Nonbeing, or to Being, to live without the earth, and without longing, without Sorrow, evermore—
>
> Above our bodies will arise the mighty flames of Truth, of Creativity of Man,
>
> And the horizon of Eternity will outline ships that carry life into nonbeing."

The poet as alchemist, making his own worlds, and as man-landscape, clinging to those that are his home, are now united in opposition to the image of Christ. The central issue seems to be man's desperate need for self-realization, through such creative power as he has, in the reality he knows around him, instead of being realized by Christ, whose death into eternity removes from man the burden and the joy of an independent act. Poetry, however, is just such an act, and therefore to be a poet is to be a rebel against ready-made salvation.

Nearly all of Niliūnas' poems stand on the borderline between man and nature in their imagery. We may remember the object-metaphors, such as the wind, which convey natural phenomena in terms of human attributes. The reverse is also often true; that is, the human figure is composed of natural objects or characterized by epithets which, in their original meaning, are descriptive of things in nature. The color of hair, for instance, may be compared to wilted grass, or eyes may become a river, or the mystery of a woman's body may be conveyed by evoking the image of an unknown archipelago, as in *The Vigils of April.* There is an intimate relationship between the human figure and the tree, established on the basis of their direct, or metaphorical, ties with the earth. A tree that stands between the heaven and the earth is fed by both, just as man lives by both his dreams and reality. Perhaps the most elegant elaboration of the man-tree analogy into an all-inclusive unity between the human body and the surrounding nature is presented in the poem "Your Ringing Ear," from *The Vigils of April*:

Of your ringing ear the lines,
Of the snail pink hieroglyphic;
Through the sea, a flying griffon
And (in fairy tale) hot night.
But your waist and then your breasts
Are a tree that blooms by the ocean;
Underneath it—mute in prayer—
Lonely shepherd of the shore.
And your shining hair—it is
Summer and the bird-filled gardens
In the winds; and streaks of silver
In the eyes; and also, grain.
And your glance is full of wonder—
It's the blood and golden sand;
It's the dead ancestral tribes,
Killing idols that are blind.

These are some elements from which the man-landscape is made. In *The Tree of Orpheus* we meet the man-landscape as the poet's alter ego, in the poem entitled "The Seventh Elegy," which is a troubled, tortured journey back to the city of the poet's memory, leading again to the fatal confrontation with Christ. The city is a limbo filled with sorrow and beauty, faithful to its children, to whom it can offer only solitude and dreams. Such children (and the poet is one of them) can only grow up to fight the darkness for an ideal they do not understand. From the perspective of time and many visions, the poet can see the magnificence of their bitter fate:

On seeing them I understood the reasons why their eyes remain forever colorless.

And why they die some day in bitter battles of a distant revolution,
Why those are blessed who fight not knowing truth,
And why their fall to dark of no return is meaningful,
And why their greatest victory is death.

The tragic fidelity of these children to a cause that promises no salvation prepares the ground for the poet's meeting in an ancient tavern with his other self, the man whose face depicts the contours of this land and who prefers to perish with the land rather than give it up as the price of hope. The attending angel of their encounter is one of the city's children:

> Along the wall still stood the table, long and yellow and unchanged,
> Unchanged, eternal, like a river running through the darkened land.
> A stranger sat behind it, but his face
> Brought to my mind the fragments of a landscape of some kind
> With lake, and little village, and the churchyard fence.
> A girl with face and hair like a golden sunflower
> (A sunflower that has never seen the sun!)
> Put down some bread and water on the table.

Then the "man-landscape, man of mud and water" begins a haunting dirge, which repeats the poet's journey through the limbo of his memories and explains the tragic and magnificent decision of this man (and thus also of the poet) to remain with the earth rather than with Christ:

And then I asked him: Who will liberate man?
If Christ were to return once more,
Would He not bring, as athletes do, the torch,

Transforming our murky fates to gold
And freeing from the trench the last few soldiers (they are we?)
But he said this:
"If He, in an unguarded moment, came again, as ordinary as the daily bread,
To put His radiant hand on this worn-out and tired head of mine,
Wouldn't it be treason then to drink His consolation?
And would it not be much too hard to give up for eternity
A hedgehog trampled upon the road
And golden oak leaves still remaining in the mirror?
Could He console us, having taken our home and joy

To have experienced in the arena the festival of triumph, or defeat.
And if we don't return along the roads which He had shown us,
If we insist upon defending our name without a shred of hope,
Will He be able to accuse us at the door, in darkness of the ages,
When He shall find us playing in His world?
If I should hear His steps, I'd tie myself, Ulysses-like, to my own home
And, having then decided not to know the truth which is with God,
I'd tell Him sadly that I'll go alone,
Desiring death and resurrection all my own."

Thus again, as in *The Symphonies of Dispossession*, the comforts of eternity which man cannot conquer for himself but must accept from the benevolent hands of God are rejected, however sadly, for in such heaven Niliūnas' poet would find himself an exile, irrevocably and forever. This is the paradox; the ultimate home of us all would be an alien land to some if it were gained at the price of the personal act of creation, even if this act were to signify despair. There is nothing new in this rebellion, for it is the same battle that Prometheus fought, and Jacob wrestling with the angel. In order to be personally meaningful, however, this struggle must forever be defined anew, throughout history, in the idiom of each given time and place, of nation and of the individual. This, then, is what Niliūnas felt he had to do.

9 Algimantas Mackus—the Perfection of Exile

Algimantas Mackus was born February 11, 1932, in Pagėgiai, western Lithuania, and died in an automobile accident in Chicago, December 28, 1964.

Mackus studied in Roosevelt College in Chicago from 1957 to 1959. He worked with the Lithuanian radio program "Margutis" (*The Easter Egg*), in Chicago from 1954. In 1962 he became the editor of the program's cultural magazine, also called *Margutis.*

Mackus published the following books of poetry: *Elegijos* (*Elegies*), 1950; *Jo yra žemė* (*His Is the Earth*), 1959; *Neornamentuotos kalbos generacija ir augintiniai* (*The Generation of Unornamented Language and the Wards*), 1962; and *Chapel B*, which came out posthumously in 1965.

AMONG the younger generation of Lithuanian writers in the West, Algimantas Mackus was perhaps the most dedicated believer in exile. Most of those who lost their country a quarter of a century ago still think of their fate as a senseless accident, going against the basic instincts of man, for it is natural that everyone should have a home. They try to compensate for this error of history either by putting down roots wherever they now are or by refusing in their minds to leave the homeland they no longer have, by continuing to live inside themselves, in their dream country, woven from the fabric of memories. Only a few can look upon exile the way Mackus did, as the fulfillment of human destiny. In his view, the natural condition of a creative writer is exile, in the largest, all-inclusive sense of the word, and the only undeniable truth he admitted to start with was his knowledge of the inevitability of death. From this point of departure Mackus strove with nobility and passion toward the perfection of man's consciousness of his solitude in the cosmic void.

This stark and tragic outlook of Mackus perhaps had its beginnings in his unusual penchant for "making strange" the world we live in by means of his poetic language in which the words and grammar seem to be constantly straining for meanings that "don't belong" to them in conventional speech, cluttered as it is with vague and comfortable assumptions about the possibility of happiness in the general scheme of things. His insistence upon precision and truth led him to deny in principle that joy of living which nourishes the inspiration of an artist who is at home in the world. "At home" here means having implicit trust in the ability of language, used conventionally, to communicate genuine relationships between reality and individual consciousness. The green blade of grass, the quick movement of a bird, can be worked into the texture of a poem because they seem parts of a reality that includes our own warm blood and extends to those intricate processes of the brain which give birth to the poetic idea. The logic of language seems to correspond directly to the logic of nature, thus encouraging the belief that ideas conceived outside the framework of material existence—such as immortality—will continue to represent objective truth. There is a sense of belonging in a universe where death has no dominion, and the very wonder at man's inheritance of eternity inspires him to the creative use of words, in imitation of God.

All this, however, would have sounded to Mackus like a description of paradise lost, or rather one that never was, because in his view the language of art, being figurative and metaphorical in principle, distorts the accepted relationships between words and reality in order to establish new ones expressive of the artist's personal perception of truth. To the extent that this truth is all his own, the artist becomes a stranger in the world. The more intense his solitude, the greater the threat of absurdity confronting him in a universe deprived of accustomed meaning by the challenge of his own imagination. Some writers are satisfied with only a partial reconsideration of experience, accepting most of the fundamental notions of reality offered by the accumulated weight of tradition. Mackus, however, was driven by honesty and pride to the extreme position of rejecting all the familiar values and beliefs, of demanding absolute freedom of artistic expression, even to the point of refusing salvation to man by denying resurrection, even existence, to God. Immortality in the reassuring continuum of nature, man, and God may seem real to others, but for him it only amounted to an illusion—a myth that signifies nothing.

In the collection *Jo yra žemė* (*His Is the Earth*) the evolution of Mackus' poetry toward its ultimate dark and tragic intensity begins with small and gradual displacements of the accepted meanings of words, culminating at certain points in some important insight—an "inner landmark"—in the geography of his poetic universe. The first poem, "Repetitions," speaks of the Milky Way repeating itself "on a late evening, near the willows." Since the poet does not, for the moment, speak of the surface from which the stars are reflected, we are left with the impression that the repetitions occur in the mirror of time and move with it across a number of evenings. This feeling of movement is then reinforced by the image of running water, while at the same time the word "evening" is changed to the related plural "nights." We now move through time, on the shore of a river, watching the galaxy reflected on its surface, with the stream, in its turn, flowing through it. But the stars themselves have now changed into "letters"—"it is enough when the shining letters / repeat themselves in the water"—producing the image of nature as an alphabet from which we must construct the words that will describe our poetic perceptions in the dimensions of time. Thus neither "water" nor "stars" nor "evenings" has quite the same meaning any more; Mackus has appropriated these words, transformed them into the building blocks of his own poetic world. In the next poem, "A Little Town in the River," he takes another step:

> I thought myself and dreamed
> And in the river's mirror watched myself.
> (All vagabonds will stand along the rivers,
> who had desires to be the earth or stream.)

The reflected alphabet now spells out the poet's own existence, possibly unreal, connected with the notion of lost and lonely wandering—the first indication of how the search for truth of personal experience will lead to solitude.

In "Life and Death of a Rice-Harvesting Girl," the image of water is transferred to the human plane by the juxtaposition of water and shining eyes. This opens all the possibilities of emotion and experience traditionally associated with the human glance. The poem also contains a reference to "glass words"—another image evoking visual comparisons with water and, to some extent, with eyes because of their glitter and transparency. Thus we can see the growth of a new frame of reference. These early poems do not aim for depth of thought greater than their constantly developing imagery can sustain, but there is a clear tendency to gravitate toward the issues relating to death and to transcendental faith. One might say that each time new image associations are worked out for familiar words, the poet "dies," in a way, to what the word used to mean to him, thus moving ever more irrevocably to radical confrontation with the ultimate visage of death. In the poem above, the girl dies after a passing shepherd boy recognizes that her eyes are "not the water of these plantations." In a sense, the poem is as much a love story as it is a tale of death and transition to a new level of experience. Similarly, in "Strange Death" the persona of the poem dies one night in spring, having seen how the dew (not grass!) turns green in the fragrant rain. The color green here blends with the substance of water (and therefore also with its previously established attendant association with glass) to produce the foundation for the figurative description of death in later poems in which death sometimes filters through the green and black stained-glass windows of a chapel, in the guise of an angel of the Lord.

This first section of the book, entitled "Repetitions," closes with a refusal to recognize God in a world not transformed by personal poetic feeling. The poem is called "Unbelief":

> Let us search no longer—
>
> we will find nothing:
> neither earth nor Spring
> written in green letters,
>
> only an evening
> and beggars playing violins
> near the cathedrals.
>
> Let us search no longer—

we will find nothing,
until we shall become
our own earth and Spring.

This poem is full of reminiscences of images developed previously. The alphabet of stars is here combined, via the symbolic green color of life, with the season of spring (as we already know, the time of death). The figure of beggar-vagabond becomes especially helpless, with his pitiful music (to be called faith?) next to the enormous, deaf stone of cathedrals —the dead and crushing mass of God, silently surviving countless hopeful generations. It is this particular God whom Mackus denounces here and in poems to come in an ever-widening circle of images.

The next section, "The Island and the Bird," continues this tight and methodical building up of images with specific meanings, valid, for the most part, only within the structure of Mackus' own poetry. Rain is transformed into fire, through the visual effect of sunlight striking the raindrops in the grass, and then again into a flood of red wild-apple blossoms. The rain contrasts sharply with the iron-heavy soul of the poet, burdened with too much emotion that has been aroused by too rapid transformation of nature from mere being to highly personal meaning through the symbolic interconnections of new images. This multifaceted, metaphorical rain pours endlessly through the poet's consciousness, forcing him to cry out, as if in complaint, "what kind of life it is / to be rained on always," and leading him finally to doubt the validity of insights brought on by a single all-pervading symbol: "Rain, I don't believe you / because I don't know if your tears are true." Mackus enunciates here for the first time his principle of rebellion as a necessary part of poetic fulfillment; if the rain is always there, will it not become a precondition for recognizing truth, something that one "must" believe, like the heavy stone God of the cathedrals? Better to doubt and go on searching.

Now the path leads to another transformation in which water, as the catalyst of emotion, is observed in the form of snow. In the poem "Snow Was White for Me as Well," the poet learns a new lesson—that true poetic feeling does not have to be embodied in the visions of water running like the heart's blood, the way it might be in romantic poetry:

and the snow was supposed to melt
and run in bloody handfuls—
I did not know that snow
is alive without blood.

For this reason, he says, it was not for him that snow was white and that the black earth began to vanish, wading into the white mass. And yet the very recognition has already enriched him so that, in the end, "the snow was white for me as well."

At this point we may note the basic colors of Mackus' poetic landscape: green (death, combined with water associations—"the green dew"—finally turning to green stained glass, in and through which we see the angel of death), red (the flood of blossoms, the blood), white (snow, alive and yet exuding the virginity of death), and black (the earth, again a bloodless principle of life, implying death as well, as does the color green, when the poet "dies" to previous levels of experience). Only a few more colors are added later, comprising a limited spectrum of poetic devices. This is also true of shapes, substances, and movements. Mackus is sparing of his means, preferring to seek profundity and richness of texture in his poetry in terms of accumulating complexity of symbolic interrelationships among his basic images as their relevance is expanded to new areas of experience.

The dynamics of movement, embodied in the shift to a new way of understanding static reality (as in the first poem discussed, in which the evening becomes poetically significant as it starts to move across its own reflections in time) evolve gradually into a kind of pilgrimage in search of poetic truth. In "March" the moment of insight is transmitted in the phrase "someone invisible has passed across," awakening the snow and water and thawing earth, filling them with the tense expectation of spring. Having perceived this change in himself as well, the poet understands that he, too, has just "walked by" through a landscape changing from winter to spring and, for him, from objects to symbols. In "Renunciation of the Earth," Mackus envisions a time when his steps will slow down completely, meeting the ultimate reality of death. Life thus becomes a descending curve, at the end of which words no longer matter and can be renounced together with the earth itself. Another expression of this finality of life is in the image of a falling bird in the poem "Island and Bird," in which the metaphor of eyes returns again. Mackus describes the heavy burden of reality transformed to feeling in the image of "enormous mountains" which fill the eyes of the falling bird; thus he ignores conventional common sense in order to operate freely with his chosen symbols in a language all his own. The enormity of the world as a poetic substance drags the bird down to death in solitude.

This precipitous meeting with death when the world becomes too much for us acquires the form of prayer in a poem so entitled in which a "stumbling and bloody shadow" is described as having passed through the earth without regret because it had never held on to it very firmly. Eternity in this poem is not so much fact as yearning: "Thy kingdom come." Thus begins a new confrontation with God, of which there will be many more in the cyclical movement of Mackus' poetry.

This particular confrontation is a paradoxical one because it results in the understanding that no meeting could take place at all. The next cycle of poems elaborates the language needed to embody this realization. The heading of this section, addressed to God, simply states: "Our Summers Have Passed Each Other By." The reason for the heading, essentially, is the insufficient image of God, or even its total absence, in the universe which Mackus had so far developed within his own poetic idiom. The section begins with a poem entitled "That My Blood Should Be in Your Wounds," in which the macrocosm of Christ on the Cross is contrasted to the microcosm of the poet's own wounds. The poet is tired (the world revealed has been too much with him); he can no longer endure suffering and thus cannot meet the challenge of recurrent sacrifice which alone could make his own blood fill the wounds of Christ. The inner drama of this poem consists, on the one hand, in the recognition that the poet, being too small, has no right to wait for God ("let us suffer separately") and, on the other, in the desire and prayer that God should approach him nevertheless, by making Himself as small as the little church in the poet's childhood, the only time he was ever happy. Of course, this is impossible; such a God can only exist within the inherited system of concepts, in the language not transformed into the poet's own and therefore meaningless to him. To accept such a God now would be the same as to cease being a poet (perhaps Mackus himself would only say: "becoming a poet"), and it is too late for that since all poetry is a journey of no return.

There is, then, no alternative except to continue to grow and be unhappy, to go on painfully developing one's insight and also the language in which it can be expressed, even at the risk of no longer being understood by those readers whose gods are still in childhood churches and who therefore have never really become exiles, no matter how far their fate might have taken them. God as a little church, or as a massive stone cathedral, has already been rejected. The poem "We Met in Rain" takes the further step of separation from God as rain. Rain has up to now been the metaphor for life and the catalyst in the creation of new and personally significant imagery, but Mackus no longer trusts rain as the ultimate allegory of truth. His feeling grows that now he needs not water but fire, the arid breath of the desert, and it is in these terms that God as water is rejected: "Under Your feet the last year's grass turns green / and under Your feet man is extinguished." This is the new turning in the road. God and the poet, if they are ever to find each other, must begin by going their separate ways:

> We part and take with ourselves
> the things that we had brought:
> You came—and there was rain,
> I came—and there was drought.

In a later poem, "Poisoned Water Does Not Bring Blessing," the growing awareness that the poet's choice of going to the desert might indeed increase his soul (as it did the souls of ancient hermits) prompts him to reproach God for having deceived him with the images of church and water:

> Why did You tell me not I'll have your blessing?
> The lonely mission chapel that I am, awaiting God?
> I would have suffered thirst,
> I wouldn't have drunk (the poisoned)
> the only water.

Then fire, the desert air, the dry and bitter solitude—the images of death, not life—will point the way to the new principle of antithesis in the construction of a personal poetic idiom. God, as Mackus says, has walked along with him to where He is not; the nonbeing of God, His passing beyond existence (a word applicable only to things that can be created), is the important discovery. From here begins the frequent and radical reversal of images, developing into one of Mackus' fundamental poetic devices. Joy, for instance, is now understood and described for the first time as "the old apostle of sorrow." The Christmas God, in fragrant hay of Bethlehem, was therefore born in summer, and so the poet's summer did not meet Him. The little world of exiles is perishing in rot because they cannot make up their minds to be reborn, that is, to die to what they were before: "We did not bring new faces / We were afraid of death." This antithetic manner of writing finally enables Mackus not only to understand the great nonbeing of God but also to come to grips with the true nature of his own physical exile. Cutting across the romantic idealism of his fellow exiles, he suddenly, and shockingly, reveals to us what we really are—the exact opposite of what we pretend to be:

> We are a dead world,
> Which should have protected things.
> We are a dead garden
> in which dead fruit trees grow.

The final section of the book, "Dedications to Death and Love," presents a recapitulation, an assessment of those moral and artistic imperatives which have emerged from the previous building up of personally meaningful imagery. The time has come for the poet to ask himself where he stands, how large is his world, and what are the things it contains. At the start he returns to the two images which dominate the beginning of consciousness—mother and father. The first poem, entitled "Mother of God," does not concern the poet's physical but his spiritual birth, that is, the birth of his God. It sums up the insight that the true concept of divinity cannot come from any outside sources, be it the traditional system of faith expressed in the image of the church, or a compelling personal symbol, such as the cross. "Each one of us," says

Mackus in this poem, "is the mother of his own God." The next poem, "Father," concerns the beginning of creative endeavor. It presents a father's testament to his son containing the inherited need for creative expression, which is depicted as tender and fragile love inscribed upon the texture of life:

> I just had time enough to pass
> to the crippled and stunted son
> the fragile love
> on the surface of wood
> engraved poem.

The concept of this inheritance is immediately expanded in the following poem, "Rain, Father, Rain," to include, by implication, the previous achievement in Lithuanian poetry. On one occasion, speaking about the Lithuanian poetic tradition, Mackus said: "What they have accomplished makes it possible for us, the younger Lithuanian bards, to do what we are doing today. We did not need to return and complete the work left unfinished by others. This is why we can be proud of the Lithuanian poetic tradition and hope that there will be time when we, too, will become a part of it." In the poem, the voice of the father (personified as a river flowing to death) speaks in the idiom of many older Lithuanian poets about fields and boats and shepherds with their horses, and ends with the following testament and plea:

> My son, I leave you nothing that has not been before.
> My waters have not been fulfilled, remaining nameless,
> my face will blend with faces in the sea before me,
> my hands will stretch toward your continent, receding now.
> My son, if you but take a single wrinkle from my face—
> I shall remain alive,
> bring back to life a single fish that swam my waters—
> and I will not have died,
> if you but hear a single dreaming girl pronounce upon my shore
> that birds, whose shadows are reflected in my waters, are alive.
> My son, I enter proud into the sea.

Not only Mackus but several other younger Lithuanian writers in exile have fulfilled this testament. Suddenly and violently exposed to the catastrophe of the Western world, they learned to survive it and to live on the brink of the possible end of all civilization. They learned to feel and understand the cold absurdity seeping into the bones of contemporary man, his loss of faith, his bleak and honest fortitude in a world without illusions. Reflecting all this in their works, they nevertheless managed to speak in terms of nature, the main catalyst of poetic experience in their own Lithuanian literary tradition. They brought to the urban and abstract modern art the feeling of soil, of growing things, of sky and water—an ancient echo of man's truthful accord with nature, a way of life so old that its image has now begun to fade from the racial memory of man. We already saw how Mackus built his own poetic language not from urban vocabulary but from names of things in nature, reaching the same truth as can be read in Beckett's back alley, from Krapp's last tape. If the heroes of Hemingway prayed to Nada in clean, well-lighted places, Mackus walks in solitude under the stars, in rain and melting snow and among wild, blooming apple trees.

Therefore, when Mackus comes to the summing up of his experience, in the poem "Dead Guests," he again uses landscape to describe his own kind of continuum from nature to man to nothing, in direct opposition to those poets who, not knowing what total exile is, still think that rivers lead to God. In Mackus' poem we see his colors of death—black and green—embodied in a green river moving toward a black forest, carrying reflections of our bodies and of our dreams—the innocence of childhood, the silver bow of the moon—both dead. As the poem proceeds, the river flows and reaches the forest; then it is already evening, the end of everything, and the setting sun, "the death of all the trees and all the forests," spreads its conflagration over the water. There is no soul in these reflections on the river's face; our souls are dead, and this is the final truth:

> In the green water
> our bodies are but fire extinguished
> and in the green water
> we are dead guests.

The basic metaphors of fire and water, developed in the previous sections, are here brought together to communicate the importance of recognizing death.

Perhaps we should remember here that death itself, the ultimate fact of life, is of no more interest to an artist than stones or trees—as facts—would be. The important thing is what the consciousness of death does to the development of poetic images. In contemplating things, we achieve an esthetic statement of emotion; in facing death, we may grasp the true nature of infinity because, while God may be a myth, death is real. It is exactly this experience of infinity, of the absolute, that Mackus strives for in his work, and the most effective means of search is, for him, antithesis. Acceptance may lead to illusions; truth begins with denial. If the true name of God is Nothing, then the true name of eternity is death. Mackus, of course, uses these terms not in their conventional context but as metaphors describing his individual experience. Nothingness can therefore be translated into conceptual language as a confrontation with God beyond disbelief in the institutionalized myth that carries His name.

If this is so, then the only real prayer may well be rebellion. The last few poems in this section of *His Is the Earth* express the terms of the artist's revolt. In "Allegory of Drought," Mackus returns to the earlier juxtaposition of water and desert. The mythology of the Crucifixion is rejected through the allegorical description of the earth drying out until the tree of the cross becomes "too dry for nails" and the bush of thorns cries out in pain without having dreamed of its destined crown. The roots of previous faith die out in the dry soil, "hearing the murmur of the last year's rain," and Veronica appears smiling, without her scarf. The poem ends with the rhetorical question "can it be that there is no king this summer, / can it be that no one has dared to be resurrected?" The next poem, "Confession," is a revolt against the implanted consciousness of sin within the framework of the established church and its laws. The Ten Commandments and the seven deadly sins demand contrition, but the consciousness of life rises up and proclaims, "I do not remember any more sins."

The book then closes (except for two or three additional poems) with a poem bearing the same title as the section heading, "Dedications to Death and Love." It enunciates the poet's faith, describing the point from which his future poetry will be developed:

> I believe in the great evangelist death.
> And for an hour of peace and joy
> I give to him my solitude.

It may be very painful to imagine how death and solitude can serve as well springs of poetic thought and as prerequisites for artistic creation, but such are the lessons of exile when a poet like Mackus makes the determined and tragic effort to understand it fully, in all its implications. His new faith may be too hard for most of us to bear, but for him no other faith is possible:

> love me, you old evangelist,
> because I now have learned to say good-bye,
> because I learned now to believe
> that solitude is the eternal father
> and that the hour full of peace and joy
> is nothing by my faith in the great evangelist.

The second book of verse, *Neornamentuotos kalbos generacija ir augintiniai* (*The Generation of Unornamented Language and the Wards*), maintains an even greater unity of structure and theme, but the basic design is somewhat different from the design of *His Is the Earth*. In his first book Mackus was mostly concerned with giving names to his very personal perceptions of reality; as he did, he created radical changes in the accepted meanings of words, which in turn, led to a full reversal in his poems of the ordinary relationship involving man, God, and infinity. *The Generation of Unornamented Language and the Wards* narrows its range by establishing the single dominant theme of exile. The book is divided into two parts. The first, "The Generation of Unornamented Language," focuses upon the poet's individual experience of exile, while the second, "The Wards," extends the insights gained to some additional situations in which innocent victims of the twentieth century are crushed by the world, which regards them as aliens.

The basic outline of "The Generation" rests upon five poems, entitled simply Parts I–V, plus an opening and a closing statement. Between these parts there are poems in which new systems of metaphors and symbols are developed and accumulated in order both to explain and to intensify the meaning of each succeeding part. For this reason "The Generation" can only be properly read as a whole; the individual poems, taken out of context, tend to become somewhat obscure. The book is also a direct progression from *His Is the Earth*, maintaining and expanding its basic figurative vocabulary and systems of symbolic references.

The brief opening statement in "The Generation" is a dialogue with an unidentified person, perhaps the poet's alter ego, about a glass coffin:

> —What am I carrying in the glass coffin?
> —I gathered all the things which I then had.
> The dead things grew their roots in me.
> —Will you not throw away the dead and cutting weight?
> When man has nothing more to bury, he becomes alone.
> —Be.

So, the inner development in what follows is the process of learning how to be completely alone. This is, of course, a reversal of the usual mental and emotional attitudes of an exile who tries to cling to his memories, to breathe life into his dead past instead of burying it.

This opening is followed immediately by Parts I and II. Part I develops an image of the poet contemplating eternal rest in a chapel with green and black stained-glass windows as if he were one of the dead things in the glass coffin, while Part II functions as a kind of antistrophe to Part I, expounding the spiritual condition of exile in a series of tense, generalized statements. Besides repeating the basic colors of death from Mackus' first book—green and black—Part I introduces a new symbolic presence, the Lord's Angel, whose shape is outlined in the window. This figure provides a focal point for emotions associated with the traditional guardian angel (always, in a certain sense, man's double) and also with the notion of man transcending himself, either as an idealized alter ego or in terms of a general humanitarian faith in man. As this figure develops in later poems, it begins to represent an illusion of hope for mankind and for the poet personally, who must learn to renounce it in order to continue speaking the truth.

In his first book Mackus worked out an extremely concise style of surface simplicity, covering complex and multifaceted implications of meaning. Here he goes a step further and increases the richness of inner content by subtle extensions of ordinary grammatical relationships among words to create almost a kind of "coded language" of his own, with an emotional impact that increases to the degree that we manage to decipher it—a task which requires not only intellectual sophistication but also a certain capacity to "feel in images." As an example we might take the middle stanza of Part I:

> I shall sleep through the Lord's Angel,
> I shall sleep through the stained glass in the chapel,
> through the face of the Lord's Angel,
> angel, through black and green,
> angel, through rest eternal.

The preposition "through," with its attendant meanings of "by means of" or "because of," is given an added visual dimension and grammatical meaning based on the transparency of glass which, in turn, recalls previous associations of glass with water and eyes, all of them implied in the face of the angel, seen both in and through the window.

The general statements in Part II describe the time and nature of exile as the poet understands it and also establish his moral-philosophical position:

> This is the time full of tension,
> the time of death unexplained,
> the cry of the lost generation,
> the resurrection recalled,
> the fingers on the stiffening body,
> and the pride before the washing of feet,
> the cry of the lost generation,
> the resurrection recalled.

The whole development of this first section of the book proceeds from the stylistic and ideological premises contained in these two poems, which are expanded and enriched with many symbolic and emotional references. Since their systematic analysis would extend far beyond the limits of this discussion, only a few matters can be mentioned here. One development is the assimilation of a new verbal texture—that of the Lithuanian folk songs—into the over-all stylistic design. It begins in a brief cycle of poems entitled "Hermetic Song," which follows Part III—in itself a culmination of ideas contained in the poems between Parts II and III. The basic points in the "Hermetic Song" cycle are that the ancient native language is dying and that this death represents only one aspect of the total and absolute mourning before the death of everything in the world. One of the dominant moods in Lithuanian folk songs is a kind of pensive, gentle, yet uncompromising accord with death which fits very well into the pattern of Mackus' imagery. He takes the typical phraseology of the songs and constructs from it a description of the closed, suicidal world of his fellow exiles:

Do not fly to the hive,
bring no more honey,
gray little bee;
the hive is destroyed,
the honeycomb empty,
gray little bee;
burn up your wings,
thrust in your sting,
gray little bee;
live for a moment,
and peace be in death,
gray little bee.

The idea of the bee stinging itself to death is suddenly and brutally intensified in the same poems by an image of total emotional and ideological cannibalism:

I feed on myself:
to my limbs—I am condor,
to my limbs—a hyena.

Dedicating the pain to myself
I dream homosexual angels,
Lesbian Theresas.

Into fire—
the blood of torn limbs—
I thrust my head.

The expressions "homosexual angels and Lesbian Theresas" at one time created considerable indignation in the religiously oriented Lithuanian press. Mackus himself had this passage in mind when he spoke on one occasion.

> What does it mean: to shock? To use in poetry a term of abnormal sexual relationships? Even when this term exists beyond sexual thought, independent in itself, to the extent that a group of sounds and letters, arranged in a certain order, is independent? . . . Perhaps these are very simple matters: a word to which some or the majority are well accustomed used in an unusual place, unusual situation, at an unusual time. Perhaps it is an unaccustomed manner of creative self-expression, an unaccustomed total effect.

This certainly amounts to more than a defense of "homosexual angels." What Mackus really describes here is his creative method, which has nothing to do with the idea of *épater le bourgeois* although there will be bourgeois to respond to his work with shock and incomprehension. What actually matters to Mackus is the freedom to handle words, sounds, and meanings according to his own inner imperative—the personal vision of truth. It is not a question of revolt against tradition or of consciously becoming a member of some artistic avant-garde, but rather of treating both reality and language as raw materials from which to shape the outlines of one's own universe. Of course, this means solitude and exile in more senses than one; it means death if life is to consist of nothing but traditionally accepted patterns of meaning, especially when murder, horror, and perversity are considered by society to be not only acceptable but even positive expressions of man's tyrannical and competitive nature. Insofar as Mackus engages in direct social protest at all, he does it by simply refusing to be a "living member" of a world gone mad:

In the green stained windows of masked gods, to mock me,
the stars of generals are lining up obediently,
to mock them—I disobeyed the orders to remain alive.

The concluding poems in this section of the book tend to bring together the symbolic imagery and the various textures of style and structure developed previously into a closing statement of the exile's position. The figure of the Lord's Angel (which, as we remember, ultimately represents an illusion—the "gods" masking their nothingness) is joined by its feminine counterpart—Theresa—in its turn a focal point of feelings associated in part with the illusionary ideal of womanhood but more importantly with Lithuania as a feminine image from the folk songs and as a victim of history and especially as the dead country carried in the "hermetical" hearts of the exiles, where it turns into an ugly pretense that it is still alive and still the "little girl" it used to be. There are echoes of Lithuanian folktales as well, especially one about Eglė, the Queen of Serpents, which deals with a young girl's exile in her new husband's home under the sea (Mackus turns this setting into the subterranean world of the dead) and her longing to return home after she has met certain conditions entailing, among other things, the wearing out of special clothing. Mackus combines this motif with his own symbols of the Lord's Angel and glass and fruits of the earth (generally signifying passion for life not transcended by renunciation and therefore illusionary) in order to create a cry of agony rising from the earth against the whole mythology of man's illusions:

> Theresa in her grave
> has grown up a big girl now
> In narrow childhood skirts
> and only that her chest
> was touched too firmly by the father's hand
> The angel in the stained-glass window in the mornings
> having heard out the prayers foreseen
> and foredoomed
> runs up with gooseberries and pears
> or apples in his basket
> Your daddy will soon send you
> a dress more spacious
> just you wear out the apples, dear Theresa,
> wear out the baskets of the gooseberries and pears.

And, angel, it's for earth that shattered glass women
farm out the bodies
of light-haired and dark-skinned daughters;
all gods are, angel, thin and angry, envious of the earth,
because of earth the heavens, angel, have been simplified
and joy castrated,

angel, because of earth
in Theresa's basket blossoms
the coarse gooseberry bush;

because of earth, angel,
the hatred of the living and the dead.

The heavy emphasis upon the earth prepares the basic conflict in the second section of the book, "The Wards," in which the young who were destroyed in the war are presented as children of the torn and mutilated earth, this "tortured plain," as Mackus calls it. Theresa, in this sense, begins to signify not only the illusions of a nobler image of womanhood but also, as a little girl, those children who in their graves grow up as big as damnation of the whole mad world. The rape of humanity is also symbolized in the "light-haired and dark-skinned daughters"—an image later developed into the tragic symbol of "Negro Mary." There is also the additional figure of orphan Jonukas, who also comes from Lithuanian fairy tales—a shepherd boy with an evil stepmother who tries to kill him. The associations of this tale—sheep, blood, victim—are transferred by Mackus to the religious context of the Lamb of God and the sacrifice of blood. Combined with images of sky and clouds, signifying the omnipresence of God, this complex of imagery results in a troubled poem, "Let Us Pray, the Summer Is Coming," presenting a challenge to the ideal of Providence as Trinity:

If I were God,
if I were God the Father, God the Son, and God the Holy Ghost,
I would be body, drinking lakes of joy
and the soft milk of new-born angels.

If I were God,
if I were God the Father, God the Son, and God the Holy Ghost,

if I were in the name of the Father, in the name of the Holy Ghost:
Pray for us, O Savior,
the herd is scattered,
the shepherd's scissors are dull,
and summer is coming.
Pray for us, full of grace—
hot is the sun of summer—
a bedding for your soul,
born from the body.
If I were God,
if I were God the Father, God the Son, and God the Holy Ghost,
I would be a vessel filled with human love,
I would be a vessel full of knife, replete with sleep.
Pray for us, O Savior,
that the edge of the knife should be hard,
that the hand should believe
in immortality of victim,
in the Trinity of God.

And if the hand—the poet's hand, the hand of the new generation—does not believe, it means the death of God the Savior, the recalling of the Resurrection.

In the closing poem of this section Jonukas speaks the dying language of his father to pronounce the "perfect death" of native land, of God, of faith in "fairy tales"—the value systems offered by the civilization which, through its own suicide, has proved that it has no values representing truth.

The second section, "The Wards," is, at least in part, an elaboration of the relevance of Lithuanian exile upon the tragic experience of humanity as a whole, deprived of its spiritual home by the events of the twentieth century. The basic structure of "The Wards" resembles that of "The Generation" since it also rests on several poems, identified as Parts I–VIII, around which other poems are built, supplementing and expanding upon the fundamental design of ideas. Unlike "The Generation," however, this part has a second center of gravity—two longer poems entitled "Ballad About the Good John" and "Jurek" which represent the dominant focus of emotion, depicting the terrible destruction that the forces of falsehood and cruelty inflict upon their victims in two widely separated places—Africa and Lithuania.

The second section begins (in Part I) from the perspective of the poet's mind contemplating the clay tablets of a lost civilization:

> from the bottom of a dead sea
> I still retrieve
> hieroglyphics, written
> on baked clay tablets:
>   the place of your grave
>   lonely—
>   without a tree
>   or bird
>   or summer.
> Just beds made up in linen cloth
> like coffins
>   on the great wide seas.

The imagery implies both Lithuanian and biblical references, and, being centered around the clay tablets, it reminds us of ancient Greece, the cradle of Western civilization, now in petrified ruins. In this way the time and space of the poem become both mythical and real, ancient and contemporary; as the poet reads the hieroglyphics, he discovers in them the eyes, frozen in horror, of the wards of his (or any) generation, seeing death, "finally terrible," written in the sun and the moon. This is the main vision of the section. Death is no longer just a poetic device designed to express a certain moral decision to renounce illusions in life and in art. Now it is real and terrible—the face of the universe reflected in the sky.

In Part II this visage of death is presented in terms of a petrified Lithuanian landscape with frozen rivers and plants and animals—the dreams of our memory, pathetically holding onto the country's old coat of arms (which, incidentally, represents a white knight, frozen forever on his galloping horse, sword raised against a blood-red emptiness). Both frames of reference, the ancient and the contemporary, are then blended in Part III through the image of modern sculpture, which depicts the rape of humanity by forcing the warm and human content into the cold and twisted abstract forms of wood and metal:

> The maidens now condemned to suffer innocence
> composed of wood and metal pieces
> at midnight sculpt anew
> their body shapes.

These tortured figures remind the poet of the twisted bodies of innocent victims in the brick and iron ruins of war—also a modern sculpture, which the wards of our time must read and understand like the clay tablets of old. The image of petrified, bloodless horror is then translated into the symbols and landscape of our time:

> In the light of black moons
> the furious silver plants are thrashing,
> and silver beasts
> lie down to claw themselves.
>
> Look close at this hour,
> son, our ward:
> silver blood
> is flowing into the new race.

The colors of black and silver are then developed in the two ballads as the basic medium of emotion—black in suffering Africa and silver in the death of a Lithuanian Jewish boy in the ghetto.

The irony of this twisted dream of modern art, resembling ruins, is further developed in "Variations on the Theme of an Ironical Dream" and in Part IV in terms of the organic principle of life, symbolized by an orange torn by the hands of both man and God. God here is the embodiment of law and hence of death (as was already established in *His Is the Earth*, in the poem "Confession" and in others, through the image of the God of stone cathedrals). As such He is the creator of the glass angels in the chapel and is also the power which turns a living vision to the frozen horror of glass, like the eyes of the wards in the old clay tablets:

Was it not beautiful, the hand of God
stroking the angel's hair,
was not the hand of God beautiful
as it thrust a glass eye into yours,
the sunbeam in the orange peel.
Chat closely together, litanies of all the saints,
enjoy the social hour, sacraments,
The sap of earth in orange peel!

As for the works of man, they are in harmony with that cold and predatory God whose laws man wrote himself:

In your hands the oranges are torn,
the continents, peninsulas, and islands.
The wards, having departed from their parents,
share their last supper.

The final preparation for the two ballads that follow is made in Parts v and vi. Part v speaks in Lithuanian folk idiom of stones and tears and the departure of white doves, while Part vi raises the threatening shape of "fierce African grass," of drums speaking the new language of the wards of our time: "in his hand a sharp machete / black will be the moon of Africa."

The choice of Africa and of the fate of Jews as the main themes might seem unorthodox for a poet writing in the seemingly remote Lithuanian cultural context. Actually, however, aside from emphasizing his new and cosmopolitan consciousness, it constitutes a very effective frame of reference against which the real tragedy of the Lithuanian exile can be properly understood. These are the two groups of people whose human rights and dignity have been most flagrantly violated in our time by the dominant, empire-building powers both of the West and of communism especially—the antithetical "heavenly hosts"—of whom Mackus writes: "Called from reserves— / Gott mit uns— / the angels are gathering." The Lithuanians, crushed by the same forces, have by and large remained cool to the fate of the Negro and the Jew, thus forfeiting their tragic birthright as victims of man's inhumanity to man. When Mackus integrates the Lithuanian references into the over-all design of the two ballads, he underscores a painful irony; claiming sympathy as exiles, the Lithuanians have no understanding of what exile really is because they have turned their backs upon their fellow sufferers. This opens the terrible possibility (at least for some) that they should think of Cain—who was an outcast, true, but not a victim—because he would not be his brother's keeper.

"The Ballad About the Good John" is an allegory of the black man's consent to submit to the God of the white empires, alternating with his revolt in the name of his own history. In the process Africa, this new "tortured plain," is itself betrayed beyond resurrection. The poem revolves around the figure of gray-haired John, "a good man and a good preacher," who did the white Lord's work in his own land, thus becoming a kind of African John the Baptist. Africa, however, had already been baptized in blood:

> John's forefather baptized
> with names of harvest gods
> the scalps of white hunters.
>
> The scalps of white hunters, with passion,
> proclaimed the whiteness of God.
>
> The hunters' bones were white,
> but the midnight was black.

There is something alien, and therefore false, about the very names of Lord and John. In the Lithuanian text they are given in English with Lithuanian endings attached, which suggests the falsity of the spiritual half-breed, an outsider in the context of the language itself and therefore in the Africa which the Lord and John are engaged in "saving." Only when John revolts, when he proclaims that God is beyond color (which implies His passing beyond the law and, in previous terms, beyond "existence") can he belong to his land and thus become a victim himself, the "ward" of the time. Yet when John is frightened by his own revolt and retreats, he again is left alone, echoing with tragic helplessness the cry on the cross: "Africa, my Africa, why did you forsake me." Having done the white Lord's work, he becomes a Judas to his land, and then his Lord, in turn, betrays him:

—Lord, oh Lord, it was You
who betrayed Judas
and flogged to death
my forefather's soul.

The poem develops in perfect balance between revolt, accompanied by the ominous beat of drums and the images of the black African moon in the silver night (returning to the black and silver colors of the earlier poem), and submission-betrayal, proclaimed by fanfares of the alien faith glorifying its twelve apostles in a song of joy which sounds very much like the end of the world:

"Twelve gates to the North,
twelve gates to the South,
twelve gates to the East,
twelve gates to the West!"

Halleluia East, halleluia North,
halleluia Jerusalem, halleluia John!

In the end John dies and a new Africa comes into being. John's friend the Lord becomes in it the greatest victim and destroyer:

—Lord, oh Lord, it was You
who brought upon yourself your fate:
in the silver sky
shines the African moon.

Tropical rains are falling
machete is sweating blood.
—Lord, oh Lord, it was You
called Judas upon yourself.

In the poem "Jurek," Mackus weeps with the Jewish mother of a murdered boy in the ancient Lithuanian capital of Vilnius. The poem opens with a powerful and stately image of the mother's total aloneness in the world, in all of history:

1. I would nestle your body in the top of a green tree,
   if I had a tree
   that was green.

I would nestle your body in the wet heaven's cloth,
if I had a bird
        that would fly.
I would raise your body to the top of starry mountain,
if I had summer sun
        that would not fade.
I would lift your body into the gray body's shadow,
if I had an orchard
        not sucked clean, not picked empty.

2. Mother asked the top of the green tree,
and the tree said to her: No.
Mother asked the wet cloth in the heaven,
and the cloth answered: No.
Mother asked the tribe of Judas, marked by the Lord,
and twelve thousand gave the answer: No.
Mother asked the tribe of Gad, marked by God,
and twelve thousand gave the answer: No.

The rhythmic repetitions of images and the phrasing of these introductory stanzas is reminiscent of the old Lithuanian songs of mourning. Thus, in their very solitude and Jewishness, the mother and her boy belong legitimately to the land they live in. Yet this land will only accept her son for burial, not for life:

Mother asked the good earth which feeds us,
and the earth answered: Yes.
Mother asked the coffin-maker who lives down the street,
and the coffin-maker said: Yes.
Mother asked of the nurse for some lullaby words,
and the nurse answered: No.

In the days of the German occupation many answered "no" to the Jews who asked for help. Very few were the killers themselves; most just stood by, so they could live and get their piece of bread from the occupiers:

Sell some bread to little Jurek, he is hungry!
You came back with the Star of David, without bread.

Give a piece of earth to bury Jurek!
You came back with the Star of David, and with a coffin.

Why did they sell you a coffin,
and to me, Jurek, they sold bread?

Following these introductory statements is a tense and tragic passage describing Jurek's death, in which the little boy appears as a helpless knight on a toy wooden horse and also as the eternal exile running forever, always remaining to die where he is:

6. Angry men came into the yard.
Jurek, ride, Jurek, ride!

Neighs the wooden horse in the yard,
pawing cement with his hooves.

How can I ride, how can I ride—
my horse is of wood!

And wood was alive, and wood cried out,
and wood ran for help!

Neighs the wooden horse in the yard,
pawing cement with his hooves.

How can I cry, how can I shout—
my speech was cut out with an ax!

Angry men came into the yard.
Jurek, run, Jurek, run!

The wooden horse fell in the yard,
tilting over toward the blood.

If the exiles of Lithuania are to deserve the name, they must first understand quite clearly that little Jurek, Star of David, was very much a Lithuanian.

An important point is made in the description of Jurek's funeral. It is that the dead should remain naïve and without hatred, even if this means that they shall not know the truth. The truth is for the living, to know the perversity of the world and to face it, so that we should have no more such dead as Jurek and as the preacher John.

—not daring to risk hatred,
in the terrible moment of recognized fate,
I closed the brown eyes of Jurek
from the stroke of sun, from sun's fury.
Let his ripe eyes maintain
the falsified image of our age.
—I shall lift his naïve body
into the silver rain,
into the pinewood winds,
so that together with trees and rain,
together with silver, the green
will murmur the heart that knew no hatred.

The poem ends with the death of Jurek's mother, who is shot in the forest. Mackus describes her death in words full of song, reminiscent of the "gray little bee" in his earlier poem, but now the bees are bullets:

—These are not shots that echo in the forest,
it is a silver swarm of bees
coming to the hive in our garden.

The final poems in this section sum up the experience and bring the Lithuanian exile to the end of his journey of conscience, toward the recognition that his land is truly lost to him and that he has gained in its stead the agony of his time:

There is no native land!
There isn't that quiet should flow the Nemunas River
and the grains of oats should ask for gentle sowing.

There is that Jurek has but green and silver,
that John should have the black-skinned dream,
that there should be the murmuring, breaking heart
in an alien land and on alien soil
before the last unction
not with sunflower oils.

A sunflower, as we know, is a plant that always faces the sun. The exile, however, must turn his eyes to darkness.

What the shape of darkness is we can see in Mackus' last book, bearing the English title *Chapel B.* It was written in response to the tragic death of Antanas Škėma in a highway accident; the undertaker's chapel where Škėma's body lay in state is called "Chapel B." Mackus and Škėma were in many ways closely related in their art. Both perceived that the gift of imagination makes the writer an exile in a blind universe inimical to man's questioning mind; both sought to express their insights in a language that went a good deal beyond conventional usage in Lithuanian; and both of them wrote, in one way or another, primarily about the thousand faces of death looking at them from every aspect of existence. Death had made itself the center of their artistic universe; with terrible irony, death, having crushed Škėma under the wheels in 1961, visited Mackus with the same violence, also in a traffic accident, in 1964. Certain passages in *Chapel B* which deal with the torn and bloody "collage" of Škėma's body are almost unbearably painful to read today, when we know that they constituted an exact prophecy of Mackus' own fate.

Chapel B presents the third and final stage in the evolution of the theme of death. First, in *His Is the Earth* and in "The Generation" section of *The Generation of Unornamented Language and the Wards*, death was mainly a renunciation of conventional attitudes in art, the means to achieve an "unornamented" language, that is, a language free from the romantic and rhetorical idiom of illusions—of all the stilted and elaborate phrases and images that had come to be identified with "poetry" in the work of some writers. In the second section, "The Wards," death became the voice of conscience, explaining how difficult it really is to bear the name of exile, what an uncompromising commitment to truth is required in order to deserve it. Finally, in *Chapel B*, the reality of death comes as a profoundly wounding human experience, bringing with it the sense of tragic and irreparable individual loss. Mackus does not, however, immerse himself in his purely personal sorrow to the extent of losing his artistic awareness that the tragedy must be related in some significant way to the chain of circumstances and events constituting the texture of our time. Quite the contrary, he makes this little spot on earth, in the Pennsylvania mountains where the accident occurred, a focal point of both past and present history of the Lithuanian exile, as well as a commentary on violence perpetrated against the "wards" of the modern age, reflected in reality—as in the present African situation—or in literature, as in the work of Federico García Lorca.

At the beginning there is an introductory statement defining several faces of death relevant to the central design of the book. Death back home in Lithuania is the gradual melting of the nation in the Russian sea:

> Death is an old and stale sunset
> over the Lithuanian landscape;
> in Spring the sun was married
> to moon, now speaking an alien tongue.

It is also the desperate, lost battle of the guerrilla-farmers resisting the new order:

> Death is fanatic tillers of the soil,
> the blinded sacrament of blood and earth;
> like wounded beasts arising from their lairs
> they shatter in the evening against cement.

Death is also the crumbling of history, like old and yellowed papers, and then it is the birth of new nations on another continent:

> Death is the names of the new republics
> in Africa, ensnared inside the trap of history;
> exhausted, Negro Mary fell to earth
> still holding a narrow amulet between her hands.

Finally, death is the imagery of glass and water, developed in Mackus' own poetry, combined with its colors of black and green, in the ancient stained glass of chapels, including *Chapel B*. Part 1 of the book (the book is actually a single long poem, although divided into parts and separate poems with individual titles; the structural unity in *Chapel B* is even stronger than in the two preceding books) is a brief and sudden cry of agony, conveyed in terms of crushing violence, of the catastrophe of the highway crash, shattering against the mass of God. Thus, ultimately, death is God. The next part is a cluster of images revolving around the concept of a restless continent, inviting us to travel in the season of death. The birth of yearning for adventure here also means the birth of the body and the withdrawal of God from reality. As Mackus develops his theme, the continent, broken up by landmarks and rivers, gradually acquires the shape of the shattered body, all blood and splintered bones. Antanas Škėma, in his death, thus grows beyond the horizon to meet the emptiness where God should be:

> The voice of the continent, at dawn, before the act, having become
> both sex and body, cries hysterically;
> on copper-plate intaglio,
> the furious God, in midst of ritual,
> recalls salvation thrown out to the crowds.

If we consider that God (at least the one that can be said to "exist" in the same way that things do) is only as alive as man, who has invented Him, then the imprint of man's crushed body upon the ground is also the portrait of his God, as if on a copper coin—the price man pays for having hoped that there will be salvation. The whole earth is then such an image of God, as Mackus makes clear in the next part, in which the Negro Mary lays down her bronze body, cut by whips, upon the soil of Africa.

The poem creates its own time and space, its own continent of agony on which the Lithuanians back home and the Negro slave Mary are neighbors and contemporaries. The specific place where Škėma died brings its own dead to this reunion—the Lithuanian and Polish coal miners who settled these places at the turn of the century and have now been assimilated, or have died out, under and above the ground. These dead also join the solemn funeral, which is really the whole book, and the little world they bring with them, including a still older image of Lithuania, of their own generation, joins with the symbol of the Negro Mary to produce a kind of hymn to death. Mary's name in it becomes a constant refrain, imperceptibly blending with the remembered image of Holy Mary of the Gates of Dawn in Vilnius—a miraculous Catholic icon, cut by the sword of Swedish invaders a long time ago.

Then follows an interlude designed to transfer the poem's references to the specific literary dimension. Mackus gives a succinct and tragic picture of the situation of Lithuanian writers in exile:

We speak the evanescent words
of our dying language.
Water flooding the boats—
our people departed in them.
Empty and broken the quai,
no one expects their return.
We speak the words we have saved
from the dead language of ours.

Turning to his Lithuanian contemporaries in exile, some of whom were envious of Škėma's talent and condemned his fierce, uncompromising challenge to their traditional values, Mackus speaks with bitter reproach:

Former citizens of the state,
think deeply of his death;
not the word became flesh,
but the flesh became word.

We scatter the foam of our dreams
with moss-covered hands,
sending angry, envious cries,
after the receding raft.

The theme "flesh became word" is elaborated further in a section directly related to Federico García Lorca's *Llanto por Ignacio Sánchez Mejías*. The refrain "*a las cinco de la tarde*" becomes "seven o'clock in the morning" in Mackus' poem; this was the time of the fatal accident in which Škėma was killed. The issue is that of resurrection. There is tension in the air at seven o'clock in the morning, because the civil guard must know where Lorca is buried and make sure there is for him no resurrection. If Lorca does not arise, the state is safe, and so is the Church, because with Lorca dead there is no God, and the rulers of the world, the "establishment," can confidently proceed to proclaim their own God and truth —the Lord of John the preacher:

And seven o'clock sharp
with fanfare of the cutting word
the representatives of faiths
with trumpets and trombones proclaimed

> there is no God!
> then congratulated the pontiff.

Yet both God and Lorca, in their word, have never died. They are now exiles, and it is into the exile that they have both been resurrected. (By "exile" we mean here a dimension of being to which neither the "establishment" nor the reality of things as a whole has any relevance.) This is where Škėma's word continues to live as well; it is a realm of no reality, if reality is the continuum of things leading to the "existing" God. Mackus then turns deliberately away from the mangled body of the deceased and from the broken pieces of sentiment and fear and envy which constitute the minds of small men—those men who would rather see Christ resurrected in body than in word. The passage is shattering in its cruel intensity, in part because, as has been noted already, the physical details of Škėma's destroyed body read like an agonizing prophecy of what later happened to Mackus himself, but especially because it contains a merciless judgment upon all those who betrayed their calling as exiles by not understanding its moral challenge. It takes a great and terrible love for a poet to speak to his own people of betrayal when they demand of him to weep with him.

The closing section is a direct antiphrase to Dylan Thomas' "And Death Shall Have No Dominion." There is a way to read Thomas in this poem as a proponent of the immortality of the life force itself, existing as love, forever in all of nature, although individual men must die. Mackus, on the contrary, wants to make quite clear that there is no such thing as cheating death by passing into the continuum of nature, by continuing to "belong." The dead are truly dead; they are exiles from all possible belonging. To Thomas:

> Dead men naked they shall be one
> With the man in the wind and the west moon;
> When their bones are picked clean and the clean bones gone,
> They shall have stars at elbow and foot.

Mackus answers:

> And death shall have its dominion.
> Dead men will no more turn around,

leaning on skeleton elbows.
The northern eye of northern moon
will shine upon what was once body.
The bones will be gathered, but not put together
like a word—one letter to the next.
The soul will remain, but there'll be no more soul.
And death shall have its dominion.

The last lines by Thomas—"Though lovers be lost love shall not; / And death shall have no dominion"—receive the following response:

And death shall have its dominion.
Never the men shall return to the house.
As clocks beyond time will keep beating
rhythm of the pulse, inside empty rooms
beds will be made for the night.
Nothing returns, and all will be gone,
the door will be shut tight forever.
Time will remain, but there'll be no more time.
And death shall have its dominion.

As we close the door on Mackus, it will serve us well to understand that his words indeed will never die. The true and and perfect exile, Mackus will always be at home, not in the perishable continuum of things but in the total and resolute renunciation of them. Immortality is precisely nothing—it is being with God forever and beyond all existence.

10 Henrikas Nagys—a Seeker of Light

Henrikas Nagys was born October 12, 1920, in Mažeikiai, northwestern Lithuania. He studied Lithuanian and German literatures and languages in the Lithuanian State University in Kaunas from 1941 to 1943, and Germanistics and art history in Innsbruck, Austria, in 1945–47. He received his Ph.D. from the University of Freiburg, Germany, in 1949. His doctoral thesis dealt with the work of Georg Trakl.

In 1947–48, Nagys taught German in the School of Applied Arts in Freiburg and, after emigrating to Canada, taught literature in the University of Montreal in 1954–56. At the present time he is working as a commercial artist.

Henrikas Nagys was one of the founders of the *Žemė* (*Earth*) group of Lithuanian émigré writers, contributing poems and literary criticism to its magazine *Literatūros lankai* (*The Literary Folios*), which came out in 1952.

His poems are collected in the following books: *Eilėraščiai* (*Poems*), 1946; *Lapkričio naktys* (*November Nights*), 1947; *Saulės laikrodžiai* (*The Sundials*), 1959; and *Mėlynas sniegas* (*The Blue Snow*), 1960. A new book of poems, called *Broliai balti aitvarai* (*Brothers, the White Aitvarai*), is currently in preparation.

UPON one occasion Henrikas Nagys pointed out that in his poetry two things were of paramount importance—the memory of childhood as a lost paradise, or perhaps as a paradise that never existed, and the creative artist's constant struggle with emotional, intellectual, and metaphysical darkness. A child's relationship to reality is important because his experience of it is poetic, that is, immediate and fresh:

> The world of childhood is, in our opinion, the true source of the primary and disinterested human condition, the spiritual state of the poet *par excellence*, when one is capable of wonder, of experiencing water, wind, and a flight of birds as they were experienced by the first man on earth. When

the round eyes of a child were a mirror and a vessel containing the amazement of the seven days of creation.

What the child's mirror reflects can be seen in the poem "Father's Yard," from the collection *Saulės laikrodžiai* (*The Sundials*).

When my bare feet the first time touched the earth,
It was warm and moist, like a mother's lips.
Far, at the foggy edge of heaven, one could hear
The drums of thunder, and the wind had the fragrance of the rain.
My bare feet felt the rounded pebbles of gravel
And they were washed by green and dewy grass. . . . The backyard
Of my father's house was wide as all infinity.

The clarity and freshness of this child's world communicates itself primarily through the sense of touch. A tactile representation is, first of all, much less burdened with the metaphors and symbols which have collected in poetic tradition around visual and auditory images, and, secondly, it conveys a much greater sense of immediacy and intimacy, since the things we can touch must be near us, must seem like the direct extension of ourselves into the texture of reality. When, further in the poem, Nagys proceeds to dreams and visions, the freshness of the opening stanza remains with them, creating the effect of wonder at the "seven days of creation" he spoke of:

I saw there twisting rivers, highways cutting through the yard.
And it was full of faraway, mysterious lands:
clear yellow forests soaking in the sun and sky,
and seas replete with shiny cottages of snails.
Long caravans of ladybugs amidst the desert sands
were bringing loads of treasures to my castle.
Black soldier ants—fleet-footed riders—
were darting in and out of silver nettles and high grass.

The childhood universe, then, comes into being through an accuracy of perception which is evocative of dreams. Both reality and vision become obscured later, for as we grow older, we do not see the world so clearly any more, nor do we know as well what our dreams may mean. The faculty of thought turns objects into symbols, and the symbols themselves turn into question marks as we confront them with the mystery of death—a force that our childhood does not know. Having reached the age of wisdom, we begin to see as through smoked glass, and childhood remembered then seems like that single bright spot in life which, at the portals of death, occupied the thoughts of Ivan Ilyich in Tolstoy's story. Those who feel this become seekers because they know that, although the innocence of childhood lives in truth, there is no way back to it. We must go on, facing the darkness, in the hope of finding some level of existence on which we can again be truthful, even with the experience of a lifetime behind us.

The commitment to such a search, in the view of Nagys, is definitely not a commitment to solitude. On the contrary, he feels that the loyalty of man to man against the darkness, against what he called "this human fear when faced with the incomprehensible ebbing of life," is the prerequisite to any hope for truth. There is a vision of friendship in Nagys' poetry which conveys the special human comfort of the heart among close comrades, the sharers of the seeker's dream:

> And now so peaceful and so glad my heart!
> As if I saw broad plains, all drenched in sun,
> When we thus sing: the seven brothers, friends
> (And even the old oak outside the window joins with us).

The thoughts expressed in these lines lead to an understanding of the statement once made by Nagys that "all our poetry was born and died at the fireside of friendship or with its ashes."

Nagys grew up and entered the world of letters with the younger generation of Lithuanian poets who were educated in the horrors of war as well as in the new trends in existentialist philosophy in post-war Europe. The urge to remain creative when everything around them denied the very principle of creativity has forged the group Nagys belongs to into a brotherhood of the seekers of light, fighters against the message of absurdity emerging from metaphysical darkness beyond the fact of death. Nagys has spoken of:

> . . . an active stance taken by the younger generation of poets toward the night, that is, toward nonbeing, toward the unanswerable, as well as toward

daily routine and the dispossessions one is subject to. In this way the poets turn their backs toward the transfigurations of paradise lost and orient themselves toward the search itself. Toward the search for answers to the puzzle of their own existence. The search for the wellsprings of the light.

The poetic image of this "generation of seekers" contains some features of the traditional romantic hero. In the book *Lapkričio naktys* (*November Nights*), Nagys devotes a whole section entitled "Brothers in Arms" to describing these poets, his brothers. This is how he addresses them:

> I speak to you, my silent brother.
> And when you cry, I cry with you.
> And when I say, I am like the tree—alone and proud—
> you also say, I am alone and proud, just like my brother.

This pride and solitude, however, is not the same as that of the great "no-sayers" of Byron who remove themselves from the humanity they despise. Nagys' brothers are not the demonic "chosen ones of evil" met in the work of the nineteenth-century Russian poet Lermontov. What they are is told in a poem called "Song About My Brothers," from the forthcoming book *Broliai balti aitvarai* (*Brothers, the White Aitvarai*). The poem is a long glance across the centuries of Lithuanian and world history, and it includes, among others, the first caveman to draw the figures of men and beasts, the explorers of new continents, the philosophers who followed the consequence of their moral conceptions unto death ("My brother drank the hemlock with Socrates"), the rebels of the Bastille, the Vikings, the persecuted Jews, and the Lithuanian and Hungarian freedom fighters. What emerges is a general picture of the seeker, the rebel, the physical and intellectual adventurer, the iconoclast and revolutionary. Nagys' brothers, in fact, are all those who cannot leave well enough alone in the established faiths, social structures, and even the given level of knowledge and morality, but feel an imperative urge, each in his own way, to extend the limits of man.

What distinguishes Nagys and his friends from the romantic pride of the nineteenth-century poets is their generous loyalty toward the little people who make up the world. There is something almost messianic about the way Nagys prays for peace and happiness for mankind while he and his brothers take up mankind's suffering to face the terrors of the unknown:

> Lord, bless them all. The galaxies
> so cold tonight, this lonely night—
> Lord, bless them all.
>
> The man with hands worn out by the machine,
> the gray soldier—he is dreaming of his home—
> and people, people in their little houses on this night,
> do bless them, ease their lives of toil . . . But us
> leave out. And give us nothing. For we search for Thee.
>
> The blood of our brothers, and their sweat, shall fall on us . . .
> And give us nothing . . . Curse us. But reveal,
> reveal at least to one of us, to one alone,
> and tell: Dost Thou exist? If not—what are we searching for?

The search itself, however, proceeds on the plane of art and not that of faith or philosophy. The insights come from images and metaphors suggested by factual perceptions which are then developed within the musical and emotional amplitudes of words. What Nagys communicates, therefore, is the artistic experience of his search for light and not a philosophical formulation of its principles. He remains, in a sense, the same wondering child he was in his father's yard, with only this difference—instead of ladybugs, there are now caravans of dark and anguished images moving across metaphysical deserts of the soul.

The will to face the unknown and the longing to recapture the childlike immediacy of perceptions are but two sides of the same coin. Children are the greatest realists, and perhaps for this reason the mystery they see in backyards and in fairy tales, far from being imaginary, represents a deep human truth, an inner reality much more genuine than the supposed voice of experience saying that there are no miracles. This is why, when we talk about the lost paradise of childhood and about the rebellious metaphysical seekers in the poetry of Nagys, we are really discussing one and the same thing; our concern is with two different types of imagery rather than with two opposed principles of life. In some of Nagys' books the dominant images convey a sunny feeling of reality, made iridescent with childish wonder and poet's dreams, while in others the tragic intensity of the seeker's existence comes through in shades of black. Various shapes of darkness and night, a kind of general "blackness of being," are especially strongly felt in *November Nights.* In this book the poet's imagination is basically romantic; the human condition is understood in terms of the dramatic contrast between fire and darkness. The poet is a lonely figure in the night, a pilgrim through autumnal landscapes, a sailor on lonely ships. Much of the general tone of the book is conveyed in the poem "The Elegy of Night":

> I lean against the black wood that my boat is made of
> and look into the whirlpools, bottomless and black—
> my heart is floating there in darkness:
> black bird, with tired, helpless wings,
> still struggling, while around there's night, and wind
> that rustles in the black and lonely churchyard wreaths.
>
> I touch the hanging sail, drooping from the mast,
> and feel as if my hand were touching mine own hair—
> my hair is cold, it rustles, like dead grass. . . .
> And mine eyes, so tired from long, confusing journeys—
> the blinded images—black stars—monotonously
> are shining in the darkened depths of midnight waters. . . .
>
> And I but feel myself and endless night—
> I feel I'm burning up in fires of mine own dreams,
> in fires of dreams unreachable and haunting. . . .
> Sometimes I feel as if a sunny plain
> would flash beyond the sails—'tis but a lie,
> enchanted lie it is—I give it birth and death! . . .
>
> I lean against the black wood that my boat is made of
> and look into the whirlpools, bottomless and black,
> I seem to see there castles of my dreams. . . .
> But when I open wide my eyes replete with night:
> a black bird is thrashing there with tired and bloody wings—
> Oh, but it is my heart which yearns for light. . . .

All the romantic emblems of deep and tragic feeling are present:

wounded birds, dream castles, lonely sails, churchyard wreaths, dark waters, and the kind of total solitude in which all visions die in one's own heart. The ruthless prevalence of blackness, however, goes beyond its standard function of conveying hopeless suffering; it seems to reach out further, toward a "black flame" of feeling which is all the poet's own. Nagys blends the blackness of death and the fire of the searching human spirit into a special vision. It begins with landscapes like the following, of a sunset over a leafless forest: "And in the tops of trees the rays of sun / like copper birds with burning wings / who can no longer fly aloft." The blackness of the tree branches, enveloped in fire, turns, at other times, into "the black torches of suffering" or into a "black flame of longing" in the poet's soul. The very blackness contains something that burns, something that flies, some special tragic-poetic passion of yearning that casts its light over much of Nagys' poetry. Combined with the childhood aura of legend and of dream, this imagery produces poems like the following, called "Dreams," from *November Nights*:

> Oh, in the morning fire, the burning forests black!
> Like kings in fairy tales, with bloody crowns,
> black mantles, and the hair so shimmery,
> like amber. . . . Kings of faraway
> bright lands—how you have charmed
> me; I cannot tear my eyes away
> from you—the dreamland kings—so wondrous strange—
> My eyes are burning from the brilliant light,
> my heart is fainting from the blue of azure skies,
> as if I sailed afloat in light, transparent ship
> through fabulously spacious, blinding palace. . . .
> My eyes are burning. O! and so my heart
> Is beating, lost and empty, and burned out.
>
> I would but like to close my eyes a moment . . .
> But in the morning fire the forests black are burning,
> like kings in fairy tales; with mantles black
> and burning crowns, they come into the valley,
> their hair, like brightest amber, sparkling so!
> I cannot close my eyes, my hurting eyes . . .

and see no more the dreamland kings so wondrous strange. . . .
How their black hands are rising from the fog!
and how they carry in their trembling fingers
the silver flower: sun, just opening! . . . When you,
O black-eyed night, did watch me sadly through the window,
I used to feel you and to long for you, but on my eyes
descended, burned, and sparkled the magic dreams of day!

This vision of sunrise over the forest has a certain naïve intensity approaching the ecstasies of our childhood, as we remember it now, when we responded directly to the touch of beauty. And yet, of course, with all its freshness and immediacy, the poem is certainly not like the response of a child—it is much too articulate and too deliberately controlled for that. A child can only see and wonder, while the poet—as a grown man—remains conscious of the void of death enveloping the beauty and wishes to fill it with words of his own creation. The black fire of Nagys is burning in this metaphysical emptiness beyond a child's horizon, shining to him as the ultimate goal of all his journeys. The only reality the poet has at his disposal stretches from the present moment to the point of death. It is a distance measurable in the unceasing movement of time. Nagys hears the inexorable steps of time in all the rhythmic phenomena in nature which are mercilessly hacking away at the shield of days and hours that protects us from oncoming death. He recognizes these deadly blows in the beating of a bird's wings—"a black bird is thrashing there with tired and bloody wings"—or in the humming of machinery "like painful rhythm of giant metal hands," or else in the nights, when millions of clocks all over the earth can be heard ticking us to death. The rhythm of the clock is then echoed back in the human heart and grows into an apotheosis of death, as in the poem "Words Spoken to the Night," from *November Nights*:

I never saw you come to me—
You're always in my room.
I raise my eyes—there, covering your face,
you wait . . . and then your heart
begins to wake up slowly in the clocks.

It beats so, ever louder, louder all around me—
it has become the heavy toll of bells—
and darkness pouring through the window
then covers my wide-open eyes, and face,
and then its black and giant heart
starts beating in the endless space, and in my breast.

The burning blackness measured in the steps of time constitutes the main emotional background of *November Nights.* This background continues, to some extent, in the other two published books of Nagys' poems, *Saulės laikrodžiai* (*The Sundials*) and *Mėlynas sniegas* (*The Blue Snow*). These later books, however, extend the poet's fundamental awareness of the deathward march of time by means of images depicting violent dismemberment of organic life or else the gradual crumbling of all things under the sun. In *The Sundials*, for instance, a landscape is described: "Into the breast of earth, split open, winds have thrown the autumn leaves, / and then the fog has covered up the broken pieces of the sun." Another poem in this collection, entitled "Spring Conquers the Metropolis," surrounds the change of seasons with pictures of violence—for example, winter:

Falling down on broken glass of lakes,
can see the fish awakening below
And in its back the shining knives of the sun.
And white the blood of Winter, running down its breast.

The themes of childhood and of the brotherhood of seekers also become suffused with the lurking presence of violent death. The sunny worlds of children's games, for instance, may acquire the nature of a funeral, as in the poem "Grammar School in the Village":

Today you place in books the crumbling leaves of trees:
the tears they wept, their dreams so green, and their red blood.
The furious rains are pouring down the windows;
they rock the weeping churchyard bells,
and, like wet ropes, they stream into the ground.

The poem "White Doves" deals with the death of a friend and with his immortality, like that of the poet's eternal brother, transcending the tragedy in a spiritual renewal of life in the realm of art. The friendship consists of the creation of poetic reality from dreams:

> Long ago, when no rivers would run through the silence of the gardens,
> you and I made a flock of white doves from the snow
> and released them to fly into huge and frost-covered heaven;
> there they flapped their white wings, settling down on the light,
> shining hands of the happy and cheerful white cloud . . .
> and the earth every morning would lift from the snow
> dove feathers, filled with the rays of the sun.

Death, on the other hand, is a fierce and screaming mechanical monster that crushes both life and dreams:

> And when we raised our heads, the trees were trembling
> and stretching out their branches toward the abyss—a fearsome
> alien sky—
> there were the warehouses, like beasts in forest, on the bottom,
> hiding their sooty snouts behind their crossed paws;
> and from their mouths, like fangs, the rails were stretching
> under the screaming wheels. . . . The blinded trains
> were flying, flying over the white doves. . . .
> My friend's heart-rending cry fell down on them, like hands.
> And on his shadow-haunted forehead blue blood of birds was
> running. . . .

In both books the color scheme of black and fire has been replaced for the most part with blue and white—the colors of yearning—which had already alternated with the blackness of *November Nights.* A poem entitled "Laterna Obscura" in *Blue Snow* (translated here by Clark Mills) combines the white and blue coloring with sharp and searing violence in a symbolic narrative describing a punitive Cossack expedition to a Lithuanian village in the days of the tsars:

> Two of us draw the child's face in the first snow.
> Beneath wild raspberry branches, my sister rocks her doll.
> Last night the workmen laid light snow on the hard earth
> and now they tar the wooden bridge over the Bartuva—
> the new-born snow, light as my sister's hair.

Through the crouched, empty town of Samogitia
the Cossacks ride. They slash with naked swords
white, breathless winter moonlight.
We sketch our brother's face in the first snow.
The epileptic daughter of the watchman
crumbles dry bread, scatters it into the ditch
for the coffin. Snow drifts over the waxen face
of the peasant woman and her pillow of pleated paper.
And through the snowstorm echo
the hoarse chant and the breathless bells.
Through the white soundless town of Samogitia asleep
the Cossacks ride. And their long whips cut
the blue winter moonlight shimmering in the trees.

No one kissed you good night. And no one wept
with you for your dead mother. No one came to bury
your father, hanged. Your land empty and naked.
Your earth a peasant's palm. For you were not admitted
into the kingdom. Gray garments fluttered
like shrouds of long forgotten funerals—
the vestments of a plague.

Through the town of Samogitia ride the Cossacks
who bear on their long lances, cut in pieces,
the blue moonlight of winter.

On a bright Sunday morning in a radiant land
the workmen tar the wooden bridge over the Bartuva.
Deep under ice, and slow, the river flows into the sea.
Under the raspberry branches, covered with snow,
my sister's doll sleeps. Two of us trace
our brother's face, asleep in the blue snow.

The harsh refrain of the riding Cossacks is, in a sense, a development of the earlier images of the shield of time being hacked to pieces by the ticking of the clocks, by the beat of the birds' wings, and by all the rhythmic movements in nature. Here the shield becomes visible as the moon, and it is blue, and the image of the moon's destruction, evoked by the rhythmic change of its phases, connects the Cossack violence with an old Lithuanian folktale about the moon cleft in half by the angry god of thunder. Thus, in the course of centuries, the moon is destroyed and recomposes itself again in an unending cycle. Against this mythological background, the theme of death in the poem becomes balanced through the presence of the idea of eternal renewal of life. This renewal actually constitutes the main thought of the poem. We can see one of its symbols in the tarring of the bridge, but most important is the brother's face, drawn in the snow. A child's game at the beginning, the drawing of the face becomes a statement of poetic faith in the end, now recorded in the blue snow of dreams after the tragedies of orphanhood and death have passed into the tombs of the past, and remaining under the snows of time like river water and like the little broken doll. On earth what can be killed will die, but the eternal renewal comes, for the poet, in the dimension of art. The very effort of artistic creation is here connected with a child's first efforts to give shape to his dreams on the white and empty surface of snow, which is the child's life, a kind of *tabula rasa*. The dream itself is again connected to the image of the brother—the figure known from other poems as a symbol of longing, rebellion, and truth.

Yet there are moments in the poetry of Nagys when even the immortality of art crumbles in the sands of time. The poem "Stones" from *The Blue Snow* portrays the disintegration of things created by man's greatest efforts to conquer eternity, those that are manifest in religion and art:

In flintstone touched by hermit's stock there opens up
the mouth of wellspring: pale stones of the moon,
the Sphinx of Egypt, walls of Carthage, Euphrates' shores,
and stone-age axes, masks of polished marble,
the gods and athletes of Praxiteles, and Michelangelo's
sad figures in synthetic stone, of children lost to us in paradise.
And mica glitters in the gravel, held in children's hands.
The rock of Genesis has crumbled. The mountains have retreated to the blue
mist. The fragile lines, their silhouettes, now melt and tremble
on the horizon. Hot the winds of Africa which sway the massive
and murky curtains of the amphitheater. Sand has covered
both bird and paradise, and also angels with their jewelled eyes.

Thus in the end we return to the same solitude in the midst of silent spaces, whether we perceive it as darkness facing us or as the blue land of poetic vision. The opposite poles of tension in Nagys' poetry seem to be at one end a great longing for the true texture of reality and at the other the irresistible call of dreams. Reality perceived with the freshness of a child's direct response to things always brings with it the excitement of the creative imagination. The dreams that are then born must shatter against the immovable fact of death. The conquest of death by the creation of a special universe of art robs the poet of his victory because his world may then be real for him alone. The land of visions does know solitude and the uncertainty to which all dreams are subject. Although we know that in the beginning was the Word, we may well find ourselves writing down nothing but what Hamlet called "words, words, words":

> In the land of blue snow there are no trees:
> There are their shadows; just the names of trees,
> put down in blind man's marks by hand of solitary hermit
> . . . .
> Only the names are left on earth of the blue snow,
> just lines and drawings, letters on the ashes.
> In the land of blue snow there is no land.

Thus the world that is so real to a child loses all substance in the visions of the poet. In realizing this, Nagys steps through the portals of modern existentialist despair into the noise of cities in which, as in his poem "Los Angeles," from *The Blue Snow*, our dreams whirl around in a kind of *danse macabre* amid the broken pieces of what we have been accustomed to call civilization:

> In coffee houses and in taverns: barefoot angels dancing.
> The angels black. And angels white. And angels blue.
> The poets resurrecting from the smoke an island of green coral,
> the homeland of the albatross. Brass trumpets in the jazz
> tear up the palm tree branches and split skyscraper stone.
> The stained-glass windows shatter, as does shopkeeper's glass.
> And artificial moons fly through the starless sky.
> On fragments of the glass, on stars, the angels dancing.

Nagys therefore belongs among those modern poets whose modernity can be defined as despair. His is the cold war generation, which survived one catastrophe only to wait for the second, and ultimate, Armageddon. At the time when Nagys wrote the poems discussed here, the world was looking at the clock of history as it drew toward the final hour without any real hope of averting the disaster of man's own making. Today the danger is still present, but there is also an awareness that somehow still another effort must be made to reprieve mankind. Some people are returning to reason, others to love, and others again proclaim their determination never to kill again. But back in 1960 the only all-embracing vision Nagys could see was that of "Mors Atomica":

> We are but animals on a deserted island.
> No room for us in Noah's ark—so we were driven here
> by arrows and by spears invisible.
> No one has sent a boat to save us.
> No one has written on the clouds in fiery letters.
>
> We wait, submissive, for the final night
> of blue and merciless sword. All ships,
> with sails raised high in panic, pass us by.
> The birds are gone. No winds. The wellsprings on the island
> went dry. Bread-bearing trees are fruitless.
>
> We feel the cold and salty sand with our lips.
> The nearness of the hair of those who've fallen next to us,
> their rhythmic breathing, chopping up eternity
> into the tiny seconds of this moment. Silence
> and the final wave washing our feet.
>
> We are the beasts of which the Scripture makes no mention.
> Driven by spears and arrows of apocalypse
> into deserted, empty coral island.
> No one has sent a boat to save us.
> No one has washed our names from naked sand.

But discussion of the work of Nagys should not end with this bleak landscape of death. There is simply too much warmth and life in what he has written; too many poems have achieved an indestructible reality of their own, to which even the *mors atomica* of all mankind seems somehow irrelevant. Particularly impressive are his visions of his native land—not dream landscapes of a country that no longer exists, but perceptions of childhood, now suffused with the music of longing, which constitute the home of everyone who has ever seen the world with open eyes. One example of such poetry is the poem "Summer Day" from *The Sundials*:

I was awakened by the whistling sound of pigeons' wings
and the flood of sunshine rising in my eyes.
Old grandma's spinning wheel is humming evenly in the light-filled room,
and swarms of bees, invisible, are humming in the neighbor's
blooming linden tree. The wind is rocking in the fragile patterns
of blue and wavy window curtains.

The trains in the railroad station catch their breath after their long journey.
The stationmaster's whistle blends with chirping crickets' song.
I run out barefoot over the white stones
into the garden full of cooling shadows. There I drown
amidst the fragrance of sunflowers, earth, and cherry blossoms.
I see there slumbering on the whitewashed brick wall
my little lizard with the half-closed eyes.
The sparrows bathe and chatter in the roadside dust.

I fall to the grass; I hear how slow my heart is beating.
How ringing clouds have touched the boughs of the apple tree.
How little ray of light that ripened in the midday sun
has fallen on my face, how it burns my eyelids. . . .

The wind is sleeping in the grass. I hear how the dull stone
of the ragged artisan is sharpening the scissors and the knives.
The crickets and the whistle of the train are chirping. Chirping sound of blade.
I hear it all in summer's humming and enormous house.
I open, then, my eyes—and all the blue with its warm clouds
is falling drop by drop into my sleeping palms.

On the other hand, the search for inner light that may have been born in childhood gardens but now must be found anew beyond the wide horizons of man's knowledge is so full of truth and passion that one cannot help but be convinced of the immortality of human hope and of the brotherhood of lonely seekers throughout the ages whose search may yet lead mankind beyond despair to resurrection. The very recognition that others have stood fearlessly at the same threshold of the unknown lends substance to the poet's own conviction that the light will some day be found. His special world is therefore real to the degree that it can be shared, and from this knowledge we are encouraged to believe in a reality that lies beyond all palpable phenomena and yet pervades them all—a reality of mind and spirit and art transcending the dimension of illusions. It is, in fact, this act of faith in the genuine existence of truth achievable by the efforts of creative imagination which in the end returns to Nagys his poet's faith in words.

11 Life as Ritual in the Poetry of Kazys Bradūnas

Born February 11, 1917, in Vilkaviškis, south Lithuania, Kazys Bradūnas studied literature in the Universities of Kaunas and Vilnius, graduating in 1943. From 1941 he worked as a high school teacher in Lithuania, and from 1944 at the Lithuanian displaced persons high school in Munich, Germany. He has been living in the United States since 1949.

Aside from teaching high school and writing poetry, Bradūnas worked on the editorial boards of several Lithuanian periodicals. He edited *Ateitis* (*The Future*), a magazine for Catholic Lithuanian youth, between 1937 and 1938, then in 1945 took up the editorship of *Aidai* (*Echos*), a Catholic-oriented cultural and literary monthly, and continued until 1948. In 1952 he became editor of *Literatūros lankai* (*The Literary Folios*), the organ of the *Žemė* (*Earth*) group of young Lithuanian writers in exile. At the present time he is the editor of *Draugas* (*Friend*), a Lithuanian-language newspaper published in Chicago.

Bradūnas' books of poems are *Vilniaus varpai* (*The Bells of Vilnius*), 1943, second edition in 1947; *Pėdos arimuos* (*Footprints in the Plowland*), 1944; *Svetimoji duona* (*The Alien Bread*), 1945; *Maras* (*The Pestilence*), 1947; *Apeigos* (*The Rites*), 1948; *Devynios baladės* (*Nine Ballads*), 1955; *Morėnų ugnys* (*Marshland Fires*), 1958; *Sidabrinės kamanos* (*The Silver Bridles*), 1964; and *Sonatos ir fūgos* (*Sonatas and Fugues*), 1967. He has also contributed a number of items of literary criticism to the émigré Lithuanian press.

WHEN, at the dawn of history, the first shepherd made his pipe, the coarse language of man began to yearn for song. During the centuries that followed, the poets learned to speak in a variety of idioms in response to the developing complexities of civilization, but among them there have always been some who, hearing the primeval call of song, continued to listen to the tune of that first shepherd, hidden deep in the racial memory of man. Such a poet is Kazys Bradūnas. He has had to live amid the deafening noise of the world's great catastrophes, but he nevertheless remains a decent man speaking good, neighborly words, still believing that it is possible to put all the horror and despair and the murderous pain of exile into the music of the shepherd's pipe. In his own way he is right, of course, because talent is always far more significant than any particular style or poetic credo. And Bradūnas' talent has the special quality of distilling hope from the witches' brew of contemporary history and of giving this drop of hope the iridescence of truth.

But there was little hope in his early book, *Svetimoji duona* (*The Alien Bread*), dealing with the first impressions of exile, because the poet's vision, darkened by pain, could see only the catastrophe of dispossession. The basic emotional experience in these poems is the intimate recognition of echoes from his own lost country in the details of life, so familiar to a farmer, seen in the alien land. The poet is like a twentieth-century Adam, remembering the trees of paradise among the thorny desert shrubs. Nothing consoles him, everything wounds him even more, everywhere he sees clear and final evidence that the homeland is now truly lost, that he is indeed an exile. In the poem "Passing By" the earth itself confirms this:

> The earth, it would seem, smells the same
> As in those sun-filled days of September,
> Only I am but an autumn leaf
> Torn from the crown of my tree, from its branch, from its roots.

It is terribly difficult for him to swallow a piece of the alien bread because, instead of taking it from the soil, he must now accept it from another man's hands. Sitting by the fire, he sees only the bloody conflagration of his homestead and desires rather to be buried in deep snow than in the ashes of his sorrow. Earth, bread, and fire figure prominently in Bradūnas' poetry as a whole, signifying the fundamental realities of life, but here they speak to him with a cold, alien voice.

This radical break from happiness "back there" to suffering " here and now" finds several avenues of expression, often by means of contrast between dream and reality, in which the fact of exile confirms itself as an awakening:

> The fragrance of flowering willows
> Floats in the air of my land. . . .
> Then I wake up. . . . 'Twas a dream. . . .
> Pale is the light in the window.

In another passage the poet complains:

> All the stars which you gathered by night
> Fall to nothingness, spilled from your hand.
>
> And you see: it's a hard, calloused palm,
> And the deadly routine of your work.
> With miraculous dreams in your wake
> You take up the day's burden and go.

Alienation becomes irrevocable when the poet, crushed by the enormity of his sorrow, withdraws even from spiritual communion with the artistic achievements of mankind and insists, painfully and stubbornly, on living only with Lithuania, listening only to the voice of his land. In a poem entitled "The Saint Stefan Cathedral of Vienna" he sees this architectural masterpiece, built to embody the magnitude of man's yearning for God, as an expression of man's own dubious greatness, and contrasts it with the humble country chapel of his memory:

> The endless reach of Gothic vaults
> Can only leave you numb with wonder.
> These aren't the prayers of the meek—
> This greatness is of man alone.
> You hear the symphony of bells,
> But in your heart you do not listen. . . .
> Instead, it seems as if nearby
> The wooden belfry speaks to you
> With sound of lonely little bell:
> A tiny church, and maple trees,
> And grain is ripe out in the fields,
> And plowman's God—thus, face to face. . . .

Consequently, Bradūnas does not accept this exile as a new dimension of creative experience but plants his roots deep in the farmer's yearning for his native soil, now left behind. What grows from this soil is not a vision of life but of death, of an eternal blending with the earth of the fathers, this time beyond all dreams and all awakenings. There are several poems in *The Alien Bread* in which the main object of longing is the soil of native churchyards; to rest in it seems equivalent to crowning one's life with meaning. However, when Bradūnas speaks of "crosses on the hill's shoulder, growing straight from the heart," he does not so much epitomize the fact of death itself as the mystery of eternity rising from the depths of the earth. His longing for native churchyards and for the graves of ancient warriors of the land leads him to deep meditations over the fate of his country, as if he were making a poetic journey back into the past, all the way to the pagan altars of his forefathers from which began the wellsprings of Lithuanian history and the mystery of the ancient religion, which, when understood, can bring him nearer to the contemporary Christian God.

Bradūnas tries to conceive of the history of his nation as a kind of ritual, an offering of sacrifice, continuing through the centuries. He has in mind not the historical events so much as the very meaning of human existence. Instead of responding to specific situations from the past, he tries to give poetic embodiment to the idea that to live means essentially to be consumed by fire on the altar of God. Things and events exist, in his view, not for their own sake but as symbolic forms expressing man's striving for eternity across the portals of death. The life of the nation in the course of centuries acquires a meaning expressed in the words of another poet, Algimantas Mackus, as a "sacrament of blood and earth." The three main rituals of this sacrament in Bradūnas' poetry are armed conflict, labor, and prayer. The earth, like a liturgical vessel, collects our blood and sweat and produces bread, the eating of which, as in the Holy Mass, is a symbol of sacrifice and thus the highest form of prayer, when God divides Himself among us. In this manner, the sacrifice of man and of God is united in the symbolic substance of bread, which is given its visual representation in the heavens, in the brilliant sun, rising like the

Host at the altar, while in the pagan world the yearning for this unity burns brightly in the eternal flame of the temples.

The ritual of war is sanctified by the deliberate decision to die for one's homeland. The killing of the enemy, the glory of victory, has never been an important theme in the old Lithuanian folk songs—the dominant theme is one of sacrifice and sorrow. Bradūnas follows this tradition by concentrating on the mystique of death instead. One of the introductory poems to his book *Devynios baladės* (*Nine Ballads*), combines both the old pagan and the new Christian worlds of the Lithuanian people in the image of death as sacrifice:

Fire and smoke of the offering climbs to the sky from the altar,
Blood of the fallen is gathered in drops; they died for their homes.
Heavy the wood of the Cross, carried through the nebulous world
On the shoulders of Christ. Your soul, embraced in His glance,
Changes to incense and bursts into flame, like dry forest grass—
Kneel on the floor of your sorrows. Die with the face of the righteous.

In the cycle "Burial Mounds," from the same book, blood and prayer sanctify the ancient graves:

The roots of the burial mound are fed
With blood of warriors, still warm.
It drops there into copper urns—
You see it glow, like buried treasure.
It is consumed with a greedy mouth
By the thirsty depths of the earth.

And you can see fresh shoots have sprung
From stumps of dry and holy oaks,
And in an ecstasy of prayer
The forests kneel before the morning star.

The earth, the blood, and the fire are transferred in this "ecstasy of prayer" into the present, to signify the struggle of the Lithuanian anti-Soviet guerrillas and to unite both the old and the new wars into a single continuing sacrifice:

The faces of the forest brothers
Look at the full moon through the earth—

The steel which came on wings of death
Is rusting slowly in their breasts. . . .

I fall crosswise onto this ground.
My burning fingers grasp the clay—
O, how the horsemen thunder on!
O, how their steeds are neighing!

It is possible by means of poetry to unite the fate of today's guerrillas and the fate of the old warriors, but this does not mean that there will be no uncertainty left in the mind, no doubt that the warlike pagan exploits can in any way be compared to the Christian offering of prayer. Hero worship, in whatever nation it is found, contains at least some elements of the Teutonic mystique of "blood, sword, and soil" which in its very essence tends to negate the idea of the Cross and consequently can and actually has led twentieth-century man back to barbarous and bloody deeds, as the Second World War confirms only too well.

In another cycle of poems from this book Bradūnas tries to understand the danger inherent in his ritual of death. The cycle is called "Apuolė"—the name of an old semi-legendary castle in western Lithuania which, tradition says, sustained some of the bloodiest fighting with the Vikings at the dawn of Baltic history. The poems develop the theme of the pagan world view, unredeemed by Christianity, leading from antiquity to the *danse macabre* of death in the present world. Bradūnas describes the tense and worried atmosphere of an ancient castle surrounded by the enemy. Everything has been done to ensure safety, but somehow it is not enough. There is betrayal in the air—the very stones speak of it. The ruler kills the guards who warned him about the lurking danger, but the stones continue to speak. As poem follows poem, the centuries pass, the language of stones turns into the ominous sound of bells and whispers, revealing itself more and more as the voice of conscience. When we see Herod murdering the babes, we understand what the pagan world was afraid of:

Pagan and Christian sacrifices
Have made the altar heavy.
The Innocent Lamb
Is murdered in my arms.

The Lamb's blood falls on the heads of our generation as we continue to perfect the weapons of mass destruction, which Bradūnas calls "the claws of the hydrogen devil." The terrible equation of the theory of relativity—a proud achievement of science—spells doom:

> At the beginning was the Word—
> But you are writing, silently,
> The formula of the end.

The gospel of science, then, becomes the voice of the new humanism, indifferent to faith, proclaiming an essentially pagan conquest of the universe, and thus just as terrible and barbarous as the ancient Nibelungen dreams:

> I'm stumbling over corpses,
> The hanged men touch my head—
> How beautiful, how pleasant,
> The spectacle of Man.

The image of man as a conqueror, whether of nature or of other men, can therefore only turn to horror if the struggle he wages is not, ultimately, a Christian offering. It follows in Bradūnas' poetry that the same threat of meaninglessness applies to man's labor—to the building of civilization—if it is not transfigured by the conception of ritual and Christian offering. In his chosen poetic role of a Lithuanian farmer, the poet further claims that any such ritual must unify man spiritually with the soil which he works. A concise expression of this can be found in *Nine Ballads*:

> The plow and the hammer and steering wheel, touched by my hand,
> Turn into things consecrated for ritual secret and ancient.
> The altar's hot stone is the earth upon which you are walking.
> Every muscle in tension quivers like dove sacrificial.

The idea of work as a ritual is developed in a cycle of poems called "Near the Breathing Earth," from the collection *Apeigos* (*The Rites*). First Bradūnas greets the everyday toil of the farmer, performed not according to the modern mentality of "agricultural businessman" but with love for the continuity of the intimate relationship between man and the soil:

> Cutting the old patch of clover, I see
> Underneath there are thousands of footprints—
> The traces of forefathers fill every furrow,
> Neither water nor time washed them out.

The earth becomes a participant in an ancient ceremony performed by both the living and the dead. When the land thus beloved is lost, we can see the full intensity of pain carried on the shoulders of the farmer-exile. The gradual understanding of the true magnitude of dispossession comes to Bradūnas through slow and deep meditation in his later books, and this is what distinguishes them from the first collection, *The Alien Bread*, which communicated, for the most part, only the immediate sorrow of parting.

Meditation leads Bradūnas to an intimate pagan-Christian religious experience which gradually comes to occupy the central place in his work. His whole structure of symbols is based on this experience. One such symbol is the elemental force of the native forests—a force which was felt and worshiped by his forefathers and which now receives its embodiment in poetry:

> Holy forest, oh, untouched and secret grove
> Stretching endlessly from East to West,
> Spreading your green carpet for the sun
> Far beyond the curtains of the dawn.
>
> Now the midday rain has washed your branches,
> Forest, streaming warmth from every tree.
> It's a huge and fragrant temple, green and ringing,
> Incense rising straight into the sky.

It is important to understand that Bradūnas does not think of the ancient Lithuanians who prayed in such forests as idol worshipers. An idol represents a deity which may become manifest in nature but actually has an independent existence of its own. The belief in this existence is rejected by Christianity as falsehood and idol worship. Here, however, the very fact that man and nature exist signifies not deity, for this would be pantheism, but a condition of prayer to the God whose work can be felt in the processes of nature and then clearly recognized in the teaching of Christianity. And so, for instance, Bradūnas mentions an earth goddess, Žemyna (reminiscent of the Latin Demeter), in some of his poems, not as a separate deity but as the name given to what happens to the rye when it grows in sun and rain. In *Morėnų ugnys* (*Marshland Fires*), the poet describes the ancient world view of the pagan Lithuanians in the following manner:

> I have no gods,
> I make no idols—
> I pray like the aspen trees
> And sing like the spruce.
> My ritual shields the forests
> From evil eyes,
> From the phases of moon.

Those who pray in this manner will come to Christianity in their own way, through communion with the earth. A poem entitled "Homestead," from the same collection, paints a landscape quivering at the threshold of the true God:

> Green hills, hemmed in by crosses,
> Begging for their baptism,
> Wade barefoot
> Into the holy lake.
> The clouds are bringing
> Communion of the Sun
> To springtime fields.
> The plowlands rise
> Filled with Holy Ghost. . . .
>
> (And just on the horizon—
> The pagan forests. . . .)

The feeling of this ancient sacral universe of the Lithuanian is conveyed with the greatest immediacy in *Nine Ballads*, in a cycle called "The Ritualistic Song." The structure of this cycle consists of two textures of language. One of them attempts to imitate the style of old folk songs in a song addressed to the earth goddess Žemyna, with the separate stanzas of the song distributed through the whole cycle. Each of these stanzas is then contrasted with a set of corresponding antistrophes in which the words of the Žemyna song are elucidated and interpreted in the imagery of the modern poetic idiom.

> And how did you then, Žemyna,
> Keep the winter rye so warm?
> Speaking potent magic word,
> Covering with snowdrifts

is followed by its antistrophe:

> Christmas snow is lightly falling,
> Seen through paling window panes.
> But stars have burst upon the heavens
> And poured their light into the blind
> Eyes of o'ergrown wellsprings,
> And these then open suddenly—
>
> 'Twas there, on hard, unyielding floor,
> My childhood knelt to pray
> And cry, all naked in the night.

The parallel between the tender shoots of rye under the snow and the poet's childhood, naked but protected by heavenly light, is given Christian meaning by the presence of Christmas with its guiding star. Then the growing of the rye appears to be also a kind of ritual expressing the life of the peasant as offered to God. Thus, through the birth of Christ the "eyes of o'ergrown wellsprings" open unto the eternal unity of earth, man, and God.

The interplay of two different poetic idioms is then expanded by Bradūnas to include contrasting sets of images which, in counterbalancing one another, produce a complex and skillfully designed structure that in the end produces a unified effect. In the *Nine Ballads*, for instance, there is a cycle of poems entitled "Stained Glass" which elaborates upon the basic structural elements of glass and of the leaden framework encasing it. This theme receives a series of metaphorical interpretations in which the strong contrast between transparent glass and its heavy frame produces tension in the imagery, successfully exploited by Bradūnas to convey intense emotion. At the beginning the poet's own "I" is subjected to the metamorphosis of lead and glass: "Let my soul be glass . . . Let my limbs be lead." Further on, in a poetic landscape, the heavy clay shore provides a framework for the river Nemunas, and then the same contrast is transferred to the plane of iron-heavy labor done by the farmers—dark figures framing the misty morning fields. The earth itself, like lead, frames a grave pit; the glass in this picture is the blue sky:

> Don't dig, don't dig any deeper—
> You'll break the crystal sky,
> The last toy of my little brother.

This metaphorical balance between frame and glass encompasses all manifestations of life, from inanimate objects to the figurative description of the breaking of bread. At times Bradūnas reproduces the effect of a painting in which thick black colors take the shape of bare tree branches, framing a flame-colored space as if it were tinted glass. In the broader landscapes the fields provide the framework for the glittering surface of the lakes. This variety of images accumulates to form an impression of the clear and fragile human soul framed, or entangled, in the heaviness of life.

Not only the separate images but the whole cycle is conceived on the structural principle of frame and glass. It is built on two series of poems, printed on facing pages. The first series describes the life and death of the poet's mother. The same four lines are repeated in the initial stanzas of each of its poems—two at the beginning of a stanza and two at the end—in this way forming a kind of frame. Here is one such stanza:

> The clay on shore has the sour smell of bread
> And an intoxicating scent of blood,
> And through the layer of thin mist, the day of Spring
> With iron-heavy feel of labor
> Weighs down the salty, sweaty earth.

Thus the imagery in the lines of the "frame" evokes the feeling of heaviness and strong, pungent smells. Between them, as a sort of "glass," is a line full of air and space and mist. This middle line keeps changing in the recurring first stanza of each poem in the series, creating the dynamic impression of passing seasons. In addition to the day of spring there is also "the stuffy, yellow Summer day" and the "red and rainy day of Autumn" and finally, as the mother dies, "the day of Advent, filled with snow." The progression of colors from semi-transparency (the mist) through yellow and red to the white of the snow immediately calls to mind the colors of a stained-glass window. The second stanza of each poem begins with variations on the same line, and the total impression produced is one of the hard, yet fruitful, life of the mother: "My mother brought me to the world"; "My mother fell in open fields"; "My mother gathered in the flax"; and finally "My mother there is now asleep."

The second series of poems describes the life of the poetic "I" as if it were a "glass" within the "frame" of the mother's life. This series does not have recurrent lines but conveys instead a number of incidents in which the dominant imagery is again built around the metaphorical structure of frame and glass.

The book *Maras* (*The Pestilence*) is a narrative work composed of separate poems describing a continuing action. The architecture of imagery in it is based on a different principle. In the first place, the presence of plot and of roughly delineated characters classifies the book as a work of narrative genre. Yet *The Pestilence* is not truly an epic because, aside from its rather limited scope, its action results not so much from the chain of cause and effect as from the logic of poetic imagery. At the very beginning, in the prologue, an old woman tells a little child about the terrible time of pestilence. Her story receives its impetus not from some event but from an image—a cemetery framed in the sunset:

> Why, granny, does the churchyard hill
> Conceal from us the face of sun? . . .
> My granny took me on her knee
> And shook her head, so slow and sad,
> And told the story of the plague,
> And broke my radiant, childhood dreams.

The prologue contains the beginnings of one of the basic image-symbols in the work—a lamp, or torch, at first conveyed in connection with glass and later expanded to signify fire in general. The child saw previously how the windows of village houses reflected the sun, as if they were lamps; now, when the old woman's story begins, his fragile dreams are broken like glass at the same time as the sun goes down, putting out the lights.

The next symbol introduced is one of scorching heat and drought; its opposite, which comes later, is water, torrential rain. The first poem following the prologue is replete with intense, dry, and fearful suffering, evocative of death: "The stones in the sun, like bleached skeletons"; "The scream of unknown birds awakens the village at night." When the first victim of the pestilence falls, the symbol of fire, having previously undergone two transformations—as a blood-red moon and as a star shattering against the sky—takes the shape of torches carried by the men looking in the night for a shepherd who has failed to return home. As the torches gather in one spot, when the body is found, the night turns into a conflagration, and with the distant voice of thunder, the terrible word resounds—"pestilence!" The earth, scorched by the sun, has produced its abundant harvest of death; the peasants die out "like lanterns late at night," when the dark avalanche of night covers everything.

The "eternal stream of darkness," as the night is called, begins the development of the imagery of water, which in the very next poem turns into a deluge of rain, torn by flashes of lightning. Fire and water are thus combined to meet the main human figure of the poem—a young girl, orphaned by the death of her mother. The poem "Maiden" begins the symbolic action of the whole narrative—the girl's journey across the dying land as death follows her footsteps: "And around her—shadows of the furious death / Searching through the earth for mystery of life." Both the girl and death are looking for this mystery, but with opposite intent. The duel between them evokes the familiar pagan-Christian imagery. There is lightning, personifying the forces of nature, before which the girl bows down "as if before an altar," and also the face of the sorrowful Mother of God. The religious symbolism culminates in an enormous heavy cross of oak put up by the dying village in the hope of gaining mercy from the heavens.

The struggle goes on relentlessly until everyone around, except the girl, is dead. By this time it is already winter, and fire and water turn into the frozen image of sparkling snow. This is the ultimate point of nothingness, after which the action reverses itself, returning to hope and to the season of spring. The girl has survived; death could not reach the mystery of life. A soldier—the former servant of death—comes home from faraway lands to begin a new life with the girl. Both the girl and the soldier inherit the gigantic power of the earth. The wheel of symbols turns around; fire and water now acquire the meaning of life:

> That evening the deer came a-running
> To drink from the life-giving stream,
> Beyond the dew-covered farmhouses
> The crickets were singing all night.
>
> And, sheltered by darkening valley,
> The smoke from the chimney arose,
> The flame was so cheerful and crackling
> And young in the life-giving hearth.

This narrative poem, describing one of the most tragic episodes in Lithuanian history, was written soon after the Second World War, which gives it an allegorical meaning—the sign of hope that the catastrophe of exile, too, will pass and that they shall return, like the soldier, back to their native hearth. This, of course, has not happened—they were all left at the frozen point of death.

Bradūnas' use of poetic language does not go beyond the traditional devices of symbol and metaphor in which the words, although used figuratively, retain the meanings assigned to them by the conventional use of language. The metamorphosis of word is only partial, going just far enough to imbue it with poetic emotion. A stylistic figure usually remains just a comparison underlining the intensity of an experience. For instance, in the book *Vilniaus varpai* (*The Bells of Vilnius*), which describes the sights and sounds of the Lithuanian capital, a cathedral built in the style of Italian Renaissance is simply compared with "A calm and noble swan, flown here from faraway South." Similarly, an apple tree in the poem "Noonday," from the collection *The Rites*, is limited in its metaphorical function to the evocation of a feeling of unity with generations past:

> With widespread boughs, as if with hands
> Of ancients, here you cover me,
> I hear their words, as if a gathering
> Of birds, in the rustling of your leaves.

The branches of the apple tree are only "as if" hands, and the words of the ancients gather "as if" they were birds. We do not see an entirely new universe but an ordinary reality intensified by feeling. Emotion and reality do not serve as "raw materials" to develop a separate world of art, but rather art and reality themselves are used as means to communicate emotion. Even the more complex poems of Bradūnas, with elaborately constructed imagery, do not depart from the customary meanings of words. The "Stained Glass" cycle in *Nine Ballads* did work out the metaphors of glass and leaden frame in a complex structure of imagery, but all the images retained their essential nature as comparisons. For this reason Bradūnas is considered to be an "easy," "clear" poet, one who places only moderate demands on the symbolic imagination of the reader. The poetic reference to emotion is immediately recognizable. When Bradūnas says that the morning "releases the soul, like a bird" into "the moist wind," we can supply a number of such mornings from our own memory. It is equally easy to participate in the poet's feeling when he says that his heart, from the great love for his native land, "has turned into a handful of the soil." The contact between the reader and the poet is direct, assured, and does not require the ability to comprehend entirely new dimensions of literary expression.

Bradūnas seems somewhat more remote from his readers, at least those who grew up in urban surroundings, when his style and vocabulary approach that of the Lithuanian folklore heritage, especially the folk songs. The difficulty arises not because the poet is hard to understand when he writes in the folk manner but because the whole frame of reference surrounding the folklore—the "little tall rye" and "little sun God's daughter" and "copper gates so fair"—has its roots in the past, which is already dead and does not mean to the contemporary man what it did to the people who, in Milton's words, "warbled their native wood-notes wild." This is why poems like "The Silver Tune" from the collection *Sidabrinės kamanos* (*The Silver Bridles*), which use musical non-sense words together with ordinary ones to create a special sound effect characteristic of the most ancient Lithuanian songs, have about them something of the musty air of a folklore museum:

> Kūkal roses ratilio
> Tatato tatato
> Who did walk amidst the rye
> Sidabro?

This is perhaps a charming yet remote echo from the ancient past, by now a cry in the desert. We are reminded of a poem in *Marshland Fires* in which an old woman dies in the middle of a folktale she is telling to a little boy:

> So who will tell now
> Where the deep well is,
> Where the busy mill? . . .

No one will, and this is the point. The little boys grow up and, while they may remember the old tales, their own language becomes quite different.

Sometimes Bradūnas makes an effort to use the ancient folk language in such a way as to express the present fate of exile in terms familiar from ancient situations. At other times he goes even further and fully transforms an old pagan symbol into a contemporary reference. In *Nine Ballads* there is a cycle called "Coffin Makers." In one of its poems a present-day undertaker in an American city is depicted as a former peasant who finds the shrewd instincts inherited from close proximity to nature quite useful in his new business:

> I used to gauge by flights of crows
> Where I should build my businesses,

Upon what deserts and what streets
To place my undertaker's sign.

Oh, only if you could have seen
My trade at dreadful time of death:
Tenacious, shiny, like a serpent
It drank from the hand of Nothingness.

The serpent drinking milk from a special dish is a very old religious symbol from the ancient pagan Lithuanians, and Bradūnas uses it to spell out his commentary upon the contemporary sense of values embraced by men who make a profession out of the holy rites of burial. Images of this type are most frequently found in Bradūnas' poetry at those times when he has his "dark inspirations" and turns his glance not just to the suffering in life but to the higher experience of tragedy as well, when he approaches the edge of precipice—the metamorphosis of reality into a strange and dreadful vision.

Bradūnas has the capacity to conceive of existence itself as a symbol of some dark, incomprehensible power. It is this element in his nature as a poet that brings him closer to the first Lithuanian mystical-abstract painter Čiurlionis (1875–1911). Bradūnas' latest book *Sonatas and Fugues* elaborates upon his "meetings with Čiurlionis" in a series of poems which constitute a kind of interpretation of that painter. Some readers might find it difficult to establish a connection between the "simple realist" Bradūnas and the metaphysical visions of Čiurlionis expressed in forms and colors related to musical conceptions. The inner tie between the two artists is to be sought in Bradūnas' deep yearning to conceive of human life as a sacred ritual that began at the ancient pagan altars and is continuing in the Christian relationship to God. Bradūnas and Čiurlionis meet on the way to a cosmic experience of life, beginning with the longing for infinity that is, to them, enchanted in the very soil of their native land.

In this last book Bradūnas seems to have arrived at the threshold of new creative horizons, presenting a challenge to comprehend the tragic vision of life and to express it in terms akin to his former simple peasant faith. Whatever direction his further development will take, the total body of his poetry up to the present amounts to a highly successful effort to reconstruct in exile the poetic essence of the native land now lost and to live in it, as if this were the return to a spiritual home—perhaps a better country than the one that actually existed at the time of his leaving.

12 Man and Nature in the Work of Albinas Marius Katiliškis

Marius Katiliškis was born September 15, 1915, in the small village of Gruzdžiai in the district of Šiauliai, northern Lithuania. After four years of schooling, his childhood and adolescence were spent herding sheep and doing farm labor. Later he traveled all over Lithuania, working as a lumberjack, on road gangs, floating timber, and in other jobs. He published his first poem at the age of sixteen and continued to write poems and short stories for various magazines and journals under a variety of pseudonyms. After military service he held a series of easier jobs, such as forest ranger, warehouse manager, and the like, finally settling down in a library, where he rounded out his education by extensive reading.

War and exile took Katiliškis to Germany. When the opportunity arose, he emigrated to the United States and now continues reading, writing, and doing manual labor. One of his jobs in the States was at a Lithuanian cemetery, digging graves for his fellow countrymen.

Katiliškis has published the following novels and collections of short stories: *Prasilenkimo valanda* (*The Hour of Passing By*), 1948; *Užuovėja* (*The Shelter*), 1952; *Miškais ateina ruduo* (*Autumn Comes Through the Forests*), 1957; *Išėjusiems negrįžti* (*Trip of No Return*), 1958; and *Šventadienis už miesto* (*Sunday in the Country*), 1963. An excerpt from *Trip of No Return* was published in English in *Lithuanian Quartet* (Manyland Books, 1962) under the title "On Whose Side Is God?" and a short story, "The Gravediggers," appeared in *Selected Lithuanian Short Stories* (Voyages Press, 1959).

HAVING spoken with his father's ghost and looked upon the frightful void of death, Hamlet explained that art should hold a mirror up to nature. This was to be a mirror with a specific purpose, namely to show the murderer the blackness of his deed, but the notion of art as a reflection of reality in general has persisted ever since, which may possibly give rise to some uneasy thoughts about what men really are. It would seem more reassuring to avoid these uncomfortable implications and say that art, per se, is something else altogether than the reality it is expected to depict. It need not be a mirror at all but rather a creation of the imagination through a process that in some ways resembles the growth of a flower. Composed of sunshine and of soil, of wind and rain, a flower is quite unlike any of these elements. It has an existence of its own, its own shape and color, and a unique beauty that is as inexplicable as a miracle.

The novels and short stories of Albinas Marius Katiliškis invite both comparisons at once. His intensely personal art grows from reality like a flower (although in his case the better comparison might be to a strong, coarse-grained oak) while at the same time it reflects, as in a tragic mirror, the deep, black void of dispossession which is called exile. In his work Katiliškis tries to resolve a very painful dilemma facing those Lithuanians who are now scattered, like so many pebbles, around the Western world. The question is how one can be an individual—unique in all eternity—and yet belong to history, that is, remain a member of a nation that has become the nameless victim of events.

The first years of exile were especially bitter because this dilemma seemed insoluble. Having left their native land, the exiles of Lithuania realized that they had also lost their human individuality, becoming nothing but a crowd of refugees while history, too, depriving them of any significance as a people, slammed its gates shut behind their backs. The faceless specter of exile haunts every page of Katiliškis' first collection of short stories, entitled *Prasilenkimo valanda* (*The Hour of Passing By*). In it the author seems to be trying to understand the fact of dispossession itself, to investigate its multiple nuances in a number of different circumstances, by playing out his plots against the enormous background of exile, which dwarfs and overwhelms his characters. Sometimes his star-crossed people are merely funny, as in the story "The End of the Lady's Piglet," in which a young matron, having lost her husband in Lithuania, must now also lose her beloved suckling pig which she was raising with such loving care in the displaced persons camp. The piglet falls into a deep cesspool and drowns, thus providing its own animal commentary on the life of the DP. At other times the laughter disappears, leaving an aftertaste of dark disturbing thoughts that perhaps the exiled lost their homeland even before they physically departed from it because they had poisoned the wellspring of its life by serving alien gods. "The History of a Well" is constructed around the central actual and symbolic presence of a deep, dark well in the depths of which the narrator, as a child, imagined that he saw the secret abode of all his purest dreams. During the German attack in 1941, which ended the first Soviet occupation, the water in this well became polluted by the rotting corpse of a Communist Lithuanian militiaman who fell into it when shot by anti-Soviet guerrillas from his own village. Thus the stuff of dreams was turned into a revolting poison, and a man became an alien in his own land.

The tragic irony remains the same in both stories; we fall into our catastrophe as into a deep, black pit. Sometimes this pit transforms itself into a wide abyss of hopeless remorse, as in the story "Along the Dull Shore," in which a husband deliberately abandons his wife during his escape from the advancing Russians because he thinks that she had been unfaithful to him. Much later—too late—he learns from the man who was supposed to be his successful rival that his wife has loved him truly and well and that his "punishment" of her was in reality a tragic act of injustice.

This whole first collection resembles a set of themes and variations on the topic of dispossession. Katiliškis seems to be experimenting with a number of stylistic devices and lines of plot in order to understand the significance of the tragic events and to develop the proper means of their artistic expression. At times he is tempted to take a shortcut to success by substituting melodrama for tragedy and by crowding in suggested meanings beyond the inherent capacity of a given story to sustain them, causing the reader to find himself wandering through a dead forest of symbols. On one occasion, for instance, he artificially slapped together a variety of literary styles, including romantic, rhetorical language, imitations of urban slang, and, curiously, authentic peasant idiom. To this were added literary echoes from Knut Hamsun and the bucolic romances, seasoned with cruel, even coarse, pathos.

All this we find in the story "The Vanishing Love," which seems intended to create a complex pattern of experiences relating to the theme of dispossession. The story line proceeds from a ludicrous starting point in the present to a melodramatic flashback and ends in an inconsequential drinking bout. Two men are wading through slush on a stormy night, fluttering across the darkness, the author says, "like two leaves driven by the wind." The men are shocked and confused because they had to leave in the middle of a gay party. This, the reader must understand, is their first dispossession; they are missing out on some marvelous cognac. Their reason for leaving reveals the second and, possibly, greater loss; this banquet had been arranged to celebrate the betrothal of one of them to a gorgeous girl, but at the last moment the girl decided she did not want to marry him and chose another suitor right on the spot.

This completes the first part. It seems hardly worth while to go on describing such a soap opera, but we must realize that the trouble is not with the author's idea but with the means then available to him for expressing it. The experience itself is deep and genuine—the total collapse of all possible hope for happiness. The means, unfortunately, are limited to the standard devices of tearful epics à la Alexander Dumas. Nevertheless, it is interesting to watch the author groping for some way to transcend his pitiful plot and come closer to expressing his true feelings. He experiments with language. Instead of the sobbing speeches appropriate for stories of this kind, his hero at first attempts to speak with a sort of brave flippancy, typical of the romantic sufferer hiding behind a mask of indifference: "One may, I say, go nuts in this devil's wedding of a night." This does not lead us anywhere, for the reader already has the impression that the whole thing is rather demented. So, the tone is abruptly changed, and the next sentence sounds like something from grand opera: "But let us hold our heads high, let us march on courageously!" Such juxtaposition of two entirely incompatible idioms makes things even worse. The author then tries another tack; he switches the whole focus of the story from the hero to his friend. This gives him the opportunity to continue in an entirely different and hopefully more plausible setting.

There is a flashback to an incident in the past life of the hero's friend, intended to illustrate his own tragic loss of love. This story is again rather melodramatic but somewhat better motivated and more complex because it has a double sting; the man lost the girl he loved for the reason that she, in turn, had already lost all her beauty previous to their encounter. In his youth the man fell in love with a mysterious, slender girl silhouetted against a purple sunset, whose face he never saw. He wrote and sent her love poems that made up in passion what they lacked in art ("I can't sleep at night and I dream / Of you, oh my unknown one"). The unknown one seemed to show no interest in getting acquainted, but one day our hero came upon her unexpectedly as she was gathering mushrooms in a grove and crying and repeating his poems to herself. This was when the tragic secret came out; the man saw that she was completely bald. It turned out that in her childhood she had been ill with typhus and smallpox, had lost her hair, and her face became as pockmarked as the lunar surface. This was why she seemed so mysterious at first, hiding her ravaged face and bald head in a huge scarf.

Katiliškis enters a more promising path when he attempts to convey the experience of homelessness and dispossession not primarily through melodramatic human emotions but through nature, through the eternal stream of life surrounding man. The issue here is that man may either feel at home in nature or else suffer from alienation, from the deadening knowledge that he is alone, that he does not belong in nature's continuum. It is precisely this belonging no longer to the native soil, this feeling of being lost in an alien landscape, that constitutes the whole tension and the pain of exile. Communicating human sorrow by depicting that fullness of life of which the hero no longer feels himself to be a part requires a rich, yet restrained, language, a style that blends together the poetic feeling and the solid concreteness of things. Katiliškis takes the first step in this direction by re-creating the remembered landscapes of home in lyrical passages like the following:

> The fog of yesteryear has covered you—my trees—from distant summer of the great remembrance. I can still see the imprint of bare feet across the cowslip meadow, where fog, like down, was rising from the valley, and where the harvesters went by with the tired evening sun splashing against the steel of their scythe blades.

There is an effort in this passage to produce a melody from the intonational rhythm of the language alone while at the same time retaining the flavor of concreteness, realism, in the vocabulary itself. We don't just see "a meadow," but cowslips in particular, not "the golden paths of youth," but a trail left by bare feet in the wet grass. The second sentence loses balance because of the effort to cram it full of all the things that make up a country evening. The artist himself has apparently been uncomfortable with it, for in a later version of the story, published in a new collection called *Šventadienis už miesto* (*Sunday in the Country*), he has simplified the last sentence and broken it in two. The trail of bare feet remains as the harvesters go by. The tired sun is smoldering in the steel blades. The calm, exhausted verb "to smolder" fits the evening mood much better than the dynamic verb "to splash." The feathery fog has been dispersed, for it would not let us see either the path or the smoldering sun. Such careful changes demonstrate that Katiliškis had learned a good deal about his trade, namely that in art the issues of thought, feeling, and philosophy must first of all be consciously confronted with the demands of syntax, vocabulary, and grammar in mind, just as in sculpture the artist's conception and form are first of all the functions of the quality of the material and of the strength of the sculptor's hand.

It is not enough, however, to be able to paint landscapes which by themselves contain the author's own emotion. A lyric poet might be satisfied with this, but a writer who works with prose needs more—a plot and a consciously acting human intelligence, a protagonist. Here, too, Katiliškis did not immediately hit upon the right approach. At first his heroes tended to exist in a vacuum of their own solitude, without relation to the flow of life surrounding them. There is a certain romantic flair in the proud aloofness of such a hero, but very soon the reader begins to tire of this silent figure who has nothing to say to him or to anyone else. We can see an example of such a man in a story called "The Hour of Passing By." The main hero is an individual without any ties to his surroundings and completely without fear because the worst thing he could possibly imagine, exile, has already happened to him. And he speaks:

> I have become covered, as it were, with a protective layer, and all water runs off me, everything which is superfluous. I can observe life for days on end, with all its manifestations, while myself remaining on the sidelines. I only need to compare that which was with what I see now in order to confirm my knowledge that all is but vanity, nothing has any meaning whatsoever.

This individual feels himself to be completely free and invulnerable because he has already lost all hope and all urge to live. Such a literary figure has its antecedents. It is Byron's Childe Harold watching the retreating shores of England with a gloomy calm. It is also Lermontov's Pechorin, from *The Hero of Our Time*, observing sleepily how his very presence brings death and suffering to other men's lives. This figure is not without interest in the romantic tradition, but it does not come naturally to Katiliškis. In his work it remains an empty shell, a bleak stranger, because it does not issue from the inner logic of Katiliškis' art. By placing the consciousness of man against the general flow of life, the author breaks the chain, indispensable to him, in which an individual is an organic and inevitable consequence of the being of nature.

The story "Misfortune" begins a different approach to the problem of placing man in his surroundings. At first it seems that its protagonist, Albinas Derkintis, is just one more figure of noble despair, unreachable and mysteriously attractive in his solitude, infinitely bored with life in the displaced persons camp. He likes to stand with his hands crossed on his chest; his hair is gray at the temples, he has broad shoulders and, paradoxically, a gentle, almost girlish smile. The difference between him and the literary cliché from which he comes is that Derkintis does understand the intimate connection between man and the forces of life in nature:

> The roots of it all go much deeper. . . . This tiny seed, having burst its shell, presses its hungry roots into the clay, penetrates rock, grows through layers of sand. And when the tree is cut, the stump continues to produce fresh shoots. And neither drought nor fire can destroy this tangled web of life down in the depths. It is vested in a safe place—the heart of man.

A world view based on the poetic notion that the deepest roots of trees grow in men's hearts opens up much larger possibilities for the development of a literary hero representing man's intimacy with nature. Having become the conscious voice of "the tangled web of life," he can be made to reflect all its power and subtle complexity. The task is to avoid the pathetic fallacy—the artificial comparisons between man and nature which lead back to the romantic, and even sentimental, position that nature, far from being indifferent, actually understands and sympathizes with man, participates in his private emotions. Instead of presenting nature in the anthropomorphic aspect of a fellow sufferer, one should do the reverse—present man as one of the many facets of life in general, as one link in the great chain of being.

Such a view is presented in Katiliškis' next work, *Užuovėja* (*The Shelter*), a collection of episodes from the life of a fictional village in Lithuania thematically united into something approaching a novel. From the very beginning the reader is aware of a new and special angle of vision from which human experience appears to be an extension of life processes in nature. It seems as if suffering, joy, or yearning are the attributes not of man but of nature itself, inherent in the shape, color, and texture of all living things. The taste of an apple, for instance, can return a man to his past in a manner reminiscent of the special magic of Marcel Proust's little cake, the *madeleine:*

> The blessedness of those hours has visited me again. Which is what I no longer believed and had given up waiting for and thought I had forgotten long ago, like the taste of a frozen wild apple, when, brought in from the frost and thawing out inside, it spreads the fragrance of a hillside drenched in sunlight.

The apple simply is, its taste is what a man feels, and the blessedness is what his feeling means to him. Man's consciousness and nature's being are seen as two identical phenomena at the opposite ends of a continuous chain. The essence is the same, only the names are different.

Sometimes what we feel can hardly be given a name but can be expressed in the descriptions of nature by imparting to them a certain metaphorical quality. Something that resembles the restless joy of early spring is implicit in "the acid smell of the bark of the spruce trees and of their needles in the wind." Similarly, when Katiliškis writes that "the village was rocking itself to sleep among the dill blossoms, melting in the incessant cricket song," we know that what has actually been described is some special feeling inside us. The "humming of so much life on the wing" has, for Katiliškis, a specifically human sound, as does "the bee-loud glade" for Yeats. In other words, a human experience does not originate within, but comes from without, through the five senses. Such descriptions are, of course, lyrical in tone, and Katiliškis retains this mood even with images that have an earthy, peasant quality, sometimes tinged with rough humor. His concern is with telling the truth without an esthete's fastidiousness, and the experience of truth is, for him, lyrical and organic, encompassing everything from the smell of earth to the dreams of children and always transforming itself into poetry in the consciousness of the writer.

The principle of continuity with nature is also extended to the structure of *The Shelter*. Its several episodes, lacking the unity of a single plot common to conventional novels, are tied together by another means. If a book does not create suspense through a planned sequence of events, it must use some kind of introductory device to transport the reader to another place and time. An easy solution would be to have several Lithuanian exiles chatting about times past around the fireplace or to have someone find an old diary, but Katiliškis chooses to effect the transfer by means of a nature image. He speaks of clouds:

> I saw the clouds rising before me from the waters. I recognized them and almost cried out for joy—at the very moment when they came into view. They were boiling up and turning and clambering from the depths, holding onto the blue with huge hands, and then slowly, bit by bit, they flattened out in the sky over the house.
>
> I was dizzy from watching them, craning my neck, and my heart was ringing like a bell. So we meet again, the golden clouds of my youth! How many ways and byways we had to travel for ten years until we met again eye to eye in a faraway corner of a foreign land! Oh, my God!

The author does not say that these are alien clouds that only resemble very closely those seen long ago at home, but directly asserts them to be the very same friends of his youth which "in those times drank the dew from our meadows and summer fields of grain." It is in this joyous moment of recognition that the past and present meet, and the transition is accomplished. The clouds are joined by the thick smoke from house chimneys and from shepherds' fires; they draw in the steam from threshing machines, they move and shape themselves into the outlines of well-known old friends, and we are now walking down an old familiar road, talking with Uncle Vaitiškis—the one with the moustache—we are home again, back in the village of Gružiškės.

Since the clouds are real, not just a metaphor, the people who come out of them also acquire a real, bodily presence. This describes one of the most characteristic aspects of Katiliškis' work; he presents a man as a personification of the surrounding reality from which he was made and then shows how this man recognizes himself to be an inseparable part of the totality of life and how this recognition flows naturally from his profound and firm understanding of the meaning of existence. In an episode of *The Shelter* called "The Thaw," we see an old man named Dryža who carefully and patiently makes his beer according to the procedures established from time immemorial and then goes out for a walk in his own fields:

> The wind kept moving the fleeting shadow of the farmer. The shadow grew and extended itself farther and farther, and Juozapas Dryža thought that perhaps there was no spot as large as he could cover with his finger where his shadow had not fallen a hundred times. On a hundred summer mornings, when the shadow is as long as it is in the evening, and noontimes, when it hardly extends to three feet, and in fog and rain, his shadow must have fallen, like the soft sound of his footsteps, like the crumbling of clods in the soil and the crackling sod, slipping off the edge of the plow. This is how one comes to own the land forever. Not by money or anything else. Covered over and over again with his shadow, passed through the fingers, patted down with bast shoes, lifted out to the sunlight every year.

It is then Dryža understands that he and the earth are the same in substance and in essence—when he touches the soil with his hand, "like a blind man would touch a beloved face." Then the exile, too, understands and is suddenly transfixed with the painful knowledge of how much he gave up when he turned his back to his native land. There is still another understanding that comes to him—to know and to accept the meaning of existence is the same as knowing and accepting death as an inseparable part of this meaning. The episode from which this quote is taken actually describes the death of Dryža, his coming back into the soil of his forefathers after living out his life "in harmony with death."

So Katiliškis reveals his essential view of man as the final fruit of the land. Perhaps "view" is not a proper term here, since it implies a conclusion, a theoretical position, a matter of principle. Actually, what we are dealing with here is a feeling akin to knowledge. This is the way it comes out, quite simply, because the wind is blowing, and the pine trees spread their fragrance, and the grain grows in the fields. Amid it all the human consciousness has its beginning, and a child is born, like the "hot summer's foundling"—little Petriukas—in the episode entitled "Summer Heat":

> The child was rolling about, all entangled in the patch of sweet peas. His voice was like the chirping of a newly hatched bird in a warm nest, in thick shrubbery, or among the roots of the rye, or in the dense grass, tangled like wool. There was this very ripening of the summer, the high noon, and the earth, like a nesting bird, covering the soft and brittle new lives hatching under its widespread wings.

In Katiliškis' work, nature, however lyrical, never becomes sentimentalized to the point of pastoral scenes in which little porcelain shepherds stand among young lambs of pure silk. Quite the contrary, it has a bittersweet taste, like an acorn; it includes aching muscles and the smell of sweat and a lurking threat of fate that follows man as a cat would, stepping softly toward a bird's nest. There is the evening darkness and the twilight of the soul and the winter frost and the hard, unforgiving heart of man. In *The Shelter* man is multifaceted, hard and tender, lyrical and grim, like nature itself, and man's joys and sorrows have their roots in the same soil from which wheat and thistles grow.

The next work by Katiliškis is a conventional novel, entitled *Miškais ateina ruduo* (*Autumn Comes Through the Forests*). In it the author attempts to build up a protagonist within the framework of a definite plot. In doing so, however, Katiliškis maintains his organic, rather than intellectual and moral, concept of man. Generally speaking, the protagonist has the qualities of a literary hero, according to criteria that are, in the last analysis, moral in some sense of the word, since of all living creatures only man is concerned with the problems of good and evil. Yet, with respect to Katiliškis' protagonists, moral judgments based on some metaphysical faith or intellectual system of values are difficult to make. When all the actions of men originate in the laws of nature, which cannot be morally judged, all values must be measured against nature itself, against the naked fact that the universe simply exists. The only action of moral value then is reconciliation with this fact—not necessarily a surrender to some Dostoevskian mindless machine or a renunciation of the creative impulse peculiar to man but rather a conscious acceptance of ourselves and the world for what we are, a decision for the organic principle of life and death, with all the consequences issuing from it. Insofar as Katiliškis operates on any philosophical plane at all, it consists of an elemental stoicism in the face of the eternal ebb and flow of life through the ages.

Watching the characters through, rather than against, the backdrop of nature creates a kind of optical illusion. It seems that man's profile, partially blended with the surrounding reality, has become so blurred as to be almost unrecognizable. Reading the novel gives the impression that living people play a much lesser role in it than the circumstances in which they find themselves. In all their intense conflicts, their many and varied adventures, tragedies and comedies, the element of independent human decision seems relatively unimportant; there is little feeling of a freely chosen fate, be it happy or tragic.

This is not to say that Katiliškis paints flat and lifeless portraits of his people. Quite the contrary, the characters are often thrown into sharp relief by the paradoxes inherent in their nature. Tilius Gelažius, the main hero of the novel, an iron-muscled young lumberjack, is so strangely weak in his heart, so blown about by the winds of fate and his own uncomprehended, uncontrolled passions, that the puzzle of his powerful yet helpless nature makes him an unforgettable, never quite fully understood figure. His chief opponent, Doveika, is defined by a different set of paradoxes. Although a lecherous and greedy old farmer, he possesses a strong, magnetic personality; he seems like a natural force, beyond good and evil, a center around which everything turns. All the riches of the surrounding country flow into him, like tributaries into a river, and so do the contempt, hatred, and admiration of men. Sharply delineated by the contradictory elements in their natures, the people in the novel nevertheless leave the impression of a uniform texture, possibly because the very paradoxes that set them apart keep repeating themselves. These people are unique individuals in the same sense that a spruce tree stands alone in a forest that as a whole looks like a single green mass. We are reminded of Sartre's words: "*Nous sommes unique, comme tous les autres.*" The inner profundity and complexity of Katiliškis' heroes are not set off against their environment but rather fulfill it in a special way. Man only expresses in his feelings and thoughts that which has been implicit in nature all the time, and for this reason he is as infinitely varied and as unchanging as the flow of life itself.

In this way, a man's life becomes the final stage of the processes taking place in nature. As long as man refrains from violating the natural state of things, does not try to change violently the direction of the great river of being, he remains strong and serene in his instinctive knowledge of all the mysteries of life. But then nothing much ever happens, and it is not possible to give life the steep incline, the dynamic change in the course of events which is often defined in literature as plot. In a sense, every novel must be the record of a catastrophe, that is, of a disruption in the normal course of things and of its consequences. The creative dynamics in the work of Katiliškis, especially in the novel *Autumn Comes Through the Forests*, consist precisely in this, that man initiates a process of change in nature and then himself becomes subject to it, most often in the direction of downfall—the logical end of his actions. At the beginning of the novel we see the lumberjacks cutting down the forest, altering the landscape while their own fate changes with it. Then comes the draining of the swamps, the building of roads, bringing further disruptions into the lives of people, disruptions which finally culminate in a catastrophe. Tilius Gelažius keeps dreaming about how he will break out of the vicious circle of circumstances and become somebody special, not just another pebble on the bottom of a river. Although the novel deals with life in independent Lithuania, the inner problems Gelažius faces are very much like those of an exile—how to be someone and yet belong with others to the stream of life, to history. Tilius cannot find a way to do it, and so, without desiring or understanding it, he does what the situation dictates—hires himself out to Doveika as a farm laborer, allows Doveika's beautiful and frustrated young wife to seduce him, abandons his former sweetheart, and in the end lies bleeding on the green grass, shot through by the jealous Doveika.

The structure of this inevitable coming of misfortune is very well controlled by the author. Carefully planning every step, Katiliškis nevertheless manages to convey the illusion of an elemental and irresistible downward movement. The dynamics of the novel consist of a slow, gradual growth of the portents of misfortune, until suddenly the lines along which the characters' passions have been taking them meet in a head-on collision. Some of the protagonists remain blind to their fate to the very end, while others are given the terrible gift of understanding all the signs and changes, like handwriting on the wall, while they themselves remain helpless in the grip of events.

At first the signs are difficult to see. Tilius Gelažius, having just agreed to work for Doveika, has no particular feelings, except a kind of vague awareness that Doveika's wife is a young and beautiful woman. But the very vagueness of this impression has something ominous about it: "Her shape seemed to be contracting, then stretching out again, as if he were seeing her through a poorly made window glass, varying in thickness and producing ugly distortions of objects and people." Thus, the "glass of fate" stands between Tilius and Doveika's wife from the very beginning, quite transparent, as if it were not there at all, but at the same time distorting their faces in the sign of misfortune.

The warnings multiply as the novel develops. Doveika is a light sleeper, and he keeps a loaded rifle handy. As in Chekhov's famous definition of action in a play, one cannot escape the feeling that the gun will go off in the end. Then there is the tender and lyrical love affair between Tilius and a pretty young girl, Agne. As Tilius continues working for Doveika, the spell of Doveika's wife takes hold of him, and he grows colder and colder toward Agne. They once took romantic little walks together through the wooded hills; now, on one such walk, their path ends abruptly in an ugly swamp.

Slowly, the evil premonition seems to spread its wings over the whole countryside. People go on working, changing their surroundings and thus increasing the bleak and threatening shadow over their heads. An old forest ranger, long accustomed to reading the hieroglyphics of nature, is very much opposed to the draining of the swamp and of the lake; he sees signs of misfortune everywhere:

> The old man could tell right now how this devilish business will end. They are going to dredge the river and drain the lake. Where, then, will the rainwater go, where will the melting snow gather in the spring? It's all right, they say. But why do the snakes leave the swamps if it is all right? He saw one the other day, squashed by a passing truck on the road. A black, screeching truck covered him with dirt and dust as he was walking along then. And beyond the patch of shrubbery, where the aspen trees grow and where begins the little swamp lake called the Devil's Eye, he saw snakes, twisting together like strands of rope, crawling down to swim across the river.

Soon the whole novel is full of the serpents of evil premonitions, and gradually the people's hearts are poisoned. It turns out that Doveika's wife had never loved her old and lecherous husband, that she was revolted by him and is now ready to fall into the arms of Tilius. Then the old prophet of doom—the forest ranger—dies, and it is Tilius who digs his grave, all the while feeling how another abyss is opening under his own feet. One day Doveika is making the rounds of his fields and finds a spot of trampled rye and his wife's comb. Suspicions are aroused, but he does not yet know that his wife and Tilius have long been spending the nights together. As the omens multiply, it seems that the whole world begins to fall to pieces. Some envious man sets fire to Doveika's forest, and the acrid smoke hangs in the air for days. Then, finally, the thunder strikes. Doveika finds out what has been going on and shoots Tilius, thus, of course, sealing his own fate.

This gloomy and tragic development is counterbalanced in the novel by the constant awareness that man is an extremely resilient animal, that he usually survives any disturbances caused by him or by some other forces, and that eventually he will live again in harmony with himself and nature. This can be surmised also with respect to the individual destinies of the protagonists. It seems that Tilius is not mortally wounded, that he will eventually recover and might even inherit Doveika's estate, as well as his wife. Agne, the girl he abandons, gradually regains her mental balance and, as the novel ends, seems well on her way to building for herself a fairly tolerable future with another man.

When the artist is in full control of the events he has created, even if they are catastrophic, the end result is always more than a mere depiction of reality. It is reality multiplied by genius, by his ability to find form and movement for his experience. There are times, however, when the outside reality itself becomes too enormous for the artist to bear, when the catastrophe simply grows beyond all measure and inundates both the artist and the world of his imagination. This is what happened in the novel *Išėjusiems negrįžti* (*Trip of No Return*). It is about the total collapse of the familiar Lithuanian world and also about the final agony of Europe during the last months of the Second World War. The author here was not able to plan and arrange the events, which followed their own incomprehensible, chaotic logic. Everything happened so quickly and unexpectedly that there was hardly time for an instinctive reaction to the events. The novel produces the impression of an uncontrolled outburst of overpowering feeling, of a human cry *in extremis*.

Whatever meaning and idea there is, is contained more in individual impressions than in the total structure of the work. An example is the very deep and painfully lyrical sorrow of dispossession. In Katiliškis' early collection of short stories much effort was expended in order to catch and preserve somehow the precise nature of this experience, but the result was sometimes hardly more than emotional rhetoric. Here this feeling emerges pure and iridescent in the intervals of quiet between shell bursts. There are brief moments of such extraordinary silence that we distinctly hear how the human heart is crying. Nor are many words needed, just a simple plea: "Remain with us." "Remain with us," says the mother of the novel's protagonist as he is about to retreat to Germany from the advancing Soviet forces; "God will protect us." "Remain with us," he hears in the whispering leaves on the old castle hill which he had climbed to say good-by to his land. These words echo endlessly throughout the novel, penetrating the noise of the world's agony. At a critical moment, when the Germans want to shoot him as a deserter, the narrator again hears these words deep inside him: "Remain with us." They wander through his mind once more at the border town of Kretinga, when he sees two Franciscan monks calmly raking the leaves in the churchyard—a counterpoint to the rattle of retreating German tanks. Thus these words become the only true answer to all the pangs of conscience, all the inner battles the refugee must fight with himself; they are like a judgment of his actions as he takes up weapons to defend his home and also when he drops them without honor and when he meditates endlessly on the complexities of the given moment in history. There was only one right thing to do—remain in Lithuania and bear whatever fate one must, even unto death.

But the raging fury of the war sometimes pushes these words into the background, and instead of their lyrical refrain comes a bitter, ironic gallows humor, a coarse, cynical outlook on the world's insanity. In the meaningless chaos of war this seems to be the only mental state that can save a man, by covering his soft heart as if with armor. And, indeed, in a certain horrible sense the situation is humorous, at least when looked upon with the eyes of a man who grew up among the quiet forests and fields, whose thoughts and feelings were shaped by a simple country life that had nothing to do with the abstract games of ideologies, principles, "isms" of various kinds. In the name of the "isms" the good earth is being torn apart and masses of people must die, and the fiercer the battle of the two giants of communism and fascism, the clearer becomes the total absurdity of it all. So, in the novel we see how our refugee looks at hanged men with the sober eyes of a farmer, saying to himself that a man must always keep his feet on the ground. And it is both terrible and weirdly funny to read how two incorrigible peasant lads explain on Christmas Eve to an honest German soldier that the candles on his Christmas tree are made from the fat of murdered Jews.

Yet at times the mask of this ghastly laughter falls off and we see what has been hidden behind it—a terrible animal cry of a mortally wounded soul, hopeless and unforgiving, an accusation hurled against God, man, and the earth. There is, for instance, the soldier Jonušas, whose "tongue was possessed by the devil himself, dipped in black burning pitch." Unable to bear his suffering any longer, Jonušas attacks a helpless seminary student who had tried to preserve his innocent faith in the middle of this black hell:

> We have been left here to undergo trial and redemption for someone's imagined sins. If everything comes from His merciful hand and is under His all-seeing Providence, then it seems to me that there is too much suffering and not enough sin. Where is God to millions of soldiers trampled in the mud, where is He to the babes, the young mothers and gray old men buried like manure in the fields? You cannot tell me because you know nothing, because your God is deaf and heartless. He sends us crashing forever into the fires of hell for just a single unredeemed sin. Tell me, is there a drop of justice in this? In a human court a man condemned to die, that is, fulfilling his punishment by his death, has paid for everything and he cannot be hanged a second time. Or if he is sent to prison for twenty years, he comes out of it clean—redeemed. But not here. There is no redeeming of yourself before God; He is waiting for you, having prepared magnificent tortures for millions upon millions of years.

For a single unredeemed sin the Lithuanian people were thrown into the hell of exile. What was the sin? It was simply that they did not listen to what the old mother said, what could be heard in the whispering trees: "Remain with us." They left their country in its tragic hour, and God forsook them in turn. Possibly, even this fury of Jonušas, these terrible, seemingly blasphemous words, amount only to a kind of prayer: "Remain with us, O Lord, for the evening is near, and the day has ended."

We do not find out from Katiliškis' novel whether God returns to man or not. It seems more likely that He does not, because one can see how in his novel man, buffeted by the terrors of war, becomes progressively smaller and pettier, is ground down like a pebble rolling about on the sea bottom through a succession of storms. He turns into his own caricature, becomes little more than an enormous, hungry, walking stomach.

His only deep inner experience is that of fear, of "hundreds of exquisite, marvelously refined variations of fear."

The saddest thing is that there is no tragic dignity in man thus defiled. In the cry of Christ on the cross, "My God, why hast Thou forsaken me!" there was already the promise of the Resurrection. But there is no resurrection for Katiliškis' protagonists in this novel. They are all trampled into mud.

Must we then come to the conclusion that Katiliškis has no faith in either mankind or the universe, that he is an incorrigible pessimist? The point is that any such judgment would be irrelevant, since faith or the lack of it are not the basic issues in his work. The source of his art is the simple existence of both men and things—multifaceted and complete, with blood and tears, blossoms and catastrophes. We have no right first to say, "I believe," and then to select from reality that which will justify our faith. If we do, we will remain liars until we learn to accept the universe in all its fullness. Only after we have consented to reality, as the old man Dryža accepted the black earth into which he must return, can the unimaginable grandeur of all that exists become apparent. The consciousness of infinitude which is then granted us has only one name —faith.

So, this may be the significance of Katiliškis as a writer. He bore witness to the reality of a small country in the midst of enormous events, surrounded by the infinitude of being. He spoke as truthfully as he could and found himself repeating the voice of nature. He did not flinch before the weakness and insignificance of men, and was rewarded by an insight into man's greatness.

13 Jonas Mekas as a Poet

Jonas Mekas was born December 23, 1922, in the village of Semenisškiai, northern Lithuania. He finished high school in 1943. In 1946–48 he studied philosophy and romance languages in the University of Mainz, Germany. During this time, he and a group of young Lithuanian writers (including his brother Adolfas Mekas and Algirdas Landsbergis) published an avant-garde literary magazine called *Žvilgsniai* (*Glances*).

Mekas came to the United States in 1949 and became interested in the art of film-making. Since 1954 he has been publishing the *Film Culture* magazine and, with his brother, producing a number of films, among them *Guns of the Trees*, *Halleluia the Hills*, and *The Brig*. He is known as one of the initiators of the "underground cinema" movement. Since 1958 he has been on the editorial staff of the Greenwich *Village Voice* in New York.

Mekas has written prose as well as verse. His prose works are *Trys broliai* (*Three Brothers*), 1946; *Iš pasakų, krašto* (*From the Land of Fairy Tales*), 1947; and *Knyga apie karalių, ir žmones* (*A Book of King and People*), 1948. In poetry, he has published *Semeniškių, idilės* (*The Idyls of Semeniškiai*), 1948, second edition, 1955; *Gėlių kalbėjimas* (*The Talk of Flowers*), 1961; and *Pavieniai žodžiai* (*Separate Words*), 1967.

THE activities of Jonas Mekas as one of the originators of the so-called underground cinema in New York have achieved a measure of recognition (some might say notoriety) on the American scene. He is known for a number of films in which a wonderful, rebellious spirit of fun combines strangely with a deadly serious and radical challenge to the values of middle-class society. He edits the stubborn and iconoclastic magazine *Film Culture* which battles the Hollywood standard of success in film industry as a mindless and hypocritical refusal to confront the demands of art and of truth in the medium of film. In addition, he has taught the art of cinema in New York, at the New School for Social

Research, and is a regular contributor to the Greenwich *Village Voice*.

It may therefore come as a surprise to learn that Mekas considers himself to be first and foremost a poet in the Lithuanian language and that in his poetry he comes to us as a barefoot peasant, carrying in his hands a conception of truth won from the earth, like a harvest, during long days of hard work and truthful thinking under the burning sun or in the endless rains of autumn. The conservative peasant mentality might seem totally unrelated to the fierce challenge of an avant-garde artist prophesying the impending death of the noisy modern megalopolis. Yet it is the marginal little world of the Lithuanian farmer that Mekas glorifies in humble and loving memory in his book of poems called *Semeniškių idilės* (*The Idyls of Semeniškiai*).

At issue here is the question of what constitutes the radical spirit. In a rural setting a radical could be one who worships the many dynamic splendors of the modern city. Conversely, an urban radical might go, figuratively and literally, back to the roots, to the natural, organic principle of life. Mekas has made a long journey from the village of Semeniškiai to the city of New York, passing through the suffering and tragedy of exile, and he may have decided on the way that most of what we call civilization is merely a superstructure of lies and illusions upon the shoulders of the simple man working the soil. When this superstructure falls, it destroys not only itself but also those who had supported and could have redeemed it. For this reason, when Mekas speaks in his poems of the special magic present in the texture of rural life, in the colors and sounds of summer rain, in the clear, cold silence of winter, in the pain in the worker's muscles, and in the rough and loving surface pine bark presents to the hand of the baby, he is being just as radical as when he throws down the gauntlet to the sophisticated hypocrites of Hollywood. It is the same challenge, for an honest film camera has the same obligation to catch the true pulse of reality, in the way, for instance, that James Agee had. Mekas' radicalism is, in a sense, reminiscent of Leo Tolstoy, and his moral insistence upon truth just as urgent, for he also feels that unless we return to being human, the hour of doom will strike inevitably.

The hero, then, is truth. For a poet like Mekas truth begins on the lowest level of intellectualization, first of all in those details of reality which have not yet been caught up in the verbal patterns of established poetic imagery. Nightingales and roses and even the Shakespearean darling buds of May have now become the prisoners of art, and it is no use turning to them in search of free and genuine perceptions of things as they are. One must raise from the soil a new poetic image of reality, and to the degree that Mekas succeeds in doing so, he is fresh and original and communicates to the reader his own sense of wonder at the rich textures of life.

The point of view adopted by Mekas in *The Idyls of Semeniškiai* is that of a farmer unacquainted with literary tradition but quite familiar with things in his back yard. The poems themselves, however, reflect, as they must, the author's own esthetic sensibilities and verbal skills. The result is a blend of strong, rough reality and fine-textured imagination which is capable of responding to the barely perceptible aura of feeling surrounding even the most ordinary, prosaic things. Therefore, in the second idyl, when springtime comes to that imaginary farmer's homestead, it has a haunting beauty composed of all the odds and ends that clutter up the rural existence:

> And there is fragrance in the yard: young shoots,
> boards drying out against the sun,
> light frost, potatoes from the open cellars,
> and the aroma of the fresh young grass.

We see these things in terms of their fresh smell as the earth is thawing out in the spring, and it is this fragrance which lends reality to the poet's longing, enabling him to recapture the past. There are many wonderful smells in the *Idyls*: the earth smells of clay and of "fish and stony fords," of pine sap, fresh milk, and of manure. The air on summer nights is full of honey and clover, and late in the evening there is the special fragrant warmth of firewood in the sauna bath.

To a considerable extent, though not entirely, Mekas is a poet of the five senses, and a good deal of his poetic magic is due to the use of sense impressions in much the same manner as someone else might use symbolic concepts or metaphors to convey a poetic feeling or conviction. If we should think of music, for instance, as a system of auditory symbols transmitting an emotional truth, then the sounds of country life in Mekas' poems acquire something of the same quality because they are described not merely to create an illusion of reality but also to speak of the author's love. The scraping noise of sod cut by a plow in the spring or the rattle of wagon wheels among the stone-hard ruts in the winter are sounds connected with meaningful peasant labor and therefore are beautiful and artistically true. Similarly, the soft tapping of a knife handle against the bark of a young sapling as a shepherd boy prepares to make a little whistle for himself is already a part of the music he will play, because it participates in the creation of beauty.

Reality in the poems of Mekas is not only heard and smelled but also touched. Its texture feels "like the coarse bark of a pine tree touched by the soft hand of a baby" or like abrasive chaff at threshing time, carried by "women, their hair over their eyes, their arms cut and bruised by the straw." This life is like stiff and scratchy homemade cloth, like the rough black bread of the peasant. It reaches through to the people in Semeniškiai, it wounds them, bruises them, it grows into their souls like the powerful roots of oak trees.

The rugged surface of reality, interwoven with the soft human presence, creates the image of an existence which, although lyrical and touching, allows no sentimentality. *The Idyls of Semeniškiai* have little in common with the bucolic miniatures of pastoral verse. They show instead a hard country landscape, whose beauty is an expression of the courage and patience of the people who live in it. It takes not only sensitivity and talent but also moral commitment to their way of life to make this beauty visible. Mekas paints this landscape in accordance with the change of seasons and the different farming occupations that accompany them. His winter pictures are sometimes reminiscent of Brueghel in their clean and rugged harmony:

> And the silence, so resonant, so cold the silence—
> Over the fishermen's holes in the ice and over the fields,
> and over the villages sunk in the snow,
> so cold the silence, so biting cold—
> and only straight up, rising high,

just a blue twisting ribbon,
the smoke climbs skyward from the chimneys.

In the autumn, Mekas' landscapes may be torn by the restless winds:

The willows weaving, wailing in the wind,
Buckling and straightening up in the gusts,
heads disheveled, tangled together.
And if with a powerful sweep the raging wind
should bare the baldheaded tops of trees for a moment,
one would see how their bark is so coarse and so gray.

Or they may come dejectedly to a stop, as if time itself were to get mired in the autumn mud:

And over the fields and shrubs, on the women spreading manure,
mud-splattered, with wide peasant scarves—over the plowlands
evenly, softly falls the cold autumn rain—
all day, all night, all night, all day.

At times the landscape of Semeniškiai seems to be put together not by the author himself but by the people born of his imagination. Mekas sketches them out in rough outline, breathes life into them, and they start walking across the countryside, piecing the landscape together as they go:

They pass the black and muddy marshes,
dark groves of black willows, yew trees,
through red saplings, flowering bushes—
a chatty, multicolored bunch of peasant scarves.
And when they wade across the last few swampy patches,
ditches clogged with mud and covered up,
it opens suddenly: green fields as far as eye can see,
they reach far out, to gray, moss-covered roofs,
to settlements, to rising tops of birches,
gray crossbeams of the water wells,
to the very edge of poor and patchy woods,
as far as clearings, trampled upon by cows and horses—
the fields of oats and peas come running

and endless blue of flax—a blinding blue,
so blue.

It is not so much a landscape as an emotion—a blue yearning which draws the poet not upward to the skies but down, closer to the earth. It is quite a different yearning than was once expressed by Bernardas Brazdžionis in his poem "Life's Nostalgia," in which he prays to the Lord to carry him away from this earth. And no wonder—Brazdžionis' earth is not real; it looks much more like a stage setting where the universe is represented by poetic symbols of reality:

And if You are a brook that flows through valleys and through mountains
And carries little boats, the down of swans, and pine needles; little boats–
We will be boats and will be feathers of white swans, and fishes—oh, we shall no more be people,
But only take us, Lord, and carry us away.

The brooks in Mekas' poems are quite different, and they carry other things:

You bring along the washerwomen's songs,
the nets of fishermen, gray wooden bridges,
and blue, warm-breathing nights,
when fog comes floating in light garlands from the meadows
and one can hear the shackled horses' steps.

Mekas does not just take one or two striking features of reality—an evening sky, for instance, or a flower—in order to build a poem by the process of expanding and interrelating the emotional values in them until they become no more than component parts of a new and complex poetic whole. His poetry deals with the sum total of all the facts of life, re-created and imbued with magic in memory. He calls forth countless details, pieces of the mosaic that was the life of Semeniškiai in days now gone, and holds them in his hands until they acquire the warm glow of his own emotion. When he replaces them, the remembered landscape is changed into a special poetic universe, no longer subject to the destructive hand of time. In a sense, this is the poetry of exile par excellence, which comes into being when the dispossessed "summon up remembrance of things past" to their own sessions of sweet and bitter thought. In another sense, such poetry contains something of the plain honesty of ordinary prose, because Mekas does not select only those aspects of reality which possess traditional poetic associations but speaks instead of everything that is true. Thus we get the picture of a hard and rugged peasant life represented in a series of plain facts, without embellishment. There are the wagons with "axle-trees that roll and splash across the muddy, torn potato patches" and the hired hand Martynas who collects milk cans and drives off to the dairy with an unholy rattle. The women "waddle" as they spread manure in the fields, they "crawl about" harvesting potatoes and sugar beets. The men "gawk" at the women weaving at the looms, and there is a dirty, muddy rain coming down the sides of the cows. Mekas' people cross his landscape of loving memory looking very real and dirty and worn out by their endless tasks:

> on narrow road, packed hard by wagons and by cattle,
> they squeak and sway, the cartloads of manure,
> lean over slowly as the horses pick their steps—
> and, wrapped so anxiously in peasant tweeds,
> his face bent down,
> as though his every step were whole eternity,
> like fate itself, the farmer walks along.

What prevents these poems from becoming a kind of versified farmers' almanac is the presence of love, of lyrical emotion that follows every configuration of the reality depicted, adding a touch of magic to the ordinariness of things. In the first idyl, "Old is the Hush of Rain" (translated here by Clark Mills), the word "old" transports reality to the poetic plane, informing it with the connotations of beauty and eternity, of humble devotion to the timeless mystery of generations that rise up from the soil and return to it, until this particular spot of land becomes a living continuum of earth and flesh and soul:

> Old is the hush of rain over the branches
> of underbrush; and the hoarse cries of the black cocks
> are old in the red summer dawn
> —old, this our speech:

of yellow fields of oats and barley,
of shepherds' campfires in the blown wet loneliness of autumn,
of the potato harvests, of the summer heats,
of winter's white glint, creak and hiss of sleighs
—of wagons log-laden, of stones in fallow fields,
of red brick stoves, of gypsum in the pastures
—and then at lamplit evening, as the autumnal fields go gray,
of wagons for tomorrow's market,
of drowned October highways washed away
—days of the potato harvest.

Old, this our life—interminable generations
that walked over the fields
and tracked their steps over the black earth
—each foot of land still speaks and breathes the fathers.
For from these cool stone wells
they watered their evening herds,
and when the clay floors of their cottages wore out
and the walls crumbled slowly,
from these fields they dug up the yellow sand,
from these pits, yellow clay.
And when we too depart,
others will rest on the same boundary stones,
scythe down the same lush meadows, plow these fields.
And as they sit beside the tables, after work,
each table, each clay pitcher, each beam in the wall
will speak. They will remember
wide gravel pits of yellow sand,
and in wind-ruffled fields of rye
the voices of our women singing from the flaxen edges
—and this first scent in a new cottage:
fresh fragrance of moss!

Old is the smell of the clover,
the horses whinnying in the summer nights,
the chirp and chime of harrows, rollers, plows,
grindstones of the mills,
the green smells from the meadow, steeping flax,
white gleam of kerchief of the weeders in the gardens.

> Old is the hush of rain over the branches
> of underbrush; and the hoarse cries of the black cocks
> are old in the red summer dawn
> —old, this our speech.

In this way reality is transformed; things, without ceasing to be themselves, become something else as well. Another factor contributing to this transformation is the dynamics of style, imparting movement and surge even to the description of colors or stationary objects. Images that would ordinarily seem static in a landscape seen from a distance, such as the first leaves of spring, are caught as they are changing to a new shade of green or as they move across the bare branches left by winter. The leaves thus "flash through the underbrush, across the pink young woods." The first winter frost is not simply there; it "gathers up the last and frozen rowanberries and cleans out the garden patch." At other times the movement is full of muscular energy and drama, like the violent spring rains coming down with a gorgeous fury:

> in large and splashy raindrops
> descending on the yard, on cowshed roof,
> howling in the wayside linden trees
> and pouring down the blossoms of the hops through garden foliage,
> in big and heavy drops
> crashing through the tops of orchards, vegetable fields,
> and slamming into falling fields of rye,
> hacking at the pea shoots, flogging
> the muddy wagon in the middle of the yard—
> and moving off, so full of wind and sudden surge,
> in misty spray across the treetops and the shrubs,
> in roaring sweep above the branches of the willows.

Then there is a slow and gentle movement, almost sensual in its sinuous flow:

> Oh, and then this water through the deeply shaded reeds,
> how you can feel it flow, how through the fingers,
> how it sweeps on and rolls, the cool blue stream.

The syntactic structure and word repetitions contribute a great deal to the retardation of movement. Fairly often Mekas slows down his language by delaying the verbs until the end of sentences or clauses—an unorthodox procedure in the Lithuanian syntax. This effect is especially striking in the example quoted earlier: ". . . wrapped so anxiously in peasant tweeds, / his face bent down, / as though his every step were whole eternity, / like fate itself, the farmer walks along." The following closing stanza of the eighteenth idyl, consisting of a single sentence, shows a similar structure:

> And in the misty open fields of autumn,
> their heads so sadly turned against the rain,
> with tufted hair and mucous eyelids,
> mired in the rain-swelled soil of pastures,
> against the wind, so slowly move the cattle.

Such language enhances meditation, invites the reader to check his own flight through life for a moment, allows for time in which to develop a poetic awareness of reality. There is also time to establish a living bond among the reader, the poet, and the peasant life passing before their eyes. This, in fact, is one of the main purposes of poetry, one of the shapes of immortality in art, because it makes an artistic experience of one time and place forever relevant to the flow of life in the future.

Mekas' concern with establishing an artistic dimension of experience which could be shared with the reader follows logically from the mainspring of his creative inspiration. However vivid and compelling is the re-created reality of woods and fields and rivers, what matters most of all in *The Idyls of Semeniškiai* is the people; the book is dedicated to them, to the farmers and to his childhood friends. This is made clear in the opening stanzas, in which the poet says that if he cries:

> it's not for you, horizons, and not you, the fields,
> my bosom friends—
> it's only for the playmates of my youth,
> and for my childhood,
> retreating in the distance irrevocably.

Mekas reiterated this point in 1957 in his acceptance speech on the occasion of receiving the Vincas Krėvė prize for the book:

> And I, the smallest one among them, bow my head before them, before the village of Semeniškiai. At least in words, with this simple little book of mine, I wish to remember them, to honor them, so that I would never forget them anymore. Because they are like saints to me.

But what sort of people do we see in *The Idyls of Semeniškiai*? For one thing, they have names: Aunt Kastūnė, Aunt Marija, the young bride Marcelė, the old man Ignotas combing the flax, Jokūbas with the new bike, and so on. Their names, however, do not separate them out as individuals. Under a different name, in another village without an exiled poet of its own, there would also be a Kazimieras wandering around "drunken, through the night," singing among the shrubbery, and an Aunt Kastūnė would still come over "from beyond the glade, to help with raking or with the stacking of rye." The poet's childhood friend, the "blond Emilija," could be running along the sandy paths of other hamlets, with books under her arm. These people are not really just the neighbors of Mekas; they are the neighbors of every Lithuanian farmer, perhaps of every man on earth. More important than the memory of particular people is the memory of man. Mekas proclaims his loyalty not so much to the peasants he knew as to the image of the farmer, the tiller of the soil—a noble presence on earth, a dream, in fact, that may have never lived. Consequently, in spite of his earthy realism, Mekas is actually an idealist and a romantic. His is a poetry of facts, written by a man of vision and of faith. It is on this level that he communicates with his readers, because we can only have faith in one who is himself a believer.

The second book of Mekas' verse, *Gėlių kalbėjimas* (*The Talk of Flowers*), is in many ways a very different book, but there is an essential continuity of spirit with *The Idyls of Semeniškiai*. A good many of the changes are superficial. The form is much simpler, and the sentences do not strain and twist like trees in the autumn rain, nor do they stretch out interminably across the native plains; instead they are brief, gentle, and fragile like the petals of a flower. There are changes in the content as well. One hears other songs—first of all, those of love:

> Let my heart,
> like words,

sing your hands,
and face,
your eyes—
your painful beauty.

The love theme is connected with the poet's interest in his own self, with personal experiences timidly, modestly veiled in presentation. The poet is, for instance, grateful for friendship, for faith in him expressed at a time when he was subjected to humiliation:

She spoke like this:
They slander you,
but I defend you
in the memory
of old friendship.

And for this reason,
heart full of song,
he walked along
talking to the night,
the rain and the wind.

Mekas now comes much closer to the people he writes about. Unlike *The Idyls of Semeniškiai*, the people here are nameless, but their presence in the flesh is felt much stronger. There is a sculptor-like interest in the geometry of the human body, within the framework of natural forms in the abstract:

The lines of the neck,
the curve of the shoulders,
are like the wheel—
the same harmony.

If Mekas tried earlier to raise a poetic reality from the soil, now he seems to be creating one in his hands, and it is a plastic and specifically human reality:

My hands touched,
like two amber pieces
turned on a lathe,
your wrists.

Another difference between the two collections is that in *The Talk of Flowers* Mekas does not reconstruct a remote and bygone world in memory but lives instead in the immediacy of the present. The book in this sense is more concrete, and yet it is also more abstract because the present is not in any particular place. Rather, it is reality in general, the basic, elemental components of it—not the earth of Semeniškiai but the experience of touching the living soil, not the rain that falls on peasant cottages but water as an element, a constant, real, and symbolic presence in the poet's consciousness. There is a great thirst for this immediacy in the book, and it is often conveyed through the imagery of water. We encounter repeatedly the metaphor of drinking, of open lips. The poet would "drink your memory like wine" if the flowers were "like lips"; he "drinks thirstily your eyes and words," as the poplars drink "rain and wind with silver lips." He tastes the earth "like wine" and sees every leaf as a "deep chalice," "filled with aroma and colors by the sun."

Water thus becomes a symbolic medium which unifies the present in *The Talk of Flowers* with the past in *The Idyls of Semeniškiai*, in which water also represented the primeval lifeblood of the earth, and with the even more remote ancestral mythology so closely bound up with water images in the ancient folk songs of Lithuania. Mekas' understanding of the universe is therefore not divisive but unifying; there is no alienation between water, flowers, and earth on the one hand and the human consciousness on the other. The poet is, as he says, "wounded again and again by the touch of things." He has a strong yearning for the concrete manifestations of life, a desire to recognize himself in the being of things, to restore the often forgotten ties between imagination and the reality from which it grows. The whole relationship of various aspects of being —among objects, body, and soul—is defined by the constant process of disruption and renewal of mutual ties. Everything is, as Mekas puts it, "only the connections; / only the connections, / and the separations." And the task of the poet is to bind, to unite.

This is why the new theme of erotic love does not signify a fundamental change in the poet's world view but an organic restitution of unity between nature and man. Open lips, open earth, open flower—all are one and the same thing:

Don't we open
so often
again for the first time,
water, earth, bread,
voice, hands and the whiteness
of body,
like an aroma?

Don't we need
to open
the eyes and lips of earth,
like a woman?

In this way Mekas resolves the issue of spiritual exile. Semeniškiai is now far away; it has certainly undergone irreversible changes, and the special world to which the poems were dedicated no longer exists. What remains is just the soil and the instinctive feeling of being of it and belonging with it to an endless continuum of life. This continuum is in essence spiritual, that is, understood and realized in thought and feeling, and as such it extends to any land the exile may visit, any reality he may touch, any flowers he may see. The poetry of Mekas is what art should always be—the conquest of man's alienation.

14 The Small People of Aloyzas Baronas and Their Great Questions

Aloyzas Baronas was born December 12, 1917, in Biržai, northern Lithuania. In the years 1941 to 1942 he studied technology in the University of Kaunas, then switched to literature and philosophy, first in Kaunas and later in the University of Frankfort, Germany, from 1946 until he came to the United States in 1949. After working at a variety of jobs in the States, he joined the staff of the Lithuanian-language newspaper *Draugas* (*Friend*) in 1955, where he remains to the present.

Baronas has written a large number of novels, short stories, satirical poems, and children's stories. Some of the titles are *Žvaigždės ir vėjai* (*Stars and Winds*), 1951; *Debesys plaukia pažemiu* (*Clouds Travel Low*), 1951; *Užgesęs sniegas* (*The Extinguished Snow*), 1953; *Sodas už horizonto* (*Garden Beyond the Horizon*), 1955; *Mėnesiena* (*Moonlight*), 1957; *Vienišі medžiai* (*The Lonely Trees*), 1960; and *Footbridges and Abysses*, 1961, published in English translation, 1965. The short story "Homecoming" was published in English in *Selected Lithuanian Short Stories* (Voyages Press, 1959), and "Dead End Street," "The Sixth Generation," and "Relay Race" in *Lithuanian Quartet* (Manyland Books, 1962). Baronas has translated works of Alberto Moravia, Carl Sandburg, Pearl Buck, William Inge, Samuel Joseph Agnon, and others, into Lithuanian.

IN the world there are people capable of both prophecy and martyrdom, but the heroes in the many novels and short stories of Aloyzas Baronas can achieve neither one nor the other, although they do speak constantly about the great issues of life and are themselves often subjected to a good deal of suffering. Their souls are simply not commensurate with the magnitude of mystery; the world for them is nothing but a puzzle, an "equation with a thousand unknowns," as one of Baronas' heroes puts it. They meander along the byways of life making vague philosophical remarks and dispensing advice the value of which they cannot honestly tell.

These people are not necessarily weak in spirit or intellectually inadequate to the challenge of living. Their predicament stems from the author's own desire to use his characters as illustrations of the hopeless confusion of man when he attempts to redefine the values of life without listening to the clear and ever-present voice of God. What happens is that man gets bogged down in words and concepts having no valid points of reference and that he must then carry his life "like a hundred-weight of unsolved crossword puzzles" in which the simple truths of natural instinct and of conscience never seem to fit the blank spaces intricately arranged in terms of abstract categories and intellectual propositions.

Sometimes the range of the issues seems fairly narrow, affecting only the personal lives of rather limited people. Even so, their problems can cause devastation if a person attempts to solve them according to some abstract notions floating in the air instead of deciding upon a course of action dictated by the inner sense of reality. In a collection of short stories called *Žvaigždės ir vėjai* (*Stars and Winds*), there is a sad tale of a young girl whose life was poisoned because of her readiness to condemn herself for not being beautiful. A boy falls in love with her, but she refuses to believe him since he is tall and handsome and therefore, according to her lights, could not possibly fall in love with a girl as ugly as she. Thus she misses the one chance of happiness in her life by surrendering to the tyranny of concepts—beauty, ugliness, the ability or inability to love—instead of responding directly to the situation and returning the affection offered her.

At other times the problems created by large-scale events become greater than any given individual's capacity to resolve them. The hero then loses himself in moral and philosophical contradictions not through any personal failure but because he has become a victim of history. In the collection *Debesys plaukia pažemiu* (*Clouds Travel Low*) there is a story about a Lithuanian army officer, Petrulis, whose life is threatened by the first Soviet occupation. The new power, determined to destroy the former officer class, is conducting mass arrests and executions, and Lieutenant Petrulis is seized among a number of others. While in prison he begins to understand his dilemma. Always a peaceful man, he had earnestly tried to live according to the precepts of his Christian religion. He would have liked to have gone on loving people, trying not to cloud their lives with the shadow of his own, but now this has become impossible. He must escape from prison, because to make no attempt to save himself is equivalent to suicide—a mortal sin in the eyes of God. Yet, when he does escape, the man who guarded him is shot for neglect of duty. Thus, in not allowing himself to be killed he has caused the death of another. Furthermore, the time comes for him to become directly involved in killing. After his recapture he feels he must make another try for freedom, and this time, in order to escape, he is forced to kill a guard with a knife. As he thrusts the blade home, his own heart is pierced by the agony of knowing that, in merely trying to stay alive, he has broken two sacred commandments: "thou shalt not kill" and "love your enemies." Thus any course of action Petrulis would take leads him to murder, either of himself or of others. Is it therefore impossible to obey God, and if so, how can there be salvation? Obviously, the dilemma cannot be resolved without the co-operation of the rest of mankind. Only if all of us renounce violence can the moral confusion of a single honest individual be resolved.

It may seem strange that such moral agonizing comes from a professional soldier who, after all, gave his consent to killing when he put on his uniform. He had already accepted implicitly the purely human notion, not proclaimed anywhere by Christ, that there are circumstances in which killing is neither crime nor sin. Baronas, however, makes no issue of this discrepancy between the inherent qualities of his hero's chosen profession and his problems, which might seem more plausible in the mind of an entirely different type of man. The complexities of Baronas' work are usually of the intellectual, rather than psychological, order, and for this reason he often feels free to treat his people not so much as individuals with certain inescapable qualities but more as extensions of his own arguments. Sometimes the gap in plausibility between a chosen character and his ideas is deliberately created to demonstrate that man in general is basically so irrational and so full of contradictions that only a paradoxical description of his behavior can approach a truthful portrayal. "Every man is *x* and *y* and the devil only knows what else," says one of Baronas' heroes.

In this light, the greatest paradox of all is man's persistence in being "logical," that is, in going against his own nature by constructing abstract propositions in the name of which he sheds real blood. Logical handling of concepts leads to complete mental and emotional confusion, because these concepts often lose relevance to reality to the degree that they become clear and compelling as structures of thought. Civilization has been built on such systems of ideas, with the result that people are now slaughtering one another in gigantic wars, with the help of precise and logical machinery and organization. Their greatest ingenuity is expended in doing a senseless and terrible thing. When the wars are over, people continue to argue among their ruins over their rights and wrongs, long after their own deeds have rendered every argument pointless and nonsensical. With an ironist's eye, Baronas perceives the idiocy of this human situation in a detail from a shattered city:

> One of the balconies was held up by two sculptures the strained faces of which were so skillfully carved that it seemed they had not been supporting a mere balcony but at least several floors. Now there were only a few bricks left on their bent backs, but the faces remained distorted by the pain of an unbearable, unending burden.

Baronas goes on describing this "civilized man's burden" in several books of short stories, always choosing limited situations in which people are made to discover the emptiness of previously held beliefs or the chaotic depths of soul which must support seemingly clear and precise patterns of ideas. As man's emotions are stirred, the structure of ideas collapses, and he is left with nothing but confusion. Some of the stories are written with subtlety and grace, resembling a beautifully made urn filled with ashes of the world's conflagration. Others seem more like exercises in the paradoxical manner of writing. Yet, as we read them, something of value begins to emerge—the growing conviction that man must liberate himself from the tyranny of abstract notions even if in doing so he at times might seem to be debasing himself. A story called "Coward," from *Stars and Winds*, illustrates this principle. In a violent and nonsensical situation, the only man of true courage is one who does not hesitate to admit to himself and to others that he is afraid, who discards the accepted notion of valor, preferring to save his life instead of "saving face." He possesses the moral daring needed in order to assert the moral truth that in dehumanizing circumstances it is false and cruel to keep up a pretense of dignity. In another story, "The Bum," we see a man who cheerfully gives up all his meager possessions, almost literally to the four winds, because he is living in a time when everything is constantly and ruthlessly being destroyed anyway. Finally he gives away even his own life to the demons of war and dies happily by the roadside, empty-handed and pure as a new-born babe. In "The Betrayal," a man whose life was saved by a Bolshevik agent during the first Soviet occupation meets this agent again, working undercover in a displaced persons camp in Germany after the war. In a bold and profoundly ethical act of faith in humanity, this man decides not to betray the agent to the authorities, giving him a chance to escape. Thus he establishes the principle that human loyalty is higher than the loyalty to an idea or even to such a sacred concept as "fatherland." There does exist, in other words, something which is truly above and beyond the call of duty as it is ordinarily understood in the abstract systems of values. This opens at least a possibility of understanding the meaning of life among human beings.

In his novels Baronas continues his appraisals of the value systems men live by. He subjects his heroes' dearly held beliefs and unquestioned assumptions to the stresses and strains of reality, which, in the period Baronas mostly writes about, the Second World War, was certainly full of catastrophic and violent distortions of the accepted patterns of life. Most frequently he chooses a group of people who had established among themselves a relationship filled with conflict and tension in the days just preceding the war or just before the mass exile of Lithuanians in 1944, and then follows through their fates in the radically changed circumstances which follow.

This relationship usually consists of a love triangle, as in the novel *Užgesęs sniegas* (*The Extinguished Snow*). In a little village on the Lithuanian-Polish border, two farmers, already placed in opposition to each other by their conflicting ethnic loyalties, fall in love with the same girl. One of the men, Kaminskas, who considers himself to be a Pole, is losing to his rival, Vosylius, a Lithuanian, in their struggle for the affections of Gražina, a girl born into a family which does not know itself what nationality it belongs to. The time is full of tension; the German occupiers are about to be driven out by the Soviet forces, and the countryside is full of Nazi troops scavenging for both material goods and people to take with them to bolster their crumbling war machine. Vosylius is caught and taken away to work in a small lumberyard in Germany. This leaves Kaminskas with a clear field to complete his conquest of Gražina's heart. Gražina herself has begun to waver in her loyalty to Vosylius for the simple reason that he, although her fiancé, is absent and there is no assurance of his return, whereas Kaminskas, who merely seems a tolerable fellow to her, is present and insistently presses his affections upon her. Vosylius, in his turn, is on the verge of betraying his beloved, because in Germany he has met a beautiful girl, Gerda, the daughter of the man he was made to work for. His dilemma is twofold; on the one hand there is the inner struggle of his heart between his old attachment to Gražina and the new infatuation with Gerda, and on the other hand is the torturous problem of whether or not he should fight his German master in some way. The German is Gerda's father and also Vosylius' political enemy and oppressor. The efforts of another slave laborer to escape force Vosylius' hand, for he cannot avoid helping him and thus putting himself in a situation that makes his own escape mandatory. Vosylius returns to his village and disrupts Gražina's life again, reintroducing himself as the third member of their triangle.

At this point the author, playing God with his characters in a time lacking all certainty, has both men caught by the Germans and transported to work in a factory deep inside Germany. Kaminskas and Vosylius have now both become losers in their rivalry; they are alone in a strange land, without Gražina. The tension between them remains, however, and finds other forms of expression related to the issue of sabotaging the German war effort. Vosylius is in an especially dangerous position, because if the Nazis find out that he escaped from them earlier, he will undoubtedly be executed. Yet he feels he must do something to give some meaning to his moral conviction that one should fight the Nazis, even though his reason tells him that any act of sabotage he could commit will not make much difference in the outcome of the war, since by this time the Germans were obviously beaten. After some inconclusive moral argument with himself concerning his duty, its futility, and the wisdom of safeguarding his own life, he nevertheless decides to try to set the factory on fire. His attempt does not succeed, and the Nazis line up the workers demanding that they tell who the would-be arsonist is; if they do not, then every seventh man will be taken out and shot. Kaminskas, who sees that he is standing seventh in line, tells himself that he must betray Vosylius in order to save his own life and also, of course, to get rid of his rival, since he still hopes to return to Gražina after the war. He is incapable of considering the immorality of betrayal and the need for sacrifice, because he has always weighed his values in purely personal terms. A chance mix-up in the counting process saves him from either death or betrayal, and both men survive.

After the war the two men find themselves facing their old problems, with a new factor added—the reluctance and fear of returning to Soviet-occupied territory. Then Gerda appears again, this time with her German fiancé, Linz, who turns out to have been one of the guards at the factory where Kaminskas and Vosylius worked during the war. Kaminskas sees a solution; he will betray Linz to the American authorities as a Nazi murderer. This will leave Vosylius and Gerda together again, while he goes back to his native village and Gražina. He carries out his plan but it does not help him much, because, in the post-war confusion, the Americans do not know whose accusations to believe or disbelieve and they release Linz shortly afterwards. The German then wounds Kaminskas in the back, keeping him from leaving for Lithuania.

While this is going on, Vosylius, burdened with a cast of mind which makes him see problems everywhere, has found a new moral issue to agonize over. Gerda still attracts him, but the longing for his lost country envelops his memory of Gražina with a nobility and beauty that stabs his troubled conscience. On the moral-philosophical plane, there is the question of justice. Should he join the former slaves who are now hunting and killing and robbing their old Nazi masters, even though, with the war over, such deeds are no longer called heroic but criminal? The difference made by law seems artificial to him, but something in his heart tells him there is a valid distinction, after all. Still doubting, he allows himself to be drawn into one such "revenge expedition" and as a result is caught and put in jail. His only chance of release is to return to Soviet Lithuania voluntarily, which he does at about the same time as Kaminskas, who in the meantime has recovered from his wound.

The events have now turned full circle. Both men are again in their native village, competing for Gražina as before, and all the experiences of the war, with all the problems, tragedies, and moral crucibles, somehow seem to have become irrelevant. The book ends with a sort of Pyrrhic victory for Kaminskas. He betrays Vosylius to the Soviets for maintaining secret ties with anti-Communist guerrillas, but he himself now cannot have Gražina, because, in moral revulsion, she turns away from him. We see how Kaminskas at every critical point in his life turns traitor in order to further the achievement of his one desire, Gražina, while Vosylius procrastinates in moral agony, always searching for a way to remain an honest man in a dishonest world. Kaminskas would therefore seem to be the villain of the piece. Yet, after all is said and done, he only wants to live and be loved, pretty much like everyone else. His mistake is in making plans, drawing up schemes to turn the flow of events in his favor. When all values become uncertain and the human response to reality unpredictable, his scheming never works out the way he wants it to, but only increases the chaos and destruction in peoples' lives.

The structural patterns of the novel thus consist of two levels of conflict, neither of which is resolved in a way that would remove the intellectual and moral ambiguities surrounding them. The issues revolve around the struggle and revenge against the enemy and around the morally permissible means of seeking happiness. The conclusion, insofar as there is one, is that, apparently, not all is fair in love and war. This is hardly a great discovery, but the people in the novel never pretend to be seekers of profound truths. "What else does a man need," says Vosylius at the end, when he is being driven to Siberia, "except to live?"

The next novel, *Sodas už horizonto* (*Garden Beyond the Horizon*), again presents two levels of conflict. One deals with romantic love, and the other with the meaning of life in general. The setting is now in peace-time Lithuania, and the philosophical quest and personal aims of the characters are not subjected to the tremendous crucible of war. There is also a love triangle, consisting of Vaičiulionis, a student who, like Kaminskas in *The Extinguished Snow*, does not try to order his life according to any particular moral principles, and his rival, Valinis, a carpenter. Valinis, in his turn, resembles Vosylius in that he tends to worry about truth and conscience as life flows by him. He has a rather muddled sense of yearning for a better station in life and thus also for a higher set of values. The two men compete for Janė, a pretty and rather foolish provincial maiden.

The basic movement of plot is also in some ways similar to that in *The Extinguished Snow*, although the circumstances are entirely different. People again start out from a small provincial place and move to completely new surroundings which upset their former ideas about the things they want from life. Valinis, who seems to be winning in the competition for Janė, leaves her in the little town and goes to the capital city to work at his trade and at the same time to try to graduate from high school. This leaves Vaičiulionis free to seduce Janė, which he proceeds to do. Then he calmly returns to the university, no longer interested in the girl. Janė, however, blandly assumes that seduction means commitment by Vaičiulionis to marry her. Since such a marriage would take her out of the province and into the glittering city, she does not ask herself any moral questions, convinced that whatever gives her a chance of future happiness is obviously good.

In the meantime Valinis meets another girl, Galina, from a rich family, and is distracted by her charms from his purpose of learning. His problems constitute a fairly good reflection of his own personality. Not truly interested in knowledge, he wants to have its rewards, that is, a higher social standing; not capable of any deep love, he dreams of the sophisticated and pretty Galina or perhaps more of entering the privileged world in which she lives. Hard work is too difficult for him without any faith in knowledge; therefore he allows himself to be convinced by Bareika, a cynical and vacuous fellow carpenter, of the futility of all human desire for achievement. Yet he does need at least admittance to Galina's social circle, which a higher education would secure, and therefore he compromises with his own conscience by attempting to buy a high school diploma—the passport to the university. This "shortcut to happiness" does not take him anywhere; he merely gets cheated by the sharks selling counterfeit diplomas in the student underground.

Vaičiulionis also meets with misfortune. Janė follows him into the city with her expectations of marriage, a thing very far from Vaičiulionis' mind. When he finally succeeds in explaining to Janė that, for him, she is nothing but a chance conquest, the girl reacts with the surprising directness of all simple minds. She takes a steak knife from the table and stabs Vaičiulionis in the stomach.

Both heroes recover eventually, but only Valinis seems to have learned anything at all from his experience, for he does decide to work honestly and earn his diploma. This is about as far as the moral lesson of the novel goes; as in the preceding book, it somehow does not seem to matter very much in the end. Baronas, apparently, tries no more than to hold a mirror up to nature—in this case, to a rather uninteresting slice of life among the aspiring bourgeoisie of a small country. As a writer, Baronas is true to life, but his heroes, who are not exaggerated, not distorted, but also not illuminated by the force of personal passion, even if it were prejudice or naïveté, do not have very much reality.

In the novel *Mėnesiena* (*The Moonlight*) we return once more to a war setting and to a love triangle which begins in Lithuania and develops, or rather falls apart, in post-war Germany. A new structural device is provided by the introduction of a metaphorical framework which tends, in a sense, to define the quality of the heroes' lives. The framework is a soccer game; the rivals in love, Abraitis and Untulis, are players on opposing soccer teams. As the novel opens, they are in the midst of a hotly contested game; as the action of the plot proceeds, the game is continued on a figurative plane. Such an approach tends to make everything that happens curiously pointless, for as we read all about the tragic and dramatic experiences of the characters, it is difficult to get rid of the persistent feeling that they are merely kicking a soccer ball around. Yet the events are serious enough, and they cause considerable anguish and suffering to the people caught up in them. Untulis is a tall, handsome fellow, interested in only two things—winning as many soccer games and seducing as many girls as possible. Lilija, his current flame, is a person capable of only serious emotional commitments, and therefore she is particularly crushed when Untulis leaves her in search of new conquests. Abraitis, on the other hand, is earnestly in love with Lilija and seduces her only in an overflow of tender emotion, with every intention of marrying her. This does not happen, however, because the second wave of the red flood, in 1944, picks these people up and throws them into far corners of Germany. Abraitis wants Lilija to go with him, but her parents will not let their daughter be separated from them. At this point no one, including Lilija, knows that she has already become pregnant by Abraitis. This fact comes out only a few weeks later, when she and Abraitis are already separated. Thus begins her personal tragedy; fiercely sheltered from temptation by her parents, she has nevertheless been loved and seduced by two men, neither of whom is with her when she needs them in her shame.

The fate of Abraitis is different. Forced into exile without Lilija, he seeks consolation in his loneliness with Irena, a girl not distinguished by any great beauty, but modest, devoted, and charming in her own way. They travel together through Austria and Germany and finally marry in a little chapel high up in the mountains. When the war ends, Abraitis and Irena descend to the ruins of Germany and meet other Lithuanian refugees, among them Abraitis' old love, Lilija. To his dismay, Abraitis discovers that he is the father of her child. In this way Baronas again impales his characters on the horns of a dilemma. Abraitis must decide which are the ties that bind—those he imposed upon himself when he married Irena or the natural bonds between father and son. Inclined to feel that fatherhood is the more important duty because it involves the future of his innocent child, he wants to divorce Irena, but the Church, in the person of a gentle and tired old monk, explains to him that marriage is a sacrament and to break it would mean committing a new mortal sin in order to expiate the old sin of adultery. Lilija refuses to break up Abraitis' family, while Irena sees a way out for everybody through her own death. Her attempt at suicide does not succeed, however, and the novel ends in a moral and intellectual limbo. The final paragraph in it is a kind of author's epilogue which permits the surmise that, for him, such limbo signifies the condition of man in general or at least of man as an exile:

> Even now, after ten years, if you should meet a man with gray temples, still in his prime, walking along the streets of Sydney, New York, Bogotá, or London, you must understand that this man is actually Abraitis. He did not wake up. He is still wandering. His life has not been resolved. He keeps walking across this pale yellow moonlight. And he will go on like this.

There are many kinds of exile, and perhaps the most painful of them is being a stranger in one's own land. We meet such a man in Baronas' novel *Vieniši medžiai* (*The Lonely Trees*). The action is set in an imaginary framework; it is 1970, and Lithuania has been liberated from the Soviets in consequence of a third world war. Having spent twenty-six years in the United States, Vytas Bruknys returns home to claim his estate. The author gives no details of the man's life in America, but it seems that he passed his days in suspended animation, more or less, doing only one thing—making money. The country in which he spent more than a quarter of a century has left no imprint on him. He did not try to learn or understand anything except, of course, the various ways of getting rich. He arrives in a big American car expecting to pick up his life where he had left it:

> He came in order to live out his life in his own land and to recapture the dream of his youth—the establishment of a model farm. Now he has a lot of money but very little time. But he will carry it through. If he gets married, there might be children. He will be seventy, and his child will be twenty.

In the meantime, the girl he once loved, for whose sake he remained a bachelor, has become the wife of a fanatical Communist, put in jail by the new regime. Bruknys used to call her, with pompous sentimentality, "my little cherry-tree top"; now she is a fat, stumpy woman in her fifties. But her daughter is the living image of everything her mother once was, and Bruknys looks at the young girl dreamily, as if she were the symbol of the past. There stands his young love, but he himself is old. To watch her smile and move about just as her mother did in the old days is already the beginning of his exile at home; it is to have and have not.

The exile deepens when Bruknys must face the problems of his estate. He came with the simple thought of repossessing everything and throwing out all the people who inhabited his home during the Soviet period when it was turned into a collective farm:

> No, they will not get anything, says Bruknys to himself, looking through the window with a dull glance. This is my land, my livestock, and everything that was brought here during the twenty-five years is mine. I'm the real owner of this place, and my dollars, my wisdom, will astonish everybody.

This is much easier said than done, however. The people, although made to live on his land illegally, have now acquired rights of their own. And they don't intend to lose them, because, now that the Soviets have gone, they have a chance to work this land for themselves rather than for their occupiers. So, both Bruknys and the former collective farmers want to have what was taken away from them, but the people have always lived here, while Bruknys is now an outsider—a nuisance and a possible oppressor in the liberated country of his birth.

The novel then proceeds to take Bruknys through a series of confrontations with various issues and persons. A new way of life must be worked out so that not only he and the other "Americans" but also the exiles who came back from Siberia and the people who never left the country will cease to be strangers among themselves. They must now rebuild the land together and make it into a home for everyone. Aside from the question of rights of ownership, the main problems arise from moral issues connected with justice and revenge. The country cannot be resurrected as long as there are people in it who are committed irrevocably to violence as the means of "purging" the land of undesirable elements. Bruknys meets two fanatical representatives of opposing ideologies who have ruthlessly fought each other during the Soviet period. One of them, Uogintas, is a long-time guerrilla who has become so accustomed to dispensing justice from the barrel of a gun that he cannot conceive of any other way of safeguarding this new and democratic

Lithuania which represents the future that he fought for. The other is Valnys, a former Soviet functionary, the husband of Bruknys' former love. He has sacrificed many lives on the altar of communism and feels no remorse whatsoever. He is convinced that his faith cannot be defeated and will survive those who fought for or against it, and therefore to him the important thing is the future Communist society, not the numbers of the dead recorded in history.

Bruknys, in an attempt to bury old hatreds and to contribute to the establishment of a new basis for human relationships, gets Valnys released from jail, whereupon Uogintas almost immediately shoots Valnys dead. When the police come to arrest him for "illegal use of firearms," Uogintas tries to defend himself and dies, as both he and Valnys had lived, gun in hand. Thus, in spite of their radically opposed ideologies, the two men really think alike and are the true representatives of the old order, the law of violence, which ruled Lithuania during the period of Soviet occupation. They "purge" each other and leave the country in the hands of those who, with all their selfish ambitions and all their doubts about themselves and the values of life, do at least understand that some way must be found to work together in peace. The paradox is, of course, that the two ruthless fighters turn out to have been right, after all, in their own way; they did cleanse society of undesirable elements by means of violence.

In some ways *Footbridges and Abysses* is Baronas' most effective novel. In his previous works the conflict between the requirements of plot and those of idea-content caused difficulty. Most frequently the basic idea in a novel is itself a developing structure, fused organically with the outlines of action leading the characters toward the achievement of some final insight or experience. Baronas, however, has basically the mind of an essayist, a commentator upon human folly, and the artistic form most congenial to him is one that permits a rather loose string of philosophical observations and paradoxical statements tinged with irony and yet expressive of tragic experience. Therefore the working out of a systematic plot with its multiple complexities involving the total human psyche rather than merely its intellectual aspects is more a hindrance than help in the embodiment of his ideas.

Footbridges and Abysses succeeds better because it has no plot at all in the conventional sense. It simply describes the experience of a group of Lithuanian slave laborers captured by the Germans to dig fortifications for their retreating armies engaged in a last-ditch effort to stem the Soviet tide in Lithuania and East Prussia at the end of the war. Neither the course of events nor the length of time covered in the book is determined by any structural considerations by the author. The work is a slice of life, an arbitrary sample of an extraordinary kind of reality. Things happen chaotically from one day to the next, and the people involved have no possibility of controlling their lives, of making independent decisions based upon predictable circumstances. Their situation itself is so unlike anything we call normal life that it becomes pointless for them to strive for any coherent system of values to live by. They can only make a series of sardonic and tragic observations upon the total collapse of the generally accepted meaning of things. Fundamental notions of life are suddenly placed in a context which makes them completely unrecognizable or worthless, and the people, turned into pitiful caricatures of themselves by their condition of slavery, experience paradoxically, a sense of relief from the moral responsibility to uphold their convictions or even their human dignity. This is how the unnamed main hero responds to his situation: " 'Column march!' The sentries bark their orders, and I feel that my existence is secure. You have been caught, and hence—free from all values that enslave—you are at liberty."

There is, for instance, the freedom from courage. Several of the slave laborers try to escape and are shot, as an object lesson, in plain view of the rest. This provides the hero with a valuable insight into the nature of this topsy-turvy world he has become a part of: "The psychological insurance against escape attempts was effective. It is not easy to risk death when, thank God, you can still be a slave." The true standards of life can be recognized as existing somewhere beyond the limits of this nightmare only by the manner in which the hero's commentaries turn into a mockery of themselves:

> Fear is a virtue. I, and not only I, can say: glorious fear, I thank you, I remained alive, for when others were distributing clandestine anti-Soviet

> leaflets, I stayed safely at home and did not touch them, and that is why nobody tortured me in prison. When the country rose against the oppressors, I did not join in the pursuit and thus I stayed alive. My honorable fear, when others spoke of liberation, I spent tranquil evenings at home, keeping all cares away; my room was warm and the rustling of my slippers whispered of peace and comfort. Noblest fear, must I even now have trust in you and wait? There have been some who waited and yet died. Fear, you can disappoint those who trust in you.

Human relationships that are supposed to transcend the horrors of war, such as love or the recognition of humanity in both friend and foe, slave and master, can only penetrate the bloody chaos by acquiring a pitiful, twisted shape. The hero sees a German soldier in a forest writing to his girl: "*Liebe Gerda.*" The nationality of a man writing a love letter, or the uniform he wears, should become irrelevant in the recognition of a common human bond with him; whoever loves is our brother. In the book this feeling acquires a peculiar quality as our slave-hero imagines his own version of the letter:

> *Liebe Gerda*, wherever you are, on the shores of the Rhine or the Main, a farmer's or a cabinetmaker's daughter, the letter will come to you from a Lithuanian forest, fragrant and verdant, a potentially charming place for reveries. Yet that soldier of yours, whom the whole world hates, may remain here forever, defiled by bullets, grenades, or bayonets. *Liebe Gerda*, all three of us are equally hapless. He's probably writing to you that some second-class people are felling timber here, yet he will never tell you that we are cursing Germans, that we swear and pray, and that our faces are tearful.

Even the philosopher's dreams of the serenity of man liberated from base desires for power, riches, and security receive their ironic fulfillment for a man sitting in a muddy foxhole in the night amid exploding shells: "Here I am, the true Diogenes. The heavenly space, and the Milky Way, and poverty, and death—they are all at my fingertips. All that a sage needs. Deliberate and dream into infinity."

The book is full of this and similar mordant observations. We read that "all roads lead home, if only you manage to walk safely past the grave" and that "the world endures only because man does not know when he must die and remains terribly greedy to the very minute of his death" and on and on in this vein. There is even a new kind of prayer: "God, give me strength, so that I can push my neighbor aside, for I want to live." The general impression is not that people are ordinarily decent and wise until they become dehumanized by the terrors of war, but that men recognize the veiled hypocrisy and viciousness of their previous life and values only after they and their tower of Babel, called civilization, have been trampled into the mud. Fighting for survival, beset by fear and greed and suffering up to the last moment of his life, man achieves the ability to recognize the truth about himself, and this is the meaning of his crucible.

One may regard all of Baronas' work from this point of view as the liberation of man from his fond illusions about himself which had made him a slave to his own base nature hidden under the pride of his intellect. This is not a new lesson. Religion has long been teaching us that the true glory of man begins at the point where he recognizes himself as mere dust. Baronas, with all his cutting wit and paradoxical convolutions of thought, is only trying to illustrate the validity of this teaching. Beyond the works of man, beyond his intelligence and logic, which have led him to proclaim that God is dead and to put himself in His place, there remains, as there has always been, truth and love and wisdom issuing from the word of God. But we cannot see them any more when we refuse to accept any truth not of our own devising. The kind of man Baronas writes about is aptly characterized in his statement that "the limits of his mind are the outlines of his God." If Baronas attempts to communicate a moral lesson to us, it is that we must recognize that the outlines of God are infinitely larger than those of any man's mind.

15 Bernardas Brazdžionis—the Passionate Pilgrim

Bernardas Brazdžionis was born February 2, 1907, in northeastern Lithuania. Between 1908 and 1914 he lived with his parents in the United States. During the years 1929 to 1934, Brazdžionis studied Lithuanian literature in the Lithuanian State University in Kaunas. Afterwards he worked as editor of several literary and cultural magazines and later, from 1937, at the "Sakalas" Publishing House. Between 1940 and 1944 he was curator of the Maironis Museum of Literature. In 1944, Brazdžionis withdrew to Germany and, in 1949, to the United States. At the present time he lives in Los Angeles and works as editor of the cultural magazine *Lietuvių dienos* (*Lithuanian Days*).

Brazdžionis has published a good many volumes of poetry, as well as stories and verses for children. Some of the most important titles are *Baltosios dienos* (*The White Days*), 1927; *Krintančios žvaigždės* (*The Falling Stars*), 1934; *Ženklai ir stebuklai* (*Signs and Wonders*), 1936; *Kunigaikščių miestas* (*The City of Princes*), 1939; *Šaukiu aš tautą* (*I Call the Nation*), 1941; *Iš sudužusio laivo* (*From a Wrecked Ship*), 1943; *Per pasaulį keliauja žmogus* (*A Man Goes Traveling Through the World*), selected poems, 1939 and 1943; *Viešpaties žingsniai* (*Steps of the Lord*), 1944; *Svetimi kalnai* (*Alien Mountains*), 1945; *Šiaurės pašvaistė* (*The Northern Lights*), 1947; *Didžioji kryžkelė* (*The Great Crossroads*), 1953; and *Vidudienio sodai* (*The Midday Gardens*), 1961.

A convenient way to introduce Bernardas Brazdžionis to the American reader might be to compare his poetry to a number of public, commonly known symbols of values which, presumably at least, constitute the core of the "American Idea." The reference is not so much to things like the Declaration of Independence or the "Battle Hymn of the Republic," because these represent heroic exploits and formulations of political thought in action. We should think more of "America the Beautiful" or "One Nation Under God" or even, perhaps, "Home Sweet Home."

We should try to remember the onrush of patriotic emotion at times of national crisis or, in the privacy of one's car, at the sudden opening of a beloved American landscape. To all such things we can find Lithuanian equivalents in Brazdžionis' verse—wayside crosses, a birch tree on the hill, a straw-covered cottage—but mostly he abounds with nobly phrased professions of love for his native land. Brazdžionis is not a Lithuanian Carl Sandburg or Robert Frost, for these men had a craggy, caustic wit, a sense of irony counterbalancing the tenderness of their emotions, nor does he much resemble Walt Whitman, who sang the universal emancipation of the self. Brazdžionis is a faithful, devoted servant of the "Lithuanian Idea"—the serenity of a pastoral way of life and the love of God, manifest and experienced in every little thing touched by the sun, and a prayerful patience and hope during the seemingly endless periods of sorrow and national adversity.

The difficulty with both the American and the Lithuanian "ideas," at least as they are presented here, is that neither one has a clearly established relationship to a changing reality. To put it bluntly, both are in danger of becoming empty clichés. This is why Brazdžionis' verse gives us the curious feeling of wandering in a verbal labyrinth that might just as easily lead to a set of hollow, shiny phrases as to deep and tragic truths of heart-felt emotion. There is, however, no doubt about his reputation with the Lithuanian reading public. For a great many people, especially those who grew up during the period of Lithuanian independence (1918–39), he is the most widely read and most beloved poet. Obviously, therefore, there must be an inner strength, a sense of value in Brazdžionis' poetry which corresponds to some realities of his nation's spirit. It is equally clear that Brazdžionis can use poetic language with sufficient skill to make his visions compelling to his readers. He should be discussed, therefore, in terms of the relationships between his poetic language and his ideas.

To begin with, we might choose four rather vague and abstract notions to be used as "compass directions" to mark off the outlines of Brazdžionis' poetic universe. We can call them, for the moment, "God," "fatherland," "yearning," and "truth." The best way to explain them is to follow their emergence from the texture of a specific poem. God, for instance, appears not so much as an entity standing somewhere outside the created universe but as an inner experience resulting from prayerful emotional response to an imagined reality. Let us take as an example a poem called "Steps of the Lord," from *Viešpaties žingsniai* (*Steps of the Lord*):

> On the rock a flower was blooming white—
> Did not need the rain or sun.
> Still it trembled, like a silver drop—
> It was You, O Lord, who passed here by.
>
> On a branch a bird was singing so!—
> Not requiring house nor clothes of slik.
> Still it trembled, like a silver drop—
> It was You, O Lord, who passed here by.

As we can see, both the bird and the flower are ideas rather than things, they come from the parables of the Gospel, and the dimension of their existence is the spirit of God perceived in the poet's prayer. We recognize this dimension as a counterpart to reality after it has been made meaningful and lyrical by the passing through of God. God is thus a transfiguration of things, as described by the poet. Consequently, the poet's own religious faith is inextricably bound with his ability to pray, meaning, in this instance, to write.

In another poem, "Life's Nostalgia," from *Per pasaulį keliauja žmogus* (*A Man Goes Traveling Through the World*), the presence of God, experienced as faith and as poetic image, is closely connected with what we have called the category of "yearning":

> Processions of the morning stars shall pass us by,
> Shall pass us by, and nobody will know,
> If there be evening, if the silver stars will shine there,
> Will there resound the prayer of the bells, the way it used to in the mountains.
>
> I feel a gentle breath of wind against my face,
> Also His voice upon the beating shore—
> It is not wind, nor is it river running down the mountain,
> O Lord, could it indeed be You . . .
>
> I know the lonely traveler's bleak road,
> I heard in darkness his complaints and prayers—

He cursed the fairy tale, his joy, the sun, and also You,
And he kept shouting "Never!" and he kept shouting "Never!"

You never, but the morning sun will rise again,
You never, but a thousand flowers will bloom.
You never . . . and this one sad voice
Has touched the earth, the flowers, and the stars and made them cry.

And if You are a brook that flows through valleys and through mountains
And carries little boats, the down of swans, and pine needles; little boats—
We will be boats and will be feathers of white swans, and fishes—oh, we
shall no more be people,
But only take us, Lord, and carry us away.

And if You are the gentle breath of wind
That lulls to sleep a tulip in the prayer of the evening bells,
Do lead us, too, where the procession has departed,
Don't let the earth, the stars, and blossoms cry.

I feel a good and gentle breeze against my face,
Also His voice upon the beating shore—
It is not wind, nor is it river running down the mountain,
O Lord, it is You calling, You . . .

The recognition of God is born of yearning for an existence beyond death. Thus an interrelationship between the two categories is established; the yearning itself is one of the poetic manifestations of Godhead, embodied here in the metaphors of wind and river, flowers, and a far-off shore.

This poem also contains the motif of traveling, which is the dynamic aspect of yearning. Life as a journey, or pilgrimage, is a constant theme in Brazdžionis' poetry, and it is always connected with a strong longing to transcend a given state of being. It lends his poems the quality of movement toward some indefinite point, at times perceived as God, at times as a poetic reality of the author's own imagination in which ideas and expressions that must in the "real" world be understood as metaphorical become, so to speak, true statements of fact. The poet's paradise is a land where evening bells do indeed lull the tulips to sleep, as in a fairy tale, and where, as in a poem called "Evoe," the dead are wreathed in a constellation made of rainbows and roses. This seems at times like a poet's narcissistic yearning for the sound, movement, and color of his own words, especially when constant rhetorical repetitions (as we saw in the poem "Life's Nostalgia") induce a kind of hypnotic illusion that reality is a closed circle consisting of only a few images turning round and round.

The religious framework of Brazdžionis' poetry has also created an inward movement which is, in a sense, a mirror image of yearning, that is, a feeling of regret. The inevitability of sin bars the way to the star-wreathed paradise, and then the longing for it becomes inverted, transfigured into a deep and bitter repentance. Here the very momentum of sonorous phrases intensifies repentance beyond what might have seemed its sufficient measure. (Brazdžionis' verse, in any case, shows little evidence of his having been a very great sinner; the erotic theme, at least, is almost totally absent.) The result is verses like the following, in the collection *Iš sudužusio laivo* (*From a Wrecked Ship*):

> Forgive me, Lord, that in the fairest morning,
> That in the blossoms of the rising sun
> I wandered without asking for Your path
> And, all in dust, came back to dust from all my prayers,
> And in Your radiance did not refresh my soul—
> Forgive me, Lord, forgive.
>
> Forgive me, Lord, because if You do not forgive,
> I'll wilt in sin as if I were the wayside grass,
> I'll fall in pain like fruit cut down by early frost,
> Of my bleak travels having reached the bitter end.
> In sorrow of my tears, in agony of groans,
> Forgive me, Lord, forgive.

The date this collection of poems was published has a significance of its own, relating to the notion of sin and repentance, because the Soviet armies first overran Lithuania in 1940. For Brazdžionis, and for many other good Christian people, this was a time of soul-searching. Belief in the goodness and omnipotence of God did not permit the possibility that there was no particular moral to be drawn from the nation's catastrophe.

It had to be, as it had been in ancient ages, a reckoning for sins. It is interesting to watch Brazdžionis' poetry develop through the years of German occupation, and later in exile, in the direction of increasing despair about the possibilities of liberation. The nation's sins had been confessed, but forgiveness was not forthcoming—the darkest night continued. For a brief moment Brazdžionis was tempted to turn to God with a mildly reproachful question, as in a poem written in 1944:

> O Lord, why do Your glances keep the vigil
> Among the galaxies, amidst the paths of ants?
> We're asking You but for a grain of sand:
> Our native land and peace in our hearts.

Such moments, however, were rare, and they soon gave way, first to a militant religious optimism—"the Lord *will* save us"—and then to a slow understanding that perhaps the path of exile and suffering was meant by God to be our nation's sacrificial destiny. In his later books Brazdžionis began to develop the image of a weary traveler driven by God's will, as if by the Furies, to be the constant witness of injustice. In this manner the notions of "God" and "yearning" blended, in eternal pilgrimage and sorrow, into the "Lithuanian Idea," the most prominent theme in the poet's work.

From the very beginning the concept of Lithuania, the native land, already contained the thematic elements of pure-hearted acquiescence to humble circumstances of life and gratitude to God for the beauty of simple things. There was also an issue of possible journeys, pilgrimages—should one ever leave this place, could happiness be greater anywhere else? An early poem from *Baltosios dienos* (*The White Days*) answers this question in the negative:

> My father went to Argentina.
> My sister to Brazil. Indeed.
> Sometimes they send a letter. Empty. Yes. No dollars.
> My father is breaking stones; my sister harvests corn; they say they live all right.
>
> I stayed at home by my mother's side.
> Oh, let them spread their wings.

Let them. Until I close her eyes,
I might as well be here.

For storms and winds can also come
Directly to my home.
And the sun is the same, shining down on them,
And shining down on us.

The joys of home are described:

> A little hut without a chimney.
> A low-slung door. And tiny windows three.
> But, oh, the happiness! Impossible to tell.
> Alas, too short, too brief a time.

In his desire to emphasize the moral power of simplicity, Brazdžionis often exaggerates the image of poverty at home, makes his country seem a lot more primitive than it actually was. The poor, plain life becomes, in effect, a poetic device, a "code signal" pointing to true standards of value, and as such it takes its place alongside the virtues of purity of heart, love of the land and of God, and the inner nobility of the humble spirit. In this way, both in spite of and because of its smallness and poverty, the poet's Lithuania becomes a priceless jewel, something quite unlike all the riches of the world. This idea can be stated in a few laconic words, as we saw above—small hut, great joy—or it can express itself in elevated language, composed in a peculiar blend of images and abstractions. Quite typical of Brazdžionis is the poem "The Fatherland of Nemunas," from the same collection:

This have I found in the fatherland of Nemunas:
The dreamland castles and the world of days now past and gone forever,
Exalted word of creativity eternal,
And, of eternal light, the sun—as strong as a hundred suns.
. . . .
This have I found in the fatherland of Nemunas:
A hump-backed evening, like the prophet's staff, leading you across the field,
So that, when night and storms and shadows pass us by,
The nation, thirsting God, should grow again into a hundred-year-old tree.

One of the characteristics of such poetic language in Brazdžionis is a lack of ordinary logic in the images themselves. In this poem, for instance, it is not entirely clear why an evening should lead one across the field in order to effect a resurrection of the country after its misfortunes. It seems an analogy is intended with the coming of the night after which there will be morning. The reader is somehow expected to step over the non sequiturs on his way to grasping the general idea. There are a good many such verbal distortions of ordinary patterns of meaning in Brazdžionis' poems. We may find such expressions as "And ears grew deaf from all the seas of lies" or "I share with him a share of his lot," the latter apparently chosen because of the sound repetitions in the original: "*dalaus dalia aš jo dalios*." Sometimes the vault of heaven is split by song "as if by old wine." And sometimes, "Like a lantern lit at night, / You shall never catch fire again."

On the other hand, the stress to which Brazdžionis subjects the logic of language often produces bold and striking images, very effective in terms of poetic rhetoric. We find such images as, "By handfuls of their hearts they drank / Inviolable festival of peace," or "They play with shadows of the storms," or "Why so pensive over plowfields, you star-spangled sorrow?" This last image also contains sound recurrences impossible to convey in English: "*Ko parymai and arimų, liūdesy žvaigždėtas*?" Such irrational images must be considered alongside the hypnotic cadences of image repetitions mentioned before and in relation to Brazdžionis' great fondness for striking sound recurrences within a given line. Taken together, such devices tend to form a very cohesive verbal texture, to create a kind of special logic which is closely related to the poet's private visions of his country and of the value patterns in them. In the end, Brazdžionis produces a poetic Lithuania entirely his own, more beautiful than anything that can be described by means of ordinary logic.

Such a country is clearly capable of existing in a dimension untouched by the reality of historical events. Thus it becomes immortal, and it can be carried in one's heart forever. In other words, it is an article of faith, a deep inner commitment akin to religious experience. On this level, Brazdžionis' faith in God and love for country meet, and a resolution is achieved; God has willed that Lithuania should become, for a time, a spiritual place, an eternal value carried in the souls of the suffering people at home, the exiles in the Siberian snows, as well as the restless wanderers in the Western world. The poet's task then becomes, in a certain measure, prophetic; he foretells the future liberation and resurrection of Lithuania. We can see the evolution of such understanding in Brazdžionis from early exile poems, in which only the pain itself was made visible, to later works, permeated with a kind of mournful inner peace. In 1945, for instance, Brazdžionis wrote:

It's hard without you, native farmsteads,
Resembling golden blossoms in the darkness of the night,
Where lilac bushes are in bloom, so blue,
And where the cherry trees cast down their petals white.

It's hard without you, darkling pinewood forests,
Without the fairy tale of gentle giants,
Where in the night the silver stars are falling
And where, in dreams, I am their happy gatherer.

It's hard without you, graying castles of old—
The living past is still in blossom there,
The music of the ancient instruments still ringing;
'Tis there I'll bow my head at any crossroad.

It's hard without you, plowfields of my home,
So full of Winter rye under the snowdrifts,
And by the roadside, Christ in sorrow bends His wooden limbs.
He's guarding you, He's guarding you—I see.

At a later date, in a collection called *Didžioji kryžkelė* (*The Great Crossroads*) Brazdžionis was ready to understand that this particular sorrow is the greatest treasure he and other exiles could possess:

I have seen so many cities on this earth,
I have stopped at many foreign harbors,
Many travelers have asked me, could it be
That our feet shall never touch the native land?

Night goes by, and it is night again, and darkness
Dwells upon the thrones of rulers, lives in the words of diplomats,

Truth is walking all across the world in tears,
And no one sees her through the curtain of injustice.

The flesh of freedom died, its spirit is now dying,
And ears grow deaf from all the seas of lies . . .
Hearts call for freedom, hearts call out for justice,
This is all the treasure of this earth we have.

Similarly, in another poem we read:

Empty hands. And radiance in the breast:
All our riches fit inside the heart!
All our riches: spirit of the fathers,
Love for freedom, works created by the living soul.

As years went by, these riches confirmed the poet's resolution to bear witness, in all the crossroads of history, that peace has not yet been achieved, that justice has not been done as long as Lithuania and other occupied countries are still in chains. The restless wanderer of Brazdžionis' poems now acquires a definite purpose, and his travels a tragic meaning. Especially significant in this respect is a poem called "The Traveler's Talisman," from the collection *Vidudienio sodai* (*The Midday Gardens*). The poem is in the form of a dialogue between a weary traveler's voice and an unrelenting echo calling upon him to persevere in his journey to the very end of the cycle of history decreed by fate, when he will come out upon the holy shores of his native land. The last two stanzas read:

THE VOICE
Not an autumn leaf . . . No, no! I'm not a corpse!
Don't make me, undertaker, any gilded coffins!
Give me a piece of bread from native soil,
Give me a silver drop of water from my backyard well—
  I wish to be alive, I wish to be alive!

ANSWERING ECHO
Sprinkle with your tears the native piece of earth.
Lily of its freedom will arise from it—
Look at all your brothers drowned in sea of gold—

Lily of its freedom grows in bloody vale.
Leave this sea and come to holy native shore,
Where your land's adorned by the catharsis of its pain.

Within such a conception of indestructible sorrow that will endure until the dawn of future freedom, the dead must also remain immortal, even in the earth on which they died. Thus Brazdžionis writes a reverent testimonial to two important Lithuanian religious and cultural figures, both of whom perished in Siberia during the genocidal Soviet deportations. The poem, called "All Saints' Mass," from *The Midday Gardens*, moves forward with a restrained tragic dignity:

Dark. It's night. Between Koshlava and Pechora. Frozen ground.
Two radiant vestments stand like pale-white shadows.
The holy word, for God's great glory, was not heard
In these bleak parts since the seventh day of world's creation.

The echo of INTROIBO flies, like legend, through the earth.
Christe eleison—Kyrie eleison answers back—
This holy Mass has reached the distant labor camp in Karaganda,
The hymn has caused the mongol guard to weep.

And piously, across bent tops of pine trees, sounds the *Dominus vobiscum*!
And then the dale is flooded with *Et cum spiritu tuo*—
The sacred sacrifice of Christ is celebrated here
By holy martyr Bishop Teofilis Matulionis,
Assisted by Professor Pranciškus Dovydaitis.

Earlier in this chapter "truth" was named as the fourth cornerstone of Brazdžionis' poetry. It is quite evident by now that faith in fatherland, in God, and in the nobility of the exile's tragic calling does in fact constitute for the poet the whole truth and the meaning of life. It remains to speak of "truth" in a different sense—as a basically structural concept, as an inner core of a given poem which represents the ultimate values and around which the poem's thoughts, images, and its dynamics of movement are organized. Quite often Brazdžionis arranges his verse to make the main thing he wishes to say appear as a single object, person, or image which either is encircled by attendant concepts and metaphors or else moves through them as through a porous texture, eventually drawing all of the reader's attention to itself. This single point, then, is the actual bearer of "truth," of the fundamental idea, and in contrast with the surrounding images it often seems to acquire both a physical and a spiritual incandescence—a glow of conviction. The basic principles of such a construction might be illustrated by the poem "Three Steps," from *The Steps of the Lord*:

Like a white and shining bird
    Your past just flew you by,
You can't catch it, like a bird,
    Nobody can try.
From its wings the silver stars
    Radiantly descend,
In its wings the sun went out,
    And a piece of sky.

Now the present—a white dream—
    Holds your heart enfolded,
Throw away this heavy net
    From your weakling heart,
Do not open up your lips
    To denounce your joy,
Make no promises to fate—
    It will promise you!

And the future, a white tower,
    Shines for you afar,
And you carry it ahead
    Like a burning torch—
Who would walk the narrow path
    And the path of thorns,
Leaves behind him radiant steps
    On the bloodied rocks.

Through the mild obscurities of the poem's language, we can see the central metaphor of time, the point of value, in three different aspects. In the first stanza it is a dynamic image—a bird in flight, surrounded by the attendant elements, the stars. As it fades away, the dying rays of sun in its wings create a nostalgic point of incandescent glow against the darkness of oblivion. In the second stanza the same white color (much favored by Brazdžionis) surrounds formlessly the central object—the heart—in its metaphorical function as the present. The future is portrayed in the third stanza as a sequence of two central images, a white tower and a torch, both of them set off sharply against their background. Now time, centralized in the image of the torch, moves across the texture of life, described in the moral allegories of the Gospel. In the end, the full meaning of a man's existence glows forever in the bloodied footprints he has left upon the tragic paths of history.

The same structural principle extends to poems dealing with a personal image of the poet as a guest, or a traveler, on earth. His yearning, a deep and lyrical nostalgia, represents a personal counterpoint to the as yet unreachable point of ultimate meaning and value in the spiritual dimension, across the barrier of death. The title of one collection of Brazdžionis' poetry, *A Man Goes Traveling Through the World*, conveys the image of a single person moving across time and space toward his final home in the beyond. Life itself thus becomes a deathward journey through a series of ultimately illusionary realities. What remains on earth after the pilgrim's passing is, in turn, presented as a nostalgic image surrounded by a wide backdrop of things and spaces. The poem "Anno Domini," from the above-mentioned collection, illustrates these image relationships:

> A grave. A cross. And Anno Domini . . .
> And the praying birch trees white.
> Oh, she will, she will walk home with me,
> The black sister, in her time.
>
> Let us go. Your hand. It's evening.
> Say good-by to all. Good-by.
> . . . .
> Light of glowing embers weakening,
> Falling star across the sky.

The shroud-like whiteness of the praying birches surrounds a single point—the grave—on which the inscription itself, the Anno Domini, is symbolic of both the hope for eternity and the passage of time. The poet's "I" then stands at a moment of transition, between the white shapes of life and the black sister death. In the second stanza two glowing specks of light in a vast surrounding darkness represent the evanescent traces of the poet's life on earth.

The rich texture of life is often treated by Brazdžionis in his religious poems as if it were a kind of sea, a swirling mass surrounding one central symbol of value—the image of God. In the poem "Procession Toward Christ," from *Ženklai ir stebuklai* (*Signs and Wonders*), such an image is the bloodied hand of Christ raised above all earthly tumult:

> Over valleys, where daisies are blooming
> And, fragrant, the caraway sways,
> Over cities with lurking Gomorrah,
> Over seascapes with yachts going down,
> And above the dead laughter of earth,
> Over steel, over fire, over cannon,
> Through the dance of the stars and the moon,
> Someone's stretching a blood-spattered hand.
>
> Down the hill run the rivers; they carry
> The thick waters of all our sins,
> Drops of blood from the upturned palm,
> Drops of blood from the quivering fingers . . .

In other poems Christ wanders alone and unrecognized across the busy vanities of earth, or else a lonely chapel in the fields becomes the focal point of the religious experience, or, in a direct inversion of the point-surrounded-by-mass principle, yearning for God is depicted as some other, all-pervading presence beyond any tangible object. During the years of exile, the religious and the political categories of experience are sometimes combined in poems that denounce both mankind's indifference to God and its unwillingness to look at Lithuania and other such small enslaved countries as living witnesses of continuing injustice. At times the author's accusatory tone becomes mixed with bitter sarcasm, as in the poem "The World's God," from *The Great Crossroads*. The poem is subtitled "Prayer to a Tree in the Meditation Chapel at the United Nations":

Perfection of Exile

If you were water
Clear as crystal, running on—
The world would say to Nero: Villain, wash in it
Your hands which bear the blood of millions whom you killed!

If you were stone,
Brought here by hands from a million miles away—
You would be tied around the neck of Genghis Khan
And he would drown, like an aged dog that has destroyed great packs of other dogs,
In the Pacific Ocean, near the Bikini Islands,
Under the hydrogen bomb!

If you were . . .
If you were Jehovah, cruel, great,
If you were Buddha, cross-legged and blessing his own peace, Buddha!
If you were mammon, ruling over governments,
If you were Christ with mustard seed of faith . . .

If you were a living tree! Growing, rustling . . .
If you were an oak from Lithuanian fields—
The flowers of the earthly paradise would bloom around you
And children by the thousands would frolic in their freedom . . .

Oh, you old tree stump you,
Are you indeed the God of all mankind?

As we can see, structurally all the elements of the poem focus upon that lone tree stump in the meditation chapel. It thus becomes an inverted symbol of value, something that should have represented God but now is dead and useless because the world has stopped believing that tyranny must be destroyed at any cost.

In the end, Brazdžionis' poetry strikes the reader as essentially rhetorical. All its main devices—constant repetitions of syntactic units, the patterning of sound textures in recurring sequences, elliptical sentences, exclamatory statements, the design of the poems around a focal point of value—are aimed at evoking the greatest possible emotional response from the reader. It could be that Brazdžionis believes in the primacy of feeling over rationality, because he holds a few basic truths to be self-evident and comprising the fundamental human wisdom. Love of country, faith in God, brotherhood of man in freedom are to him ideas which a poet can elaborate upon in the language of emotion and thus entirely fulfill his calling. And it is, perhaps, a tragic thing after all that not many doors will open in our day to receive a pilgrim bearing such a message.

Index

(Page numbers in italics indicate important, continuing discussion of a work)

PERFECTION OF EXILE was printed on paper which bears the watermark of the University of Oklahoma Press and which has an effective life of at least three hundred years.

University of Oklahoma Press

Norman

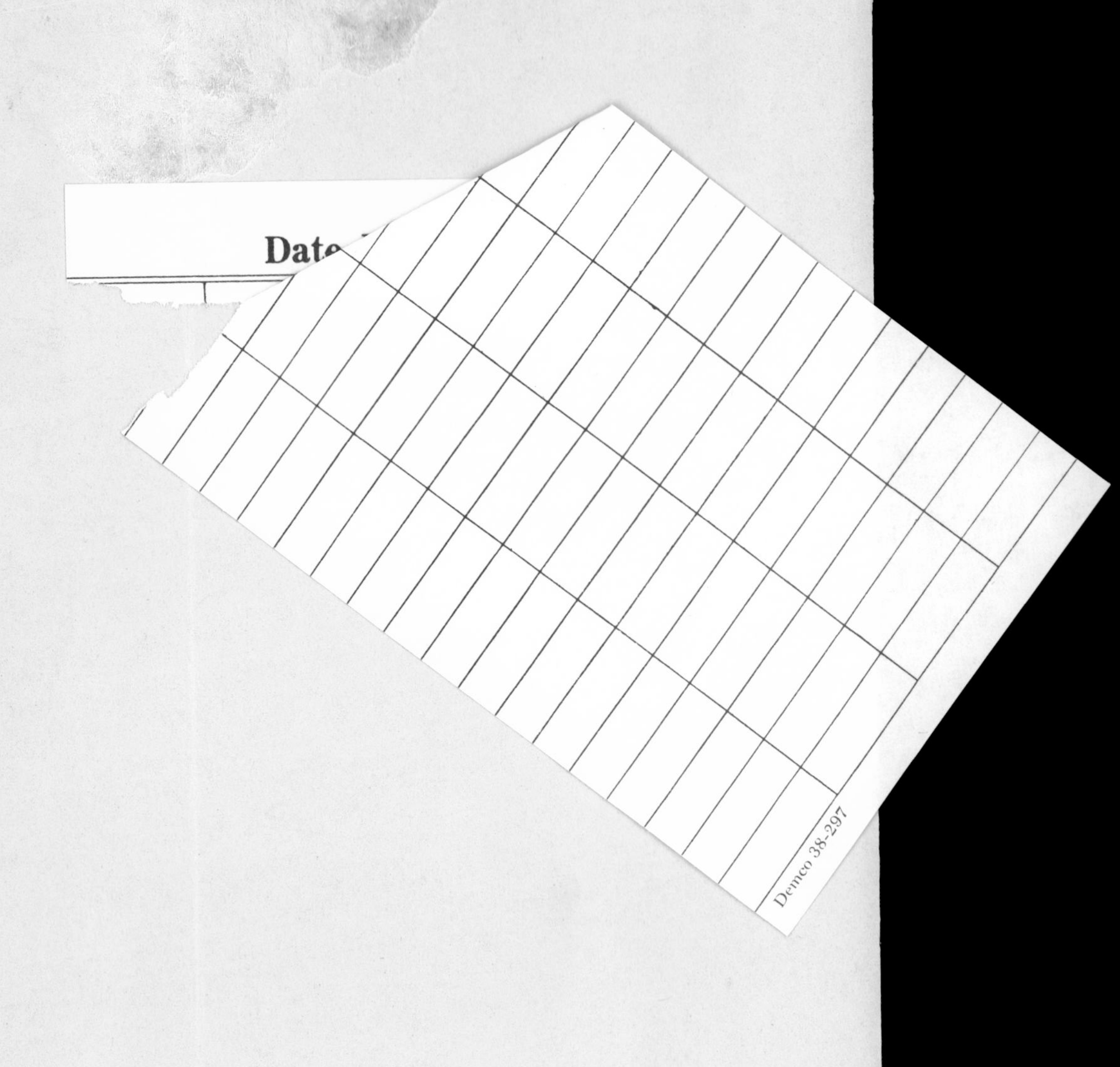